How To Make A Forest Garden

Patrick Whitefield

Permanent Publications

Published by:
Permanent Publications
Hyden House Limited
The Sustainability Centre
East Meon
Hampshire
GU32 1HR
England
Tel: 01730 823 311
Fax: 01730 823 322
Overseas: (international code + 44 - 1730)
Email: enquires@permanentpublications.co.uk
Web: www. permanentpublications.co.uk

Distributed in the USA by:
Chelsea Green Publishing Company
PO Box 428, White River Junction, VT 05001
Tel: 802 295 6300 Fax: 802 295 6444
Web: www.chelseagreen.com

First published 1996
2nd edition 1998, 3rd edition 2000, revised 2002, reprinted 2007, 2008, 2009, 2010, 2012, 2013, 2016
© 2002 Patrick Whitefield

The right of Patrick Whitefield to be identified as author
of this work has been asserted by him in accordance with
the Copyright, Designs and Patents Act 1988.

Edited by
Madeleine Harland

Designed and typeset by
Tim Harland

Line drawings by
Tricia Cassel-Gerard

Printed in the UK by
CPI Antony Rowe, Chippenham, Wiltshire

Printed on paper from FSC certified mixed sources

British Library Cataloguing-in-Publication Data.
A catalogue record for this book is available from
the British Library.

ISBN 978 1 85623 008 7

CONTENTS

This book is dedicated to

Chris Hoppe
1966 - 1996

Permaculture designer and teacher,
mover, waker and shaker,
tree planter,
friend.

THE AUTHOR

Photo by Ian Cherry

Patrick Whitefield (11th February 1949 – 27th February 2015) was an early pioneer of permaculture, adapting Bill Mollison's teachings with a strong Southern Hemisphere bias to a cooler, maritime climate such as the British Isles. He wrote a number of seminal books, *Permaculture in a Nutshell* (1993), *How to Make a Forest Garden* (1996), a new edition of *Tipi Living* (2000), *The Living Landscape* (2009), *How To Read the Landscape* (2014) and his magnum opus, *The Earth Care Manual* (2004), an authoritative resource on practical, tested, cool temperate permaculture. *How to Make a Forest Garden* was the first book to explain how to design and plant forest gardens in cool temperate climates and was quickly adopted as a key text.

Patrick was born on 11th February 1949 in Devizes, Wiltshire and brought up on a smallholding in Somerset. He qualified in agriculture at Shuttleworth College, Bedfordshire and after several years working in agriculture in the Middle East and Africa, he settled in central Somerset.

Patrick has appeared in several BBC TV programmes, made popular YouTube videos and was a consulting editor of *Permaculture* magazine since its launch in 1992. Patrick taught many permaculture and other practical courses with his wife, Cathy, and was one of the first teachers in the world to develop an online Permaculture Design Course.

After Patrick's death, there were obituaries in *The Telegraph*, *The Guardian* and on BBC Radio 4, and tributes to him from all over the world on social media. Patrick Holden from The Sustainable Food Trust wrote, "It is only towards the end of his life that the wider significance of permaculture ideas began to emerge... the true significance of Whitefield's ideas was not adequately acknowledged during his lifetime, but his influence will survive him..."

Maddy Harland, FRSA
editor of *Permaculture* magazine and co-founder of Permanent Publications
February 2016

ACKNOWLEDGEMENTS

I owe a great debt of gratitude to Robert Hart, the pioneer of forest gardening in temperate climates. Without his work this book would not have been conceived. Indeed there would be no forest gardens at all. I am also grateful to other forest gardeners who have shown me their gardens, shared their experiences, and provided photographs for the book.

I would also like to thank Andy Daw, whose help and support throughout this project has been considerable, and Phil Corbett, who read the manuscript from a technical point of view and made some useful suggestions. However I take full responsibility for the contents.

Thanks too to Tricia Cassel-Gerard, who illustrated the book, and whose garden features in the second part of Chapter 10.

My special thanks go to my publishers, Maddy and Tim Harland and Glen Finn. Working with them is a truly co-operative venture, full of mutual support and genuine friendship. I hope and trust that the quality of our relationship is reflected in the all-round quality of this book. *PW*

FOREWORD

by Robert A. de J. Hart

We all have the forest in our blood. Deep down in the subconscious of each one of us are dim race memories of a time when our ancestors were dependent on the wildwood and its inhabitants for the essentials of life – food, shelter, clothing and the soul-food of beauty. Millions of people, when they can, seek solace in woodland areas from the discords, artificiality, pollution and sheer ugliness of the urban environment. But, tragically, the number of such areas is declining throughout the world as civilisation, in its destructive march, fells more and more trees for motorways, airfields, housing and industrial estates, cornfields and cattle pastures, while exploiting the trees for timber and pulp. Such devastation, promoting the greenhouse effect and other severe environmental problems, threatens the very survival of humanity.

Is there anything that we, the ordinary people, can do to reverse this suicidal trend? Obviously, few of us are in a position to restore the forests, and protests and demonstrations seldom have much effect in influencing the powers that be. But tens of millions of us have gardens, or access to open space such as industrial wastelands, where trees can be planted. And if full advantage can be taken of the potentialities that are available, even in some heavily built-up areas, new 'city forests' can arise that would compensate for the destruction of the countryside. Patrick Whitefield's excellent book gives numerous practical details of the steps that many of us can take to realise this alluring vision. I know Patrick as a dedicated and enthusiastic permaculture lecturer, who writes with authority based on intensive study and experience.

Permaculture is a modern adaptation of a system of land-working and a way of life that has existed since time immemorial. The first horticultural activities of our earliest ancestors consisted in learning to *manage* the constituents of their forest home. By carefully observing the habits of their animal neighbours, they learned to recognise which plants were good to eat and which could be used to cure their ills. They then learned to promote the growth of these valued plants by freeing them from encroaching 'weeds', by opening up the forest canopy to enable more of the Sun's rays to penetrate them, and possibly by diverting the streams to water them. Later they learned the mysteries of reproduction by seed and vegetative propagation. The next step was to make clearings in the forest by the use of fire and stone tools, to prepare the land, to sow seeds and plant cuttings. These were the first forest gardens. In the remotest parts of Africa, Asia, Latin America and the Pacific Islands, the indigenous inhabitants are still making similar gardens.

Ever-increasing concern is being expressed about the wholesale extermination of tropical rainforests with all their myriad inhabitants: strange and beautiful plants, insects, birds, animals – and human beings. It is a vast man-made disaster that affects us all, though we may not be immediately aware of it. In the first place, plant-life absorbs carbon dioxide which is responsible for the greenhouse effect, the creeping environmental malady that could, in time, so alter the climate in every part of the world that many forms of life would no longer be sustainable. Secondly, plant-life exhales oxygen, that basic necessity of life. Thirdly, the destruction of so much beauty, such a diversity of complex life-forms, must inevitably have a deleterious influence on the collective unconsciousness of all humanity.

Most conservationists are making devoted efforts to preserve the Earth's remaining forest cover. But mere preservation is not enough. The forest is a vast and infinitely varied resource that should be developed for the sake of humanity, not in an exploitative but in a sustainable way. And here we have much to learn from the forest's indigenous inhabitants, because, for thousands of years, they have been doing just that. Many of them have acquired an encyclopaedic knowledge of the qualities and uses of forest plants.

In fact, a new science of ethnobotany has been evolved to tap this knowledge. While doing everything possible to preserve and promote the growth of the most valued trees and other wild plants, many forest-dwellers have planted, under their protective shade, useful economic plants such as bananas and coffee bushes, pineapples and peppers. These they have used, not only to enrich their own diets but also to sell for cash, so that they can acquire some of the genuine boons of civilisation, such as small machines and radio sets.

The fact that I quote the example of 'primitive' tribal people does not mean that I advocate that we should all return to primitive lifestyles. Obviously it would not be right to jettison the genuine technical advances of material progress, which the present century has produced in such bewildering abundance. Computers and television networks, jet-planes and genetic research, as well as many other devices and disciplines, have legitimate roles to play in a wisely regulated post-industrial order. At this most crucial period in the history of the world, when the future of all life is at stake, it is our most urgent task to work out a new way forward, integrating the best of the old and geared to the total well-being of living organisms rather than dead systems.

And in this greatest of creative enterprises the new-old sciences of permaculture and agroforestry have fundamentally important roles to play. Their most significant feature is that they combine conservation of the environment with methods to produce most of the basic necessities of life. By means of constantly evolving new techniques, they make it possible to grow not only an abundance of nourishing foods and beverages, but also medicines, fuels, fibres, timbers, oils, resins – most of the things that are needed to maintain a reasonable standard of living for all.

The creation of a permaculture plot on any scale, from a town patio to a large rural area, is a fascinating and satisfying task. It is a way of restoring the intimate relationship with nature, with Mother Earth, with Gaia, for which every human psyche is programmed. Just as much as any plant, the human being is intended to have roots in the natural environment, if she or he is to achieve spiritual security and all-round self-fulfilment. After a few years of relative self-sufficiency in food-plants and possibly medicinal herbs, one comes to realise that the products of one's own soil have a quality that attunes them uniquely to one's own metabolism. One then experiences a process that goes beyond satisfying the appetite and healing minor ills to the enfoldment of positive health. A new vitality, a new life-force enters one's being.

The process of creating a permaculture garden is not like making an ordinary garden, because one's every activity has a meaning, an aesthetic-technical significance, that transcends mere enjoyment and utility. This is because it is part of a new way of life that must be developed, if people are to achieve root-solutions to the colossal problems of the present era. It helps one to gain the realisation that all life is one. One becomes a participant in the innumerable interactions that constitute the harmony of a diversified ecosystem.

In my own garden, a majestic edible rowan seems to exhale a beneficent influence over human beings and other plants alike. In the summer and autumn of 1994 a nasturtium and a runner bean that I had sown at its foot entwined it in what seemed like affectionate embraces that spiralled almost to its summit.

The study of plant interrelationships is a science that is still in its infancy. Intensive research has been undertaken into the nitrogen-fixing capacities of members of the pea family, which benefit not only the plants themselves but also their neighbours and successors, and also into the mycorrhizal associations between certain fungi and plant roots. But there is a vast lore of traditional biochemical reactions that awaits confirmation or rebuttal in the laboratory. One thing is certain: the mutual aid that Kropotkin postulated as the prime motivating power in evolution is a far more potent force than antagonism in the multi-species plantation that is a forest garden.

Hence its profound symbolical significance for the modern world.

Many visitors comment on the peaceful atmosphere of my forest garden. I am inclined to attribute this to the fact that it is believed to be the site of a Celtic Christian mixed monastery, an outpost in the primeval forest that once clothed the Welsh Borderland. Such an atmosphere, as I know from experience, can often be detected in potent places, such as stone circles or Iron Age hill-forts, where powerful emotions have been felt in the distant past, and I feel a warm sense of kinship with those early pioneers. But I hope and trust that my garden's peaceful atmosphere owes something to the present as well as to the past: to the numerous beneficial relationships between different plants, which – dare I say it? – love each other.

Especially prominent in the traditional lore of companion growing are more aromatic plants, not only trees such as the balsam poplar, the delicious scent of whose young leaves can be wafted over distances exceeding half a mile in early spring, but also bushes such as the blackcurrant, which is believed to have a special affinity for plum trees. Herbs, however, such as the many species of mint, each of which has the characteristic odour are the principal plants credited with the ability to ward off pests and diseases from their neighbours and stimulate their growth. Herbs are one of the constituents of the ground-storey of a forest garden, and they contribute to a physical, as well as a spiritual atmosphere.

This is just one facet of the comprehensive answer which permaculture puts forward to the problems of industrial blight. Faced with the challenge of the vast toll of environmental degradation which industrialism has inflicted on the countryside, thousands of ordinary people in many countries are creating new landscapes, more beautiful and more diverse than the old, that are also capable of supplying a multitude of useful products. And many of the landscapes will doubtless incorporate forest gardens. I am very grateful that Patrick Whitefield has become such an eloquent advocate of the forest garden.

Right: Robert Hart, pioneer of the temperate forest garden, with all the tools he needs to maintain his famous garden in his wheelbarrow. (Fransje de Waard)

INTRODUCTION

What is a Forest Garden?

FOREST GARDEN OR WOODLAND GARDEN?

Robert Hart coined the term 'forest garden' when he invented this new way of gardening. Personally I prefer to call it a 'woodland garden'. To me, and many British people, the word forest suggests either the king's hunting preserve or a huge plantation, dark and monocultural. A woodland is something more diverse, more natural and usually on a smaller scale. I can more easily imagine having a bit of woodland in my back garden than a patch of forest.

But 'forest garden' has gained wide currency, both here and overseas, and is perhaps more understandable in international English. So to avoid confusion I have used the accepted term. But, dear reader, forgive me if I occasionally lapse into my own vernacular and call it a woodland garden. The two terms mean exactly the same thing.

A forest garden is a garden modelled on a natural woodland. Like a natural woodland it has three layers of vegetation: trees, shrubs and herbaceous plants. In an edible forest garden the tree layer contains fruit and nut trees, the shrub layer soft fruit and nut bushes, and the ground layer perennial vegetables and herbs. The soil is not dug, and annual vegetables are not normally included unless they can reproduce by self-seeding. It is usually a very diverse garden, containing a wide variety of edible plants.

Many gardens contain the same things as a forest garden, but usually each is grown separately, as orchard, soft fruit area, vegetable patch, and herb bed. What distinguishes a forest garden is that all are grown together on the same piece of ground, one above the other.

Gardens like this have long been cultivated in many tropical countries, and still are in places as far apart as Central America, Tanzania and the Indian state of Kerala, to name but three. But in Britain they are a new thing, at least in the full three-layer form. Two-layer combinations, such as fruit trees with soft fruit, and hazel nuts with vegetables, have been grown in the past. But the modern trend to monoculture has seen the end of them. (It was largely the introduction of poisonous sprays that put paid to them, as the spraying regime for one crop would be incompatible with the other.) If there have been complete three-layer forest gardens in this country in the past, history is silent about them.

The pioneer of forest gardening in Britain is Robert Hart. He has spent much of his life as a farmer and gardener, searching for a way of growing food which is harmonious with the Earth, healthful for people, and compassionate to all living things. The forest garden he has planted at his home on Wenlock Edge in Shropshire is the result of this search. It provides him with a high proportion of his food with a minimum of external inputs, including no animal manures. Many people have been inspired by his garden to plant forest gardens of their own. But it takes time for a garden containing trees to mature, and as far as I know his is the only fully-grown example of a complete forest garden in Britain.

There are no hard and fast rules about what a forest garden should be. In fact every one should be different, tailored to the needs of the individual gardeners and their family, and to the unique environment of each garden. Some may consist of only two layers rather than all three. Others may include annual vegetables, especially in the early years, before the tree roots have grown to occupy all the soil. But they all share one thing in common: they are modelled on the natural climax vegetation of Britain, which is woodland.

Forest Gardening and Permaculture

Permaculture is an approach to food growing – and many other aspects of life – which takes natural ecosystems as its model. People sometimes assume that permaculture and forest gardening are one and the same thing, but this is not so.

Although both learn from natural ecosystems, the learning is much more of a direct copy in the case of forest gardening: a forest garden looks like a woodland, but a permaculture system may not look like a natural ecosystem. Permaculture is not modelled on the outward forms of ecosystems, but on the underlying principle which makes them work. What makes them work is a web of beneficial relationships between the different plants and animals, and between them and the rock, soil, water and climate of their habitat.

For example, different plants specialise in extracting different minerals from the soil, and when their leaves fall or the whole plant dies these minerals become available to neighbouring plants. This does not happen directly, but through the work of fungi and bacteria which convert the minerals in dead organic material into a form which can be absorbed by roots. Meanwhile the green plants provide the fungi and bacteria with their energy needs. Insects feed off flowers, and in return pollinate the flowering plants. In desert ecosystems every plant and animal is adapted to minimise the use of water, while in very wet ones plants are adapted to cope with waterlogging, and so on.

Natural ecosystems can be very productive, and they don't need all the inputs of fossil fuels and other materials that are needed to support our present-day agriculture, industry and infrastructure, nor do they emit any pollution. Permaculture seeks to create systems which have all the desirable characteristics of natural ecosystems but which provide for human needs. The key to achieving this is to set up a network of beneficial relationships between the different elements we need in a garden, on a farm or in a whole community.

So the things you find in a permaculture garden may not be radically different from those in any other garden, but they will be placed so as to create as many beneficial relationships between them as possible. For example, there may be a greenhouse, but it is unlikely to be a free-standing greenhouse. It is much more likely to be a conservatory placed along the south side of the house. The waste heat from the house keeps it warm in winter and spring, while it in turn contributes to warming the house. Young seedlings grown in the cons-er-vatory get maximum care and attention from the gardener without the need to even step outdoors. Here is a simple web of beneficial relationships involving house, glasshouse, plants and people.

Although forest gardening and permaculture are not the same thing, there is much that they have in common. Both are about putting components together in a harmonious whole, so both have a strong element of design, and both are firmly rooted in a sense of ecology. But permaculture covers a much wider field than gardening, including farming, forestry, town planning, financial and social structures and much more. A forest garden may be a component in a permaculture design, but it is most unlikely to be the whole thing.

Forest gardening is also much more than just a part of permaculture. It is a way of gardening, indeed the basis for a way of living, which arose quite independently: it can be practised by anyone who has access to a little land, and the desire to try something that is quite new – and yet as old as life itself.

Chapter 1

WHY GROW A FOREST GARDEN?

Introducing the main themes of forest gardening

There are many good reasons for growing a forest garden, and no two people who are attracted to it have exactly the same set of reasons. But the main one for most forest gardeners is that it is the most natural way to garden.

A NATURAL WAY OF GARDENING

Wherever you are on Earth the most sustainable and Earth-friendly way to grow food is the way which is most like the natural vegetation of that area. In each part of the world a different natural vegetation has evolved over the ages to fit perfectly with the climate and other local conditions. In Britain it is woodland.

Fields of crops and grass can be made to work here, but the land is forever trying to get back to woodland. If a field is abandoned it is soon colonised by brambles, blackthorn, gorse or other shrubby plants. Little trees grow up through this protective layer, and if they are left long enough they grow into the tall canopy of a new woodland. It takes a constant input of energy from humans or from our grazing animals to stop this natural process of succession from happening.

By planting a forest garden we are working with the natural inclination of the land rather than struggling against it. This saves us a great deal of energy. But more than that, it takes us closer to the kind of vegetation which the process of evolution has found to be best suited to the conditions here. There is no doubt that this kind of vegetation will be the most healthy for humans, plants, animals and the whole Earth organism, and the easiest to sustain over long periods of time.

In other parts of the world, where the natural vegetation is different, the model for the most natural way to grow food is different. For example, on the Great Plains of North America the natural vegetation is prairie, a mixture of perennial grasses and herbs. There

is a movement afoot there to develop 'domestic prairies', mixtures of these plants which yield human food. This would not only save the enormous amounts of energy involved in growing annual cereals, but would be a cure for the terrible levels of soil erosion which are still common in North America.

It may be that domestic prairies have a place in Britain, and forest gardens on the Great Plains – if only so that people living in both places can have a more complete diet from local sources. But each will always be most harmonious when grown in its own home. It is interesting to note that both systems have two important things in common. The first is that they are composed of perennial plants and the soil is rarely, if ever, ploughed or dug. The second is that they are composed of intimate mixtures of plants growing together, not segregated blocks of different crops, as in a conventional garden or farm.

Plate 1.1 An example of natural succession, as woodland re-establishes itself on an abandoned pasture in Devon. Bracken and bramble grow up through the grass, while gorse, blackthorn and willow spread out from the hedgerow. In the background stands an oak, seed parent of the trees that will succeed these pioneers. (PW)

Global Benefits

As well as being suited to its locality, a forest garden has beneficial effects that are global in scale. Possibly the greatest single ecological problem we face is climate change caused by the greenhouse effect. This is no longer a threat but a reality; it has already started to disrupt world weather patterns. As it intensifies, not only will many species become extinct, but much of the world's food-producing capacity will be lost, as many present agricultural areas become semi-desert. Moving production to new areas cannot be done overnight.

The increase of carbon dioxide in the atmosphere is the biggest single cause of the greenhouse effect, and much of the carbon dioxide comes from the destruction and burning of forests around the world, including tropical rain forests. Growing new trees is one way to take carbon dioxide out of the atmosphere, by turning it back into living wood. Indeed Robert Hart's pioneering work was to a great extent inspired by the desire to do something to compensate for global deforestation.

On the first page of his book *Forest Gardening* he records how the idea of the forest garden first came to him:

> *Those who are concerned with the full implications of the ecological crisis which we now face generally agree that urgent steps should be taken to plant many millions of trees... It occurred to me that there was no reason why many of the desperately needed new trees should not be fruit-trees planted by the owners of town and suburban gardens, who would gain the bonus of growing nourishing fruit. If one could persuade 100,000 Londoners to plant just ten fruit-trees each, that would be a million trees – quite a forest! And if tree-planting programmes were pursued in urban areas around the world, a new worldwide City Forest would arise which would go some way towards compensating for the devastation of the tropical Rainforest.*
>
> *I had a vision of mini-forests in millions of back-gardens.*

His forest garden was started as a demonstration of what could be done in these millions of back-gardens.

The ecological benefits of trees do not stop at being a sink for unwanted greenhouse gasses. They also enable the soil to store more water and then to release it slowly, preventing both flood and drought. They protect soil from wind and water erosion. They give shelter from wind and Sun to us, our buildings and domestic animals, and help to moderate excessive heat and cold.

They form part of the habitat of wild plants and animals. In their falling leaves they recycle soil nutrients and provide soil organic matter. They prevent excessive build-up of salts in the topsoil of irrigated land. The list goes on.

Not all of these benefits will apply in every urban, suburban or rural back garden where we may think of growing a forest garden. But some of them will apply in every case. As a rule of thumb, if we have a choice between feeding ourselves by growing trees or by another means, it is likely that we will do more good to the Earth by choosing the trees.

To put it another way, growing a forest garden is a way of preserving the health of the planet and getting food and other benefits for ourselves into the bargain. But how much food can we expect to get from a forest garden, and what kind of food? Is it a worthwhile use of land from a purely productive point of view?

Plate 1.2 Michael and Julia Guerra's multi-storey food garden, Welham Green, Hertfordshire. Although only 10m by 4m, this tiny back garden produces a significant proportion of their food – the annual equivalent of 15 tonnes per acre with only 4 hours work a week. (Michael Guerra)

YIELD OF FOOD

To answer this question we first need to look at where our food comes from now. Simply, it comes out of an oil well.

A Problem ...

Our food production system has become so dependent on oil that, by the time the food arrives on our plates, for every calorie of energy in that food, approximately ten calories of fossil fuel energy have been expended to produce it. This includes the energy used to run the tractors, to manufacture them and all the other machinery, and to make the fertilisers and other chemicals. It also includes transporting the food, processing it, wholesaling, retailing, driving to the supermarket and back, and cooking it.[1]

This ratio of ten to one is an average. It has been calculated that the energy cost of a Kenyan mango, eaten in London, is 600 times the amount of energy contained in the fruit.

This is not just a prodigious waste of a finite resource, it is a major cause of global warming. Every bit of fossil fuel we burn means more carbon dioxide in the atmosphere. In addition, each stage of the food production process also has its own pollution cost, from the nitrates that get into the groundwater in intensive farming areas to the excessive packaging in supermarkets.

As well as the energy and pollution costs of our food, there are other ecological and human costs which are often not considered. Some of our food comes from the tropics. As well as exotic fruits, much of this consists of soya beans and other protein foods which we feed to farm animals to provide ourselves with meat, eggs and milk. Often this food is grown on land which could be providing food for the local people. They are then forced to migrate to urban shanty towns, or to start cultivating steep marginal land which suffers severe soil erosion as soon as the tree cover is removed, leaving both land and people destitute. Much of the soya crop is grown in South America on land that has just been cleared from forest.

This is not to say that the food business is more ecologically destructive than any other. But food is one thing that we cannot do without, and one which many of us have some opportunity to produce for ourselves.

... And a Solution

All of these costs can be avoided by growing food in our own back gardens. We don't need to aim for total self-sufficiency, but every bit we grow means that much less passing through the destructive process of industrialised food production.

But how can gardening seriously hope to replace farming as a major food source for urban people? An answer to this is suggested in an interesting report called *The Garden Controversy*, published in 1956.[2] The authors found that the production of food from an average acre of suburban London was worth the same as that from an acre of above-average farmland. This was a comparison of cash values; the weight of food from the suburban land was half that from the farmland, but it was valued at retail prices, whereas the farm produce was valued at farm gate prices.

Nevertheless this was a remarkable finding, especially as only 14% of the housing area was used for growing fruit and vegetables, the rest being taken up by houses, lawns, flowers, paths and drives. This means that the gardens were out-producing the farms by three times, in terms of weight of food per area of land actually used for food production. If a larger proportion of the area had been used for food the suburbs could easily have out-yielded the farms overall. Gardening is inherently more productive than farming because of the greater amount of attention that can be given to smaller areas.

These days, in recently built suburbs, the situation would be quite different because houses are now built at much higher densities and the modern garden is a miserable scrap of land compared to the generous tenth of an acre that was typical in the heyday of suburbia, the 1920's and 30's. There is still plenty of scope for growing food in smaller gardens, but obviously a higher proportion of the garden must be devoted to it in order to grow a reasonable proportion of the family's food.

Modern British agriculture is often described as being efficient. But this is only true when you measure efficiency in one very specific way, by output per worker employed on the farm. If you include all the workers involved in producing the machinery and chemicals and in processing and distributing the food, it begins to look a lot less efficient per worker. As we have just seen, if efficiency is measured in terms of output per area of land cultivated it's actually less efficient than back gardens. In terms of output per unit of energy employed it is so inefficient that it actually uses up ten times as much as it produces. Even from a money point of view it cannot be very efficient, as British Agriculture is subsidised to the tune of £10 billion each year.[3]

Gardening begins to look like a much more efficient

1   See *Meeting the Expectations of the Land*, eds Wes Jackson, Wendell Berry & Bruce Coleman, North Point Press, San Francisco, 1983.

2   Best, Robin H, & Ward, JT, *The Garden Controversy, a Critical Analysis of the Evidence and Arguments Relating to the Production of Food from Gardens and Farmland,*Dept. of Agricultural Economics, Wye College, Kent, 1956.

3   See *Our Food, Our Land*, Richard Body, Rider, 1991.

way of producing food when you look at it from more than one limited viewpoint.

All this says a great deal for gardening in general, but what about forest gardening in particular? How does its productivity compare with that of other kinds of gardening?

As yet we don't know for sure. Any useful comparison would have to be based on looking at the yield of a number of gardens over a number of years. Woodland gardening is so new to Britain that such a comparison will have to wait till the gardens which are being planted now become mature. But a look at how forest gardens work can give us a good idea of what to expect.

HOW A FOREST GARDEN WORKS

A Natural Woodland...

A forest garden works the same way as a natural woodland does in our climate.

Although there are no wholly natural woods left in Britain, there are still some semi-natural woods, where human activity has been confined to taking a regular harvest of timber and other produce, but where we have never grubbed out the existing trees and replaced them with species of our own choice. These woods usually have a structure consisting of three layers: the canopy of tall trees, a lower layer of shrubs and coppiced trees, and a layer of mainly herbaceous plants at ground level.

If you visit such a wood in early spring, say the first week in April,[4] you will see that all the growth is taking place at ground level. There may be a green carpet of wild garlic, bluebells or dog's mercury, making the most of the spring sunshine to manufacture food in their leaves. The mercury, along with celandines, wood anemones and violets, will also be taking advantage of the bare branches above them to flower and set seed.

If you come back towards the end of April you will see more green in the shrub layer, as the hazel, hawthorn, guelder rose and other shrubs take their turn at the sunlight before the canopy leafs up.

This happens some time in May in most woods, depending on the kinds of trees present in the canopy. For example lime usually comes into leaf in late April, while the last few ash trees are still bare as May turns into June. As the shade deepens some of the herb layer plants, like wild garlic and bluebells, give up trying to catch any sunlight at all. They leave flowering to the last minute, just as the tree leaves are expanding to close off the last gaps. Then their leaves disintegrate, the food they have manufactured during the spring is passed to the underground bulbs and to the seed, and the plants wait for next spring to start growing again.

Plate 1.3 A semi-natural wood in May, with the shrub layer in full leaf and the canopy just starting to leaf. (PW)

Other woodland herbs continue to grow at a low rate throughout the summer. Some of these are genetically adapted to cope with low levels of light, or able to adjust themselves to it. Others tend to grow where some extra light is let into the wood, such as where a tree has fallen or on the woodland edge. Primroses can use both of these means. They prefer to grow on a woodland margin, where some light can come in from the side, but if they are in a shady place the leaves expand to something like twice their normal size to catch as much light as possible.

By its multi-layer structure, a woodland makes use of the three dimensions of space in order to fit a large number and diversity of plants onto a single piece of land. The tendency of each of these layers to come into leaf in sequence makes use of the fourth dimension, time, to ensure that they all get their share of the Sun's nourishing energy. It also means that the fullest use is made of the sunshine, from early spring to late autumn.

It almost seems as though each layer is being charitable to the one below. Surely it would profit the trees to come into leaf as early as possible and get all the sunlight? The reason they don't is because their leaves are not frost hardy. Any protective mechanism which gives a plant resistance to an adverse influence, like disease or freezing temperatures, takes energy. If the plant can do without that mechanism it means that much more energy is available for growth. Thus the trees have sacrificed a few weeks sunshine in return for freedom from the need to protect themselves from late frosts.

The herbs don't have that option. They must come into leaf early in order to get their share of the sunlight before the shrubs and trees begin to shade them, and that means being in leaf when there is still a high probability

---

4   The dates given here are for southern England. They will be a little later further north.

of frosts. They must invest part of their hard-won energy in frost-resistance.

The herbs are occupying a different niche from the trees. An ecological niche is the role a plant or animal has in an ecosystem and the way in which it makes its living there. For a plant this includes how it gets enough sunlight, water and mineral nutrients, what conditions it needs to reproduce, which parasites and herbivores feed on it, what climate it needs, how it competes or co-operates with neighbouring plants and so on.

One aspect of the niche of the trees in a wood is being tall, frost tender and relatively late-leafing. This combination enables them to get enough sunlight and to avoid frost. The corresponding aspect of the herb's niche is to be short, frost-hardy and early leafing. The shrubs fall somewhere between the two extremes.

...And a Forest Garden

A forest garden works in the same way. First the vegetable layer comes into leaf, then the soft fruit, and finally the top fruit. Some extra light coming in from the side is usually needed too, but having at least one of the layers in full leaf throughout the growing season means that the garden can make maximum use of the available sunlight in a way that a conventional vegetable garden or single-storey orchard cannot. The growing season starts much earlier in the spring, as the perennial vegetables, which have overwintered as mature plants or rootstocks are able to put on rapid growth early in the spring when annual vegetables are still seeds in the packet, or at best seedlings in the seed tray.

Plate 1.4 A two-layer planting of fruit in May, with blackcurrants in full leaf and apples in blossom but only just leafing. Carol Jacobs' garden, Wiltshire. (PW)

As above ground, so below: the wide variety of plants in a forest garden gives a wide variety of root systems, each of a different size and shape. This means that the whole volume of the soil can be used without the plants competing unduly with one another for water and nutrients. The taller plants can also reduce the water requirement of the shorter ones by creating a more humid microclimate beneath their branches. Competition for water is also lessened by the fact that plants do not consume water when they are not in leaf, so the succession of leafing times has its part to play here as well.

In short, a forest garden can make much better use of the available resources, both above and below ground, than can a single-layer garden because more niches are filled. So the potential yield is clearly much greater.

Although we can't yet put a figure on this, there are some interesting indications from the world of agroforestry, the practice of growing trees and farm crops on the same land. For example, ash trees can be grown for timber over a pasture, making a double-layer system not unlike a traditional orchard. It has been calculated that the grasses do 60% of their year's photosynthesis – that is the production of food, for which they need sunlight – before the ash trees come into leaf. As pasture grasses are not woodland plants this figure is very encouraging. We can expect that the vegetables and shrubs of a forest garden, whose wild ancestors came from the herb and shrub layers of wild woods, will do at least as much of their photosynthesis before the canopy closes.

The important point about all mixed plantings is that we are not looking for maximum yield of a single crop; we are looking at the combined output. Although the yield of grass in a pasture with ash trees may be slightly less than the yield of grass in a pasture without trees, the total output – grass plus timber – will be greater.

The same is true of a forest garden. It will almost certainly yield less top fruit than a simple orchard, less berries than a pure stand of soft fruit bushes, and less vegetables than a simple vegetable garden. But it will produce more in total than any of the single layer plantings.

WHAT KIND OF FOOD?

A Varied Diet

There are three main products from a forest garden: fruit, nuts, and leafy vegetables. This may not sound like a complete diet, but then we do not usually expect our home gardens to produce everything we eat. If we are going to grow a proportion of our food at home there are some very good reasons for choosing just these products.

Agriculture is a very recent invention on the timescale of evolution. People have only been eating an agricultural diet, based on grains, for some two or three hundred generations, and perhaps half that time here in the northern part of Europe. This is a short time in evolutionary terms, a tiny fraction of the time that we and our hominoid ancestors have been on Earth, almost certainly too short a time for our bodies to have evolved to suit the new diet. It is most likely that we would be healthier if we ate more of the foods which our bodies have been 'designed' by evolution to live on.

Fruit, nuts and leaves, supplemented by some animal protein, is probably very much the diet of our stone-age ancestors. Hazel nuts were certainly a staple during the middle stone age in Britain, judging by the large numbers of hazel shells found around habitation sites of that date by archaeologists.

Certainly it would be good for us to eat more fruit than most of us do now, especially raw fruit straight from our gardens.

Shop-bought fruit may look brilliant, but that visual perfection is a sure sign that it has been sprayed over and over again to prevent the slightest blemish. A typical commercial orchard may have been sprayed 15 times or more during the growing season, including herbicides, insecticides and fungicides, and the fruit itself sprayed again in storage. Much of this spraying is purely cosmetic and has nothing to do with increasing yield. Organic fruit is hard to find in the shops, and expensive.

The fruit we buy in shops is almost all imported. Even the apples and pears that used to be grown in Britain are now mostly from overseas. By the time the fruit gets to us what vitality it ever had in its chemically-cultured orchard is very largely gone. What is more, only a very few varieties are commonly available in the shops. These are not the ones with the best taste or nutritional value, but the ones that best catch the eye on a supermarket shelf, or the thick-skinned ones that travel best.

Such fruit bear no comparison to juicy gooseberries eaten fresh off the bush, or the perfect plum, picked at the peak of its ripeness and popped straight in your mouth.

Robert Hart is a great believer in the health-giving properties of fresh green leaves. "My whole life has been a struggle against ill-health in my family and myself, and for me the forest garden has been part of the culmination of that struggle," he writes in *Forest Gardening*. He has revived the old word 'sallet' to describe the kind of salads that were eaten in days gone by. "Our forefathers made no distinction between vegetables and herbs," he says. "Anything that was edible and green, cultivated or wild, was liable to be included in their 'sallets'." He notes that John Evelyn, writing in 1699, listed 73 plants that were commonly eaten raw in his day and added that many more could have been included.

This level of diversity sounds remarkable. But both archaeology and studies of modern-day hunter/gatherer peoples suggest that it is what we have been used to throughout our evolutionary history. It is our simplified twentieth-century diet which is unusual.

We may not manage to grow over seventy different food plants in our forest gardens, but certainly we can grow many that are not found in a conventional vegetable garden, and any increase in the variety of our diet must be good for health.

Many of the plants which are suitable for a forest garden are either taken straight from the wild or have only been slightly modified by plant breeding. Wild plants are on average much higher in protein, vitamins and minerals than conventional vegetables. They may also contain a variety of organic substances which are good for our health in ways which present-day nutritional science is not aware of.

Annual garden vegetables, on the other hand, have been intensively bred over many generations for high yield and other commercial qualities. Nutritional value has not been selected for, and has withered away by default. Perennial vegetables have not on the whole been as intensively bred as annuals, and they retain much of the nutritional value of wild plants.

Most of the produce of a forest garden, whether fruits, nuts or salads, can be eaten raw. Most of us would probably benefit from having a higher proportion of raw food in our diets. What's more, eating it raw saves us both the trouble and the energy cost of cooking it. A quarter of the ten calories of energy expended in putting a calorie of food on our plates is spent in the home, and this is mainly in cooking. The more raw food we eat, the less energy we use, the less global warming and acid rain we cause. The beneficial effects of our forest gardens spread out over the Earth like ripples from a stone dropped in a pond.

A Varied Garden

Although there are many good reasons for eating more of the foods that grow in a forest garden, this does not necessarily mean we should do away with our conventional vegetable gardens. Most of the plants grown in a conventional vegetable garden are Sun-loving annuals, and would not fit into a woodland situation. A kitchen garden which is partly woodland and partly conventional will give more variety than either alone.

The two parts of the garden complement each other in three important ways:

- Firstly they enable us to keep growing food throughout the year. The vegetable yield from a forest garden is seasonal. It is at its peak in spring, and begins to decrease just as the annual vegetables are beginning to come ready in the summer. In the autumn many of the perennial greens in the forest garden retreat below ground to spend the winter as rootstocks. Then the hardy members of the cabbage family – like sprouts, kale and savoys – come into their own, providing greens through the dark days of winter. On the other hand, some of the salad plants in the forest garden stay green through the winter, when conventional salads are hard to find.

- Secondly, there are some things which are hard to get from perennials in our climate. Bulk carbohydrate is the most obvious one. There is no real alternative to the potato at present (though there are one or two herbaceous perennials which could rival it if they received attention from plant breeders).

- Thirdly, and not least, we like to eat what we know well. Although I personally take great pleasure in exploring the new tastes of unusual vegetables and making exotic salads from unexpected plants, I would be loathe to give up the pure joy of the year's first picking of broad beans, lightly boiled and served with a knob of butter!

However, most of us are not trying to grow all our own food. Most gardeners grow what they enjoy growing, or find easiest to grow, and enjoy eating, and buy the rest from the shops. In that case there is no reason why the whole area should not be put down to forest garden, plus some lawn and ornamentals. In any case, the yield of food is only one reason for growing a forest garden.

THE EASY LIFE

Another reason for forest gardening is that it does not take much work. To some extent the amount of work depends on the inclination of the individual gardener. You can go for an intensive approach, with intensively pruned trees, masses of mulch and careful nurturing of individual plants, or a more extensive one, with minimal pruning and mulching, and a sink-or-swim attitude to plants. The extra work should yield extra produce, but you can choose your style according to your priorities.

Nevertheless, there are some basic characteristics of a forest garden which make it less laborious than an annual vegetable garden, however intensively you choose to cultivate it.

A No-Dig Garden

The first of these is that there is usually no digging involved. There is not much scope for digging in a garden full of trees, shrubs and perennial vegetables. But even where it is possible, there are some very good reasons for not disturbing the soil.

Bare soil is rare in nature; there is almost always a cover of living or dead plant material on the surface. Disturbed soil is also rare. Barring ice ages and earthquakes it is mainly caused by the action of animals, either burrowers like moles and rabbits, or rooters like badgers and wild pigs. Although these animals may be common in some ecosystems, the soil disturbance they cause rarely affects more than a small percentage of the area at any one time. We are so used to the idea of ploughing or digging every piece of land on which we hope to grow some food that we think of it as the norm for productive land. But it never was the norm till we humans invented agriculture, and that, on the timescale of evolution, was an instant ago.

Soil is not an inert mineral substance. It is an intricate blend of mineral, air, water, organic matter and living organisms. The relationships between these components are so complex, and so hidden from our view, that we really know very little about how the whole intricate system works. What we do know clearly shows that there are some quite specific ways in which digging or ploughing the soil disrupts its natural fertility.

- Crumb structure is one important element in fertility. In an undisturbed soil it can be quite complex, and it provides the essential crevices through which air, water and plant roots can penetrate the soil. It is severely disrupted when we dig or plough, and it is destroyed in a frequently cultivated soil unless steps are taken to restore it. On a farm scale it can be restored by alternating arable crops with temporary grassland which remains undisturbed for a few years to allow the structure to recover. On a garden scale it can be maintained by incorporating a lot of organic matter into the soil. But in a forest garden it is not disrupted in the first place.

- The micro-organisms in the soil are the powerhouse of soil fertility. A myriad of essential chemical processes are going on all the time down there, including the cycling of plant nutrients and the conversion of raw organic matter to humus. These processes are carried out by bacteria, fungi, algae and other micro-organisms. They are so numerous that in a salt-spoon full of healthy soil there are more living beings than there are humans on Earth.

  Digging destroys many of them. 80% of these organisms live in the top 5cm of soil, and they die if they are buried deeper. Others are killed by exposure to sunlight, and many which are not killed are unable to continue with their natural cycles because the soil is suddenly swamped with an unnaturally high level of oxygen. This excess of oxygen can lead to a rapid loss of organic matter and plant nutrients from the soil.

- A bare soil is exposed to erosion. In this country erosion is rarely catastrophic, but it is often insidious, carrying off a small fraction of the soil each year. It is always the most fertile fraction, the organic matter and clay particles, which goes first. We then have to replace this lost fertility. Water erosion, caused by rain hitting bare soil, is much worse on sloping land than on the flat. So growing a forest garden can be a good option for steep land, which would need to be terraced if annual crops were to be grown there without causing erosion.

To dig or to plough is to forgo the natural gifts of the soil, and to commit ourselves to providing them ourselves. We may feel we can do this better than Nature can, by mechanically aerating the soil and providing nutrients with manures or chemicals, but it will certainly involve us in a lot more work.

Of course there are some good reasons for digging, otherwise people wouldn't do it.

- One is to control weeds. In a forest garden mulch plays an important part in weed control. But there are not so many weeds in this kind of garden anyway, firstly because digging is the main thing which encourages weed seeds to germinate in the first place, and secondly because any plant which is useful in one way or another is welcome in a polyculture. Many wild plants are edible, and deep rooted ones work at bringing mineral nutrients up from the subsoil.

- Incorporating manure and compost is another reason to dig. But in a forest garden the material is just placed on the surface as a mulch and taken down into the soil by the earthworms. (This also saves the work involved with composting, as organic matter which is applied on the soil surface does not usually need to be composted, as it does when it is dug in.)

- Another reason for digging is to prepare the soil for sowing seeds. This is not strictly necessary, as there are many successful annual vegetable gardens which are run on a no-dig system. But in a forest garden, where the plants are perennials, there is no need to prepare a seedbed each spring.

Perennial Plants

Any gardener who has grown both annual vegetables and fruit will know which takes the most work! It may take more work to get the fruit established, but once that is done the biggest job left is harvesting the produce. In a forest garden this applies to the vegetables too, because they are perennial also. There are some maintenance tasks to be done, but they are pretty light compared to the sowing, planting, thinning and so on that are a never-ending round in a conventional vegetable garden.

Annual plants are much less common than perennials in nature, as they usually need a patch of bare soil in which to germinate and establish themselves. Most are pioneers, able to establish themselves quickly on a newly available piece of ground, but unable to maintain themselves once the perennials get established. A community of perennials is more stable than one of annuals. It can keep going much more easily without our help.

As far as the vegetable layer of the garden is concerned, perennialism has another advantage which saves the gardener a great deal of bother. It avoids much of the problem with slugs. Slugs are undoubtedly the most destructive garden pests in Britain, especially in the wetter west of the country. Plants are most vulnerable to slugs when they are young. Once they get past the small and tender stage they can usually outgrow a slug attack, and perennial vegetables only go through that stage once every five years or so, not every year. In fact many perennials can be propagated by vegetative means – detaching part of the parent plant which will grow into a new one – rather than by seed. These young plants are bigger than seedlings and can usually grow away from slug attack more easily.

Diversity

The diversity of a forest garden helps to keep it free from serious levels of pest infestation. This is not just a matter of having three layers instead of one, but also of having a rich mixture of species and varieties within each of the layers.

Where many plants of the same kind are growing together, pests and disease organisms are surrounded on all sides by more of their host plants, so they find it easy to reproduce rapidly to epidemic proportions. Where each kind of plant is mixed in among many other kinds it is much more difficult for pests and diseases to build up, and they usually stay at a level that does little harm.

In addition to the benefits of general diversity, there may also be specific interactions going on. For example some plants provide food for insects which are predators on plant pests. But it is not always necessary to know precisely what the relationships are between plant and plant in order to benefit from the principle of health through diversity. We can be pretty sure that the greater the diversity of plants and the more they are intermingled the healthier the garden.

OTHER BENEFITS

Beauty

A forest garden does not have to be totally dedicated to food production. For many people the beauty of the garden is just as important as its yield of food. Fruit trees make a magnificent display with their blossom in the spring, and there is no reason why some trees, shrubs and herbs should not be chosen more for their appearance than their edible produce. Some purely ornamental plants can be included too. The balance of priority between food and beauty can be struck just where the individual gardener wants it to be.

The rigid separation between the edible and ornamental parts of a garden which we think of as normal is really only a convention. It is quite a recent one too, dating back to about the middle of the last century. When we free ourselves from it, whole new vistas of garden design possibilities can open up before us.

A Backyard Ecosystem

As well as the purely visual beauty of the garden, there is a fascination in being a witness and participant in the growth and development of an ecosystem. Strictly speaking any garden is an ecosystem, and there is interest and pleasure in watching its development. But a forest garden is so much closer to a natural ecosystem than serried ranks of Brussels sprouts – more complex and less predictable.

This is partly due to the timescales involved. As well as the annual cycle that every garden has, a forest garden has the much longer cycle set by the lifespan of the trees. In fact it is more complex than that because different trees and shrubs grow at different rates and have different lifespans. Perennial vegetables also have their lifecycles, spreading and shrinking in response to age, competition from neighbours, different seasons, increasing or decreasing shade from trees and shrubs, and interventions from the gardener. Add to this the wild plants and animals that move into or out of the garden as conditions change, and you have a kaleidoscope of changes unfolding as each year unfolds.

Wildlife Gardening

Looked at like this, forest gardening can seem very close to wildlife gardening. In fact there are many similarities between the two approaches.

Wildlife gardeners may start out with the main aim of providing a haven for wild plants and animals, and forest gardeners with the aim of producing food in an Earth-friendly way. But the solutions they come up with are often very similar. Some of the plants are the same, as many native plants are edible, but the two kinds of garden are also alike in structure and in technique.

Chris Baines, in his excellent book *How to Make a Wildlife Garden*,[5] suggests that the ideal shape for a wildlife garden is one modelled on a woodland glade, with trees and shrubs round the outside in a crescent or horseshoe and lower vegetation in the middle. This is also one of the best configurations for a forest garden, as we shall see.

In the same book he made the classic statement: "In a good, healthy bit of garden wildlife habitat there will be hardly a leaf that has not had a bite taken out of it." Exactly the same goes for a healthy forest garden, or any garden grown along permaculture or organic lines come to that. All these approaches lead to the same end. The differences are only ones of emphasis, and an interest in wildlife can be as good a reason for growing a woodland garden as any.

Personally I would go further than that and say that we have no right ever to design a garden without making provision for wild plants and animals. We humans are only one species on the Earth, and all the others have as much right to thrive and prosper as we do.

This does not just mean setting aside a little area for wildlife in the garden. It means working with our gardens – and farms, woodlands, townscapes and so on – so that wildlife can thrive in the main productive areas, not only in a bit labelled Nature Reserve. It also means choosing a low-impact lifestyle overall. Our patterns of consumption, transport, and waste disposal all have direct and indirect impacts on wild plants and animals. In fact the need to create nature reserves is an admission that we have failed to keep the rest of the land in a healthy condition, or our own appetites for material goods at a reasonable level.

Playspace

The main use of many back gardens is as play space for children. Parents often say that they need to keep a large area of lawn because the children play on it. But the average lawn is too small to make a really usable open space, one big enough to ride your bike or play football. Cutting it down to half its size may make no significant difference to its value as a play space.

---

[5] Published by Elm Tree Books, 1985.

The other half can be planted up to something much more attractive to most children – a shrubbery.

There is so much more you can do in the three-dimensional space created by shrubs and trees. You can climb the trees, make dens and tunnels, imagine yourself to be thousands of miles away in the jungle, or create a whole secret world, one that is not visible from adult eyes at the kitchen window!

Using a forest garden as a play space will greatly reduce its potential for food production. The soil will get compacted, the herb layer trampled, and it is not conducive to maximum fruit yield to have children climbing all over fruit trees. But within these limitations there is no reason why at least some food cannot be grown in a shrubbery where children play.

The balance between food and play can be struck wherever it suits the individual family. It could mean a play-shrubbery that contains just a few fruiting trees and shrubs. Any food harvested would most likely go straight into the mouths of the children. Why not? It's an excellent way for them to experience at first hand the relationship between plants and people, something that many children today never experience at all.

At the other end of the spectrum, perhaps with older children or ones who want to take an active part in growing food themselves, there could be areas which they agree not to trample, where a vegetable layer could grow and soft fruit bushes could live in uncompacted soil.

Whatever kind of shrubbery, from pure play space to forest garden, one thing can be reasonably sure – maintaining the shrubbery will be a lot less work than constantly mowing the lawn throughout the summer.

HOME GARDEN OR MARKET GARDEN?

There is an assumption in all the above that a forest garden is a domestic garden, not a commercial one. In fact there does not have to be to be a hard and fast distinction between the two. Many a home gardener sells a bit of surplus on a roadside honesty stall or the local WI market, and often this amounts to a significant supplement to their income. This can apply to a forest gardener as much as any other. But is there a potential for using the principles of the forest garden to produce food as a principal source of income?

The main problem is one of harvesting. The home gardener may be quite happy to spend five or ten minutes wandering through the forest garden, picking a leaf here and bunch of berries there, to come up with enough food for a meal. But commercial growers need to be able to pick large quantities of produce in a reasonably short time. Profit margins on organic market gardening are very low, and a large part of the cost is work time, whether that of paid helpers or the gardeners themselves, and the biggest job is picking and packing the produce.

If you have orders for a dozen boxes of this and five nets of that you need to be able to get your head down and pick a large quantity of each crop at a time, not to have to look here and there amongst trees and bushes for plants which are scattered around amongst other kinds which you have no orders for that day. The amount of diversity that is possible on a market garden is limited by this need for efficient harvesting.

Nevertheless, it may be possible to incorporate some of the principles of forest gardening into a market garden, albeit in a modified way.

No-dig gardening is sometimes practised on a commercial scale, usually on the raised bed method. Long no-dig beds are alternated with narrow paths, with the beds sufficiently narrow that all work can be done when standing on the paths. This means that it is never necessary to tread on the beds, so the soil does not get compacted, thus removing one of the main reasons for digging or ploughing. It is hard to mechanise a garden laid out like this, so all planting, weeding and so on is usually done by hand. A no-dig market garden is hard work, but feasible.

A certain degree of diversity is possible on a commercial scale, though much less than in a home garden. It may be necessary to grow each crop by itself for ease of harvesting and other operations such as sowing or planting out, but the area of each monoculture can be restricted. For example, on a raised bed

Plate 1.5 A raised bed in an organic market garden, showing long narrow beds alternating with paths. Montague Organic Garden, Shepton Montague, Somerset. (PW)

system each bed may contain only one kind of plant, but no two adjacent beds contain the same. A compromise, but certainly an improvement on the wide expanses of a single crop sometimes seen on chemically-grown market gardens.

In fact simple mixtures can work commercially. Two crops may be interplanted on the same bed, if they complement each other rather than compete. Leeks and celeriac is one combination that works, the tall thin plant and the short bushy one using different parts of the three-dimensional space available. Cabbages can be interplanted with lettuces, the quick-growing lettuces being harvested before the cabbages expand to their full size. Both of these combinations will give a higher yield per square metre than one of these crops on its own.

No-dig, diversity and intercropping are ideas used by many gardeners, and are no way unique to forest gardening, though they are very much part of it. If there is one distinguishing mark of a forest garden it is the combination of tree fruit, bush fruit and vegetables on the same piece of land, and this is perhaps getting a bit too complex for commercial growers.

Two-layer systems can be successful. In the nineteenth century rows of soft fruit were often planted between the rows of trees in commercial orchards, and vegetables were grown in commercial hazel plantations. These kinds of combination are rare now, but I have seen a combination of tree fruit and annual vegetables in an organic, no-dig market garden.

One part of the garden has young standard apple trees planted out in it at orchard spacing. I asked the gardener why he had planted them there and he said, "I don't think I'll want to go on doing this for the rest of my life. By the time I'm ready to retire these trees will have grown up and I'll have an orchard instead of a garden." As yet the trees have virtually no effect on the yield of vegetables.

Overall it seems that while there is some scope for market gardeners to move in the direction of forest gardening, this is severely limited by the low prices paid for produce, even when organically grown. To a great extent prices are set by the growers who can produce at the lowest cost. Any growers who adopt methods that increase their labour requirement must pay for it out of profits which are already slim.

Marketing Diversity

Nevertheless, there are two specific markets which could well make use of the vegetable layer of a forest garden without much increasing the cost of harvesting: salad bags, and veggie-box schemes.

A salad bag is a mixture of salad vegetables and herbs of a set value but variable contents. A typical bag may cost say 50p, and contain a mixture of whatever is in season. Growing the plants in a mixture could actually make it easier to fill the bags than having each one growing in a separate block. The fact that all the vegetables are perennials or self-seeders would mean that the work of sowing and planting out is largely eliminated. For salad bags, forest garden-style growing might work out cheaper all round.

Of course salad bags only make use of one layer of a forest garden. The commercial salad bag producer may find it more convenient to grow the tree and shrub layers elsewhere, if at all, and simply grow a bed of mixed, mulched perennial vegetables for the bags. Strictly speaking this is not a forest garden, but it's getting closer to it.

A veggie-box scheme is one of the kinds of marketing setup which comes under the general heading of community farming. It is a way of making a direct connection between growers and consumers, avoiding the cost, waste and excess packaging and transport involved in selling through the supermarkets.

Each customer agrees to buy a box of produce once a week at a standard price. They form themselves into delivery groups of about ten, the growers deliver all the boxes to one member of each group, and the others collect from that person.

The growers have an assured outlet, at something over the wholesale price, while the consumers have a supply of food they can trust at about the same price they would pay for non-organic in the shops. Transport is kept to a minimum and all packaging can be returned. The consumers are usually encouraged to visit the garden or farm to see what is going on there and sometimes social events are organised.

The essence of a box scheme is that the consumers commit themselves to accept a mixture of what is in season, and this can include fruit as well as vegetables. So the mixed nature of a forest garden could be an advantage rather than a disadvantage in filling the boxes.

Neither salad bags nor boxes are usually the only output of a market garden. Nor will either of them be filled entirely with produce from a forest garden, especially the box, as the consumers are likely to want a range of conventional annual vegetables. So it is unlikely that a forest garden would be more than a part of a commercial market garden.

Closing the Circle

Although there may be ways of using the forest garden idea in a commercial setting, doing so will always be something of a compromise. A forest garden is first and foremost a home garden. This is not just because it's difficult to make use of it on a commercial scale; it is also because the fact that the garden is right outside your back door is, ecologically, as important as the style of growing.

All of nature is based on cycles, circular flows of materials through rocks, soil, water, air and living things, driven by the power of the Sun. Only by constantly cycling the elements needed for plant and animal growth can life be sustained indefinitely.

By contrast, our present agriculture is based on linear flows. Plant nutrients, for example, follow a well-defined path from source to sink: they are mined from limited mineral reserves or extracted from the air by processes using a great deal of fossil fuel, transported to farms as chemical fertilisers, transported to us in the food, flushed down the sewers and dumped in the sea, where they become pollutants.

Organic growing replaces much of this linear flow with cycles, but some linear flows remain: fertility may be bought in the form of manure from neighbouring farms; the food is usually consumed far from the place where it is grown; and the sewage still ends up in the sea. Home gardening eliminates all transport, and allows for the return of all the nutrients in the food, by means of composting, directly to the soil that grew that food. It is indefinitely sustainable.

In fact it is an axiom of permaculture, or any truly ecological way of living, that where we do things is at least as important as how we do them.

The Kitchen Window

This applies to the flow of human energy just as much as it does to flows of fossil fuels and plant nutrients. The biggest single factor in the success or failure of any garden is usually the amount of attention it receives. There is an old Chinese proverb which says 'the best manure is the gardener's shadow'. A more recent version of the same idea is the Kitchen Window Principle, which says that the most fertile soil in any garden is that which can be seen from the kitchen window. Nothing makes a garden grow better than giving it the attention it needs when it needs it.

A forest garden does not need a lot of work, but it does need attention. Though it can stand the odd spell of neglect, if it only gets attended to in occasional bursts of energy a few vigorous plants will take over the lower layers and much of the food will go unharvested. It needs someone to wander through it regularly to see how it is getting on, to cut back a rampant plant here, add a little mulch there, pick those tender little leaves or juicy berries before they go past their best. In short it needs someone to inhabit it.

Many of us have not got the space for a forest garden outside our own kitchen windows, and have to

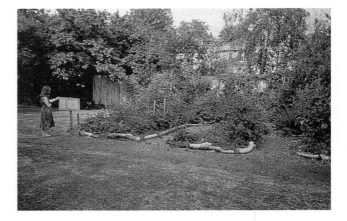

Plate 1.6 The forest garden at the Sutton Ecology Centre in Surrey is looked after by the staff of the centre. It is an educational asset, as well as a productive garden. (Martin Evans)

look at planting one on an allotment, or in a public place such as school grounds or an unused piece of municipal land. A forest garden can succeed in these situations, but only if there is someone, or a number of people, interested in spending regular time there.

This can happen without effort if the garden is at the gardener's workplace, or somewhere along the way to work. Unemployed or retired people may have the time for frequent visits to a forest garden on an allotment or public site. But where attention can most easily be given in large but infrequent instalments, such as on weekends, it may be better to think of another use for the piece of ground in question.

Main crops of potatoes, beans and so on are ideal for allotments which get infrequent visits from their otherwise busy tenants. For public land a traditional orchard is an option worth considering. There are a number of successful community orchards around the country, both old ones reprieved from destruction by local enthusiasm, and newly planted ones.[6] All the work in an orchard can be done in short bursts. Pruning days and picking days can be organised, and many hands make light work.

However if a successful forest garden can be grown in a public place it becomes a demonstration of what can be done. Even a garden grown in a private back yard can be made open to interested visitors. This is what Robert Hart has done, and many people who have visited his garden have been inspired to go home and start planting their own – the first steps towards the fulfilment of Robert's dream of 'mini-forests in millions of back gardens'.

---

6   There is currently a grant from the Countryside Commission for restoring old orchards.

Chapter 2

THE FOREST GARDEN COMMUNITY

The main components of a forest garden:
trees, shrubs and vegetables – their size, shape and structure

THE LAYERS

Although we think of a forest garden as having three layers – trees, shrubs and vegetables – in practice the distinction may not be as clear as that. There are small trees and large shrubs which are much of a muchness, and it may not be possible to say whether an individual plant is a tall member of the shrub layer or a short tree.

Sometimes the difference between a tree and a shrub may be more a matter of how well the plant tolerates shade than of its potential size when mature. For example, it may be more worthwhile to prune a hazel or an elder into a low shape underneath a taller fruit tree than to let them grow up to their full height. Both hazels and elders can grow to the size of a standard apple tree, but they are equally happy as a low spreading bush, and they are also fairly tolerant of shade. If the aim of forest gardening is to grow many layers of food plants on one spot, shade-tolerance is an important quality, not to be wasted on a canopy tree.

The difference between the shrub and vegetable layers is more clear-cut than that between trees and shrubs: shrubs and trees have woody parts, while vegetables and herbs do not. The perennial parts of the vegetables and herbs are their roots. The top growth usually dies down each winter and is renewed each spring, though there are some which remain green all year. (There are a few plants which we think of as herbs which have perennial woody stems, such as rosemary, but strictly speaking these are small shrubs.)

On the whole the herbs are smaller than the shrubs, but there are exceptions to this too. Lovage, for example, can grow more than two metres tall, and in summertime it out-tops most shrubs, and even some of the trees if they are on dwarfing rootstocks.

Our attempts to split the natural world up into neat categories are inevitably a bit artificial. In practice all three layers of a forest garden merge into one another, just as they do in a natural wood.

There is in fact a fourth layer, the vertical one. This consists of plants which occupy all three horizontal layers, including climbers, cane fruit such as raspberries, and trees and shrubs which are trained up walls and fences. Climbers, including grapes, kiwi fruit and roses, are included with the shrubs in this book, except for nasturtiums, which are included with the vegetables.

A Two-Layer Garden

A forest garden without trees sounds like a contradiction in terms. But many people are not able to plant trees on the ground they have available, or do not want to.

Some allotment sites, for example, do not allow trees but do allow fruit bushes. In some urban gardens it may not be possible to plant trees without shading the house, or the neighbour's house or garden. Also, many of us these days move house frequently, and may not feel like leaving a legacy of expensive and carefully tended fruit trees, just about to start bearing, to the doubtful ministrations of the new occupants.

There is no reason why people in these situations should completely deny themselves the joys of forest gardening. Most of the ideas in this book can be put into action quite well in a garden of fruiting shrubs and perennial vegetables. It is not that difficult to take a two-layer garden with you when you move, either. Most perennial vegetables will move quite well, especially if they are dug up when they are not growing actively – autumn and winter for most kinds – and many fruiting shrubs can be propagated from cuttings.

THE TREE LAYER

One of the most important requirements of a tree in a forest garden is that it should not cast too much shade. Very heavy shading trees are not suitable, even if they do produce a useful yield of food. But much can be

Plate 2.1

Plate 2.2

The effects of heavy- and light-shading trees, as seen in a semi-natural woodland. These pictures were taken from the same spot, facing in different directions. Notice the almost bare ground beneath the sycamores (Plate 2.1) compared to the abundant growth of hazel, bracken and other herb-layer plants under the oaks (Plate 2.2). (PW)

done to let light into the lower layers by the overall design of the garden and by adjusting the size and shape of the individual trees.

The size and shape of fruit trees vary enormously: from the standard pear or cherry that is taller than a house, to the little apple on a very dwarfing rootstock; from the spreading, unpruned cider apple tree, to the tightly disciplined cordon tree – a single upright spike with no side branches.

The trees are very much the framework of a forest garden. All the other plants are fitted into this frame-work, which dominates them and is a major influence on the conditions in which they grow.

There are a number of factors which affect the size and shape of fruit trees. The most important ones are:

- the rootstock which it is grafted onto;
- the soil it grows in;
- the variety;
- how it is pruned.

Not all of these factors affect every kind of tree, for ex-ample some trees are grown on their own roots instead of being grafted, and others are often grown unpruned. But all trees are affected by one or more, and most of the fruit trees commonly grown in our climate – apples, pears, plums and cherries – are usually affected by all four.

Rootstocks

Most fruit trees are propagated by grafting a living piece of the desired fruiting variety (the scion) onto the roots and lower stem of another type (the rootstock).

The two fuse together to make a tree which has the fruiting characteristics of the scion and an overall size characteristic of the rootstock (*see Figure 2.1*).

The primary reason for doing this is that most tree fruits do not breed true. If you sowed a seed from a Worcester pearmain apple the resulting tree would not be a Worcester pearmain. It would be a new variety, with some of the characteristics of a Worcester, and some completely different characteristics which might not be at all what you want. This is because the Worcester cannot pollinate itself and has to be pollinated by pollen from a tree of another variety – not just another individual of the same variety.

So the seeds are always a cross-bred, a mixture of the mother tree and the tree which the pollen came from, which must be genetically different from the mother. The only way to ensure that the daughter trees are the same as the mother is by vegetative reproduction, taking a part of the mother plant other than a seed and inducing this to grow. As fruit trees do not take easily from cuttings, the preferred way of doing this is to graft a piece of the required variety onto a specially grown rootstock. There are exceptions to this. Some varieties can pollinate themselves, many plums for ex-ample. But most kinds of tree fruit

*Figure 2.1
A graft*

cannot, and this means that at least two varieties of each fruit must be grown together to ensure pollination. (Pollination is dealt with in detail in Chapter 6, Choosing Plants.)

The second reason for grafting, and the one which directly concerns us here, is that the rootstock has a major influence on the size of the tree. A variety grown on a vigorous rootstock will grow into a bigger tree than the same variety on a dwarfing rootstock. Trees on dwarfing rootstocks also come into fruit sooner in their life than those on vigorous ones, and have a shorter life expectancy.

Dwarf Trees

The advantages of dwarf trees are that:

- you can fit more of them in a given space and thus grow more varieties;
- they produce less fruit per tree, avoiding overproduction of non-keeping kinds of fruit;
- they come into bearing much earlier than more vigorous trees: two or three years for dwarf apples, compared to the five to ten of vigorous trees;
- they are easy to reach for harvesting, pruning etc.

On the other hand, they are delicate things and need a lot of looking after. This particularly applies to apples on the 'very dwarfing' or 'extremely dwarfing' rootstocks, M9 and M27, and to some extent to plums on Pixy. (There are no really dwarfing stocks for other fruits at present.) These little trees:

- need staking all their lives because their roots are brittle;
- are normally grown in a circle of bare soil throughout their lives because they cannot stand competition;
- are short-lived, with a productive life of around 35 years.

If one of the aims of forest gardening is a low-maintenance system where plants largely look after themselves, it is hard to see a place in it for really dwarf trees. It has been suggested that they could form an intermediate layer beneath standard trees and above the shrubs. This is not a very practical idea. For one thing they are not much bigger than many fruiting shrubs; for another they could not survive for long, let alone produce fruit, beneath standard trees. The root competition from bigger trees and the shading would both be too much for them.

However, the advantages of these trees should not be ignored. They have a place in gardens where space is a limiting factor, or on south-facing edges far enough away from other trees to benefit from their shelter, rather than suffer from their competition. But they will always need more care and maintenance than larger trees.

Moderately dwarfing trees, classed as 'dwarfing', 'semi-dwarfing', 'semi-vigorous' and so on are probably the best for most forest gardens, combining some of the advantages of both vigorous and dwarfing trees.

Soil

The less fertile the soil, the smaller the tree will be. So the choice of rootstock must always be balanced with the soil fertility. If you are planting fruit trees on an infertile soil you will need to use more vigorous rootstocks to get the required size of tree than you would on a fertile soil. Indeed the more dwarfing ones will only do well on good soils, and should not be used on infertile ones.

The ideal soil for most kinds of fruit is a deep, well-drained loam, slightly acid at about pH6.5-6.7. But fruit can be grown on a wide range of soils, and to the degree that the soil differs from the ideal the trees will be less vigorous. For example an apple tree will grow less vigorously in either a heavy clay or a light sand than in a medium loam.

Climate also has an effect. Cool or wet conditions reduce the vigour of a tree, and a more vigorous rootstock is needed to compensate.

Variety

The vigour of the scion has an effect on the size of the tree. In most cases the effect is small. Most varieties grown side by side on the same rootstock in the same soil will turn out much the same size, but at the extremes a very vigorous variety could be twice the size of a very weak one.

The choice of variety can also affect the shape of the tree. Pears and plums can vary greatly in shape from one variety to another, some being tall and upright, others low and spreading. Apples generally show less variation in shape.

Pruning

While the combination of rootstock, soil, variety and general growing conditions together determine the potential size of the tree, its actual size and shape is modified by the kind of pruning regime adopted.

The conventional reasons for pruning are:

- to influence the shape and size of the tree;
- to form a strong framework of main branches;

- to remove overcrowded, diseased, broken or dead branches;
- to stimulate the formation of new flower buds or shoots;
- to increase fruit size and saleability.

From a forest gardening perspective we could add:

- to decrease shading of the lower layers.

There are three main approaches to pruning:

1. No pruning at all.
2. Open-grown forms.
3. Restricted forms.

1. No Pruning

Yield
The no-pruning option is usually ignored by fruit experts, though often practised by default in people's back gardens! But it has its advantages. Obviously it reduces work, but more surprisingly it can lead to higher overall yields. A study of bramley apples in the early part of this century found that unpruned trees yielded more than hard-pruned ones: three times as much in the first five years of production, and twice as much in the second five years. Yields of moderately pruned trees fell between the two.

Fruit Quality
So why do commercial growers bother with pruning if they could get higher yields without? Mainly because pruning increases the size of the fruit, by reducing their number. There is a limited market for small-sized fruit, so the yield of *saleable* fruit from a pruned tree is usually greater than that from an unpruned one.

However there are some fruit trees which do not produce larger numbers of smaller fruit when unpruned, and these are the tip-bearing kinds. Fruit trees can be either spur-bearing or tip-bearing (or a mixture of the two). Spur-bearing trees are those which produce fruit on little shoots which grow out of branches two years old or older. Tip-bearing trees produce fruit on the tips of one-year-old branches.

An unpruned spur-bearing tree has virtually no limit on the number of fruiting spurs it can produce, whereas a tip-bearer is restricted to last year's new shoots. So an unpruned spur-bearer will produce masses of fruit, while a tip-bearer will produce fewer, larger fruit.

Spur-bearers produce fruit behind the canopy of leaves rather than out in the sunshine as the tip-bearer does. If this outer canopy is not pruned the fruit of spur-bearers does not get the light it needs to ripen properly. This means the evenness of colouration is impaired, and this too reduces saleability.

Most apple and pear varieties are spur-bearing, but some are tip-bearing. All plums are tip-bearing, and they normally get little pruning once the shape of the tree has been formed during the first three years of growth.

To sum up, if you don't mind having more but smaller fruit, and are not too concerned about colour, spur-bearing varieties can be left unpruned as well as tip-bearing ones. But there are other disadvantages.

Tree Structure
Some of these arise because all the fruit on an unpruned tree is borne near the ends of the branches. As the tree gets older the fruit is borne further from the trunk and from thick branches which will take the weight of a ladder, and so it becomes increasingly difficult to pick it. The tree will probably grow taller than it would do if pruned, requiring a longer ladder, and there will be a thicker mass of twigs and foliage to contend with.

The distance of the fruit from the trunk also means that its weight puts the branches under greater strain. Branches can sag right down to the ground, and even break off. A sagging branch can be propped up with a crutch made from a forked stick or a couple of fencing stakes tied together in an X. After many decades the whole tree may become recumbent, with branches running along the ground for a space before they lift their fruit-filled heads in the air. There are often such trees in old, untended cider orchards. They make wonderful seats and climbing trees for children, and may still yield reasonably well. But they are out of place in a productive woodland garden which has limited space.

Biennial Bearing
Another disadvantage of not pruning is that some trees tend to become biennial, bearing a heavy crop every other year and very little in the intervening ones. Apples are particularly prone to this, though some varieties are more so than others. It comes about because the hormones produced by the fruit have an inhibiting effect on the formation of the fruit buds which will bear the following year's crop, so a really heavy crop in one year can lead to a really light one, or none at all, in the next.

Biennial bearing is the trees' own way of preventing themselves from producing a bumper crop year after year, which would lead to utter exhaustion and early death. By regular pruning we can encourage trees to produce a moderately heavy crop every year, which avoids the need for the tree to rest, and provides us with a yield which is more regular, and probably greater in total. It is much easier to prevent biennial bearing by regular pruning than to cure it once it has set in.

Shading

In our climate light is the main limitation on multi-layer growing, and more light can be let into the shrub and vegetable layers by judicious pruning. If you want to get the maximum yield of food from your forest garden pruning is probably necessary. It may reduce the yield of the canopy layer, but it may enable you to increase the total yield from the garden. On the other hand, if the low-maintenance aspect is more important to you than yield, the no-pruning option is one to be seriously considered.

2. Open-Grown Forms

Otherwise known as unrestricted forms, these are the forms used for free-standing trees. They are normally pruned in winter. They include:

- standard;
- half standard;
- bush;
- dwarf bush;
- spindlebush.

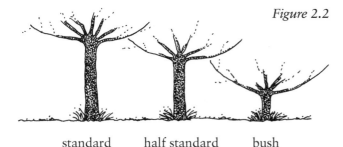

Figure 2.2

standard   half standard   bush

- The **standard** has a clean stem up to 2m tall and a crown of branches pruned with an open centre, or unpruned. It is the traditional orchard tree, originally designed to allow cattle to graze beneath the trees without damaging them. A vigorous rootstock is used, and standard trees are too large for all but the biggest gardens. But where there is room for them they leave plenty of space for large shrubs, such as hazels, beneath them.

    The yield per tree is very high, but the total yield of fruit per square metre may be less than a larger number of smaller trees. They take longer before they start producing fruit than smaller forms, eight to ten years for a standard apple. But the tree is much longer lived – a standard apple can produce fruit for well over a century. Pruning and picking can only be done from a ladder, or with very long-handled equipment. Spraying, which is sometimes done even in organic fruit growing, is very difficult.

- The **half standard** is the same shape as the standard, but the stem is shorter, around 1.2m tall, and the whole tree is smaller in proportion. It has the same characteristics as the standard, somewhat scaled down. Perhaps it was originally designed for an orchard to be grazed only by sheep.

    Being closer to the ground they are somewhat easier to work with than standards, yet there is still enough space beneath them for all but the tallest shrubs. But it is still a largish tree for most back gardens, and choosing this form may restrict the number of trees, and thus varieties, which can be grown.

- The **bush** tree has only 60 to 90cm of clear stem below the branches, which leaves less space for underplanting. But the branches go up at an angle of something like 30 to 45 degrees, so there is space for an understorey of shrubs near the edge of the tree's canopy, with low-growing vegetables nearer the trunk.

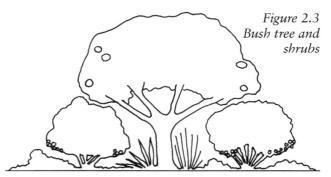

Figure 2.3
Bush tree and shrubs

A bush tree is really just a standard with a short stem. It is the form most often recommended for planting in large gardens, because it is easier to get at for pruning, picking and so on than the standard and half standard. It may start bearing at five to eight years.

- A **dwarf bush** is a bush grown on a dwarfing rootstock. It is the form normally recommended for small gardens.

The **spindlebush** is a conical shaped tree, quite the wrong shape for underplanting, so it need not concern us here.

3. Restricted Forms

These are mostly forms which are grown against a wall or along a specially constructed fence of posts and wires. They are pruned in summer. They include:

- cordon;
- fan;
- espalier;
- dwarf pyramid.

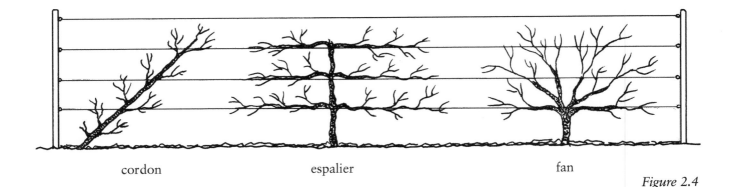

cordon   espalier   fan

Figure 2.4

The two-dimensional forms have their advantages and their drawbacks. On the one hand they:

- allow tender trees to be grown in the favourable microclimate of a sunny wall;

- make excellent use of space in a small garden, generally giving a greater yield per square metre than open-grown trees;

- cast less shade than open-grown trees;

- restrict the size of the tree; this allows trees for which there is no really dwarfing rootstock, e.g. sweet cherries, to be grown in small or medium gardens;

- can look attractive.

On the other hand they:

- yield less per tree, which means more trees must be bought to get the same output;

- need a framework of wires to be trained to, whether they are grown in the open or along a wall;

- need more intensive pruning, and suffer more than unrestricted forms if this is neglected.

Tip bearing varieties are less suitable for restricted forms, and cannot be grown at all as cordons.

- The **cordon** is a single straight stem with fruiting spurs growing directly from it. Sometimes more than one stem is grown, using a more vigorous rootstock, in which case they are grown parallel to each other. Apples and pears are the fruits most commonly grown as cordons.

Cordons are often grown at an angle of 45 degrees. There are two reasons for this. Firstly, a taller stem can be grown up a wall or fence of a given height when grown at an angle than if it was grown vertically. This means that a smaller number of larger plants can cover the same area at the optimum density. Secondly, it increases the number of fruit set by reducing the inhibiting effect of the terminal bud.

This effect, known as apical dominance, is caused by hormones which are passed down the plant by gravity from the terminal bud. The hormones reduce the activity of buds lower down the stem. (Under natural conditions this helps to keep the number of fruit down to a level which the plant has the resources to nourish. But under garden conditions we provide extra nutrients, so the plant can successfully nourish a larger number of fruit.) Reducing the angle of the stem reduces the flow of hormones and thus allows more fruit to be set.

Although cordons can be grown to a great height up the walls of houses, this is difficult, and rarely done. They are usually small plants on moderately dwarfing rootstocks grown in small gardens where space is at a premium. The advantage of cordons is that a greater number of varieties can be grown than with larger forms, and yield per square metre can be very high. The disadvantage is that you need to buy more plants in order to get that yield, so the initial cost is more.

For example, a dwarf bush apple may be 2.5m wide and yield 20-25kg of fruit, while cordons may be planted 75cm apart in a row and yield only 2-3 kg each.

Multi-stemmed cordons are of course larger, and so they reduce the cost per area covered.

Not to be confused with the cordon is the ballerina. Whilst cordons get their shape

Plate 2.3 A young cordon apple tree in blossom. (Andrew Daw)

and size from pruning and rootstock selection, ballerinas are fruiting varieties which are like that genetically. In other words they have been bred to have no side branches other than fruiting spurs and a restricted height. Having said that, some ballerina varieties have turned out to grow on up and up – apparently quite unaware that they are genetically programmed to stop at two or three metres!

We also hear that the fruit doesn't taste that good. There may be some future in this kind of tree, but at present they seem to have more value as a novelty than anything else.

The minaret, which at the time of writing is being marketed as something new, is little more than a vertical cordon.

- The **fan** is grown up a wall or fence with its branches radiating out like the ribs of a fan. This is the restricted form usually used for plums, cherries, peaches, apricots and figs. Apples and pears are rarely grown in a fan. The fan makes a tall tree, so it is better suited to growing up a house wall than a garden fence, unless you can increase the height of the fence with extra trellising.

- The **espalier** has a central stem with pairs of horizontal branches coming out from it at right angles. It is usually used for apples and pears. Espaliers can be grown short or tall to fit the vertical space available, with more tiers of branches on the taller ones than the shorter.

- The **dwarf pyramid** is the only free-standing restricted form. It is too short and the wrong shape to allow a shrub layer to be planted underneath it. Although there may be a chance of fitting the odd one or two somewhere in a forest garden, it is not really a form for a multi-layer system.

Family Trees

It is possible to graft more than one scion onto a single rootstock. This gives a tree which bears fruit of two or more varieties, known as a family tree. They are an alternative to cordons for small gardens where space is limited. One tree can provide a succession of fruit and ensure good pollination.

Although they can be grown in unrestricted forms, they are not a low-maintenance alternative to cordons. A family tree has to be pruned as faithfully and skilfully as a restricted form tree. Some varieties are more vigorous than others, and careful pruning every year is necessary to prevent the more vigorous crowding out and killing the less vigorous.

To some extent this can be countered by choosing varieties with a similar level of vigour. Many off-the-peg family apple trees include a bramley, a very vigorous variety which can eventually crowd out the others altogether, even with careful pruning. This kind of tree should be avoided.

Nurseries which supply family trees will usually make them up with the customer's own choice of varieties, but of course this will involve a wait of a year or two, and is more expensive. Even a family tree from stock may cost twice as much as a similar single-variety tree.

If the varieties are carefully balanced, and the tree is carefully pruned over its first few years, a family tree can survive with less attention once it is mature. The fewer varieties on the tree the more true this is. Two-variety trees can sometimes be seen growing happily in orchards which have not been touched for years. With three or more varieties the tree is more likely to need continuing attention in its later years. But part of the pleasure of growing a family tree can be the satisfaction of successfully growing something which is both unusual and slightly difficult.

The rootstock and scion do not need to be the same species in order to graft together successfully, though they do need to be closely related. So it is possible to have family trees with more than one species on them. Thus we have such oddities as the Fruit and Nut tree, composed of two plums and an almond.[1]

THE SHRUB LAYER

The most commonly grown shrub fruits are known as soft fruit. They are divided into bush fruits, including currants and gooseberries; and cane fruits, including raspberries, blackberries and hybrid berries. The bush fruits are the right shape to fit under the tree layer, while the cane fruits are taller and more vertical in habit and are more suitable for growing alongside the trees.

Figure 2.5

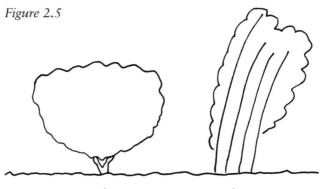

gooseberry   raspberry

---

[1] Supplied by Deacon's Nursery. See List of Suppliers.

Soft fruit are both shorter lived and quicker to start bearing than top fruit. Cane fruits start to bear in the second summer after planting, bush fruits usually in the third year. Most kinds have a productive life of 10-12 years, but gooseberries can go on for 25 years or more.

All soft fruits normally receive regular pruning, for much the same reasons as tree fruits. But if low maintenance is more of a priority than high production it is possible to get away without pruning bush fruits and many hybrid berries. Raspberries and blackberries really do need pruning, though.

There is not the same scope for manipulating the size and shape of the shrubs as there is of the trees. Shrubs are very rarely grafted, so rootstocks do not come into the picture, while the scope for variations in pruning is limited by the growth habit of the shrubs. Getting a range of sizes and shapes in the shrub layer is mostly a matter of choosing a range of different shrub fruits.

Some shrubs, including blackcurrants and raspberries, are multi-stemmed from ground level, and so cannot be trained into a standard, cordon or fan shape. A few, including red and white currants and gooseberries, do have a short length of single stem at the base, and so can be trained as a fan, or even a standard. But they much prefer to remain as bushes, which is their natural shape. Hazels also have a single main stem at ground level, though it branches out very low down and the trees sucker freely from the roots. Fan-trained hazels are possible, though rare, and standards are not normally grown.

Light and Shade

The best way to get an understanding of the light requirements of the shrubs is to look at their natural history.

Edges

Most of the shrubs we can grow in a forest garden are cultivated varieties of plants which grow in the shrub layer of natural woodland. Woodland is their ancestral home, so they have evolved to cope with a certain level of shade. Most of them can survive in quite deep shade but need more light for flowering and fruiting.

Producing flowers and fruit takes energy, much more energy than producing leaves and stems, and

---

COPPICING

If you cut down a broadleaf tree it does not die but regrows from the stump in a multiple stemmed form. It can be cut again after a few years to yield a crop of poles, and this cutting can be repeated at regular intervals of years. The roots continue to grow, but the top growth is kept small by the repeated cutting. This way of working with trees is called coppicing. A woodland treated like this is known as a coppice, and an individual tree as a coppice stool.

Most traditional woods in lowland Britain had a three layer structure consisting of scattered standard trees over coppice with a herb layer beneath (*see Figure 2.6*). Often the coppice layer would consist of trees which would grow to the same height as the standards if not coppiced regularly.

At first sight coppicing might seem like a good way to get large trees to fit into the shrub layer of a forest garden. Sweet chestnut, for example, is a useful nut-producing tree which is much too big for all but the biggest gardens when grown as a standard, and one which is often coppiced for poles. Hazel is another nut-producer which is often coppiced, and is too big for small gardens.

Unfortunately nuts are not produced for a number of years after cutting. In order to keep a chestnut small enough to fit into even a large garden it would be necessary to cut it again before it had started bearing. The same would be true of a hazel in a small or medium sized garden. Thus there would be no nut output from coppiced trees in a woodland garden. There would be a yield of sticks, but this is a low-value product, needing very little care and attention. It is certainly not the kind of thing to grow in an intensive forest garden.

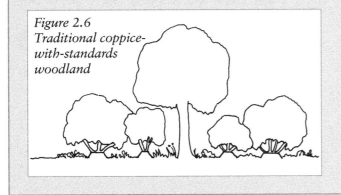

Figure 2.6 Traditional coppice-with-standards woodland

plants can only get energy from sunlight. Insect pollinated shrubs also need a fairly sunny environment at flowering time to encourage the insects, and later in the year at least some direct sunshine is needed to ripen the fruit.

In the wildwood which covered Britain before our ancestors started farming, the shrubs probably spent most of their lives in a vegetative state, growing slowly, not flowering or fruiting, waiting for a gap in the canopy to appear. This would have occurred when an old tree died and thus stopped casting shade, or when one was blown down by the wind. Then the shrubs would have their chance to flower, set seed and reproduce.

An exceptional storm, like the one that struck south-east England in 1987, would have been a boom time for the shrubs. They would have blossomed and set fruit all over the areas where the trees were laid flat by the wind, until the new generation of trees grew up through them and gradually shaded them back into a vegetative state, to wait for their next opportunity.

In the modern landscape woods are little islands in a sea of open country, so a relatively large proportion of each wood is composed of the woodland edge, where sunlight can penetrate from the side as well as from above. Indeed woodland shrubs are often referred to as woodland edge species. This does not mean that they only grow at the edge. They can be found inside the wood, where they make use of the spring sunshine,

before the trees come into leaf, to stay alive and well. But they do not do much in the way of flowering and fruiting, nor do they grow very fast. On the edge of the wood, however, they grow strongly and flower profusely every spring, producing a rich harvest in autumn for all the creatures, including humans, who care to partake.

Succession

If a piece of grassland is left to its own devices and neither grazed nor mown it will regenerate to woodland. Before the trees become dominant it passes through a scrub stage in which all kinds of shrubs can grow and reproduce. Many of the shrubs which are found in scrub, such as gorse and broom, are specialists at colonising open ground, and eventually die out once woodland has re-established. Others, such as brambles and hazel, live in woodland as well as scrub and can live on to become the shrub layer of mature woodland.

Another place we can observe regeneration of woodland is in a coppice wood after cutting. In the first couple of years the woodland wildflowers – the equivalent of the vegetable layer in a forest garden – grow vigorously and flower profusely. Then brambles may take over, and for a few years there can be a heavy blackberry crop. Hazel and other coppiced trees and shrubs grow up through the brambles, and towards the end of the cycle, when it is almost time to cut them again, they will produce a crop of nuts and berries. As each stage in the succession grows it shades the previous one back into a semi-dormant, largely vegetative state.

Forest Gardens

As in natural or semi-natural woods, so in a forest garden, shrubs fruit best either on an edge or in the early years of the garden before the trees grow big. If the garden is to go on producing soft fruit once it is mature it must be designed with plenty of edge to let in light.

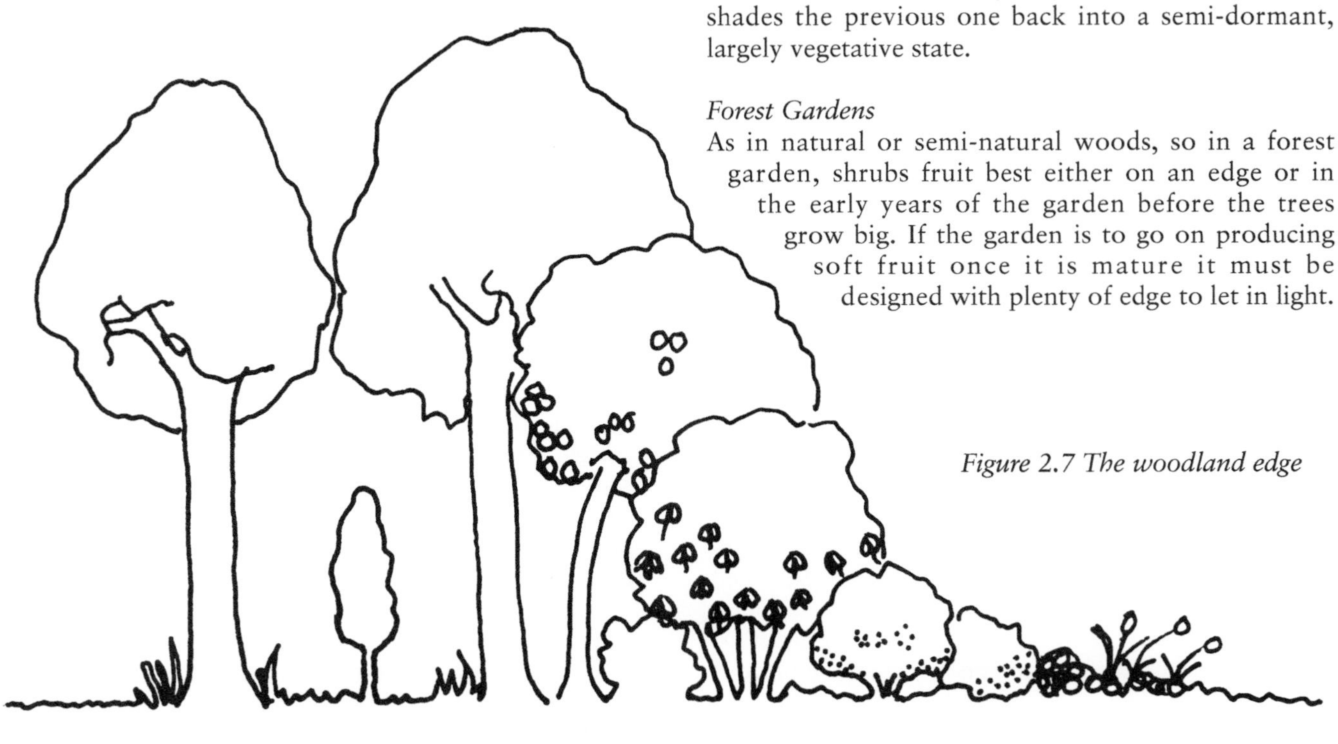

Figure 2.7 The woodland edge

Climbers

The idea that food-producing climbers can be trained up food-producing trees is an attractive one. It would mean that we could increase food production on the patch of ground occupied by the tree, and save ourselves the trouble of constructing a trellis for the climber.

In the tropics this arrangement is common and successful, because light intensity is so great that climbers can do well in the shade of a tree, indeed some actually need that shade. But whether the same can be true here is open to question.

If a grape vine is trained up a standard apple tree the two plants compete for the limited light which is available in our climate. One of the two outgrows the other, and although the weaker partner may survive quite happily, it will not fruit well, if at all.

It should be possible by careful and skilled pruning to keep the two in balance so that they both produce a moderate yield. But would the total yield be more than if they were grown separately? And would it be worth the extra trouble? Pruning a grape which is growing through the crown of an apple tree cannot be very easy.

Some climbers can be grown successfully up standard apple trees, but only as long as the apple is already well grown when the climber is planted. This will mean a wait of at least ten years in most cases. Roses and hops have both been grown like this. Both can stand some shade – which grapes certainly cannot – and both need to be kept to the lower branches of the tree by regular pruning. Once they get up into the crown they will start to rob the tree of light.

It is not the easiest thing in the world to make this relationship work, and the best place for climbers in a forest garden is probably on walls and fences.

THE VEGETABLE LAYER

Perennials

How strictly a forest garden is kept to perennials only is up to the individual gardener. There is really no reason why annual vegetables and flowers should not be grown between the developing trees and shrubs, though once the trees are mature there would be neither the root space nor the light for them.

The two things that distinguish perennials from annuals in the garden are: that the soil is not disturbed each year to grow them, and that they propagate themselves from year to year with little help from us. There is another group of plants which share both of these characteristics – the self-seeders.

Self-Seeders

These are plants which can reproduce themselves by seed. All the gardener needs to do is to allow a few plants to go to seed and to see that there is a suitable soil surface nearby for the seeds to germinate in.

Annual and biennial plants – i.e. those which complete their life-cycles in one or two years respectively – can only reproduce by seed. Those which are able to self-seed, such as bittercress and chard, are suitable for a thorough-going forest garden where no digging, hand-sowing or planting out is done on a regular basis. Some perennials self-seed, for example sorrel and Good King Henry, and a few of the self-sown plants can be allowed to grow on to replace their parents as necessary. (Other perennials normally reproduce by vegetative means, in which some part of the parent plant like a bulb or a root runner becomes detached and forms a new plant.)

Garden plants vary greatly in their ability to self-seed. There are those which never do it, and those which 'once you've got them, you've got them for life', with every shade of difference in between. Most wild food plants are strong self-seeders. But some of the most prolific ones are conventional, if unusual, vegetables, like lamb's lettuce and winter purslane.

Gardening with both self-seeders and perennials is not quite as straightforward as growing only perennials. Some soil needs to be left bare or only lightly mulched for the seeds to germinate in, and where self-seeders can germinate so can unwanted plants. So some weeding is necessary, and also some thinning. If only perennials are grown the whole garden can be kept tightly mulched and life is much simpler. A tightly-mulched perennials-only garden may involve as much work as one containing self-seeders as well, because it probably needs more mulch and that mulch has to be grown or collected from somewhere. But it does not require so much attention.

Self-seeding is also more difficult to maintain over a number of years. It is easy to get a good self-sown stand in the first year after hand-sowing or planting out, but less easy as the years go by. Self-seeding is more a technique for the early years of the garden than for the mature garden with a thick stand of perennial vegetables.

Root Crops

Amongst the range of perennial vegetables which can be grown are a number of roots. But if the forest garden is strictly no-dig surely there is no place for root crops, which by their very nature can only be harvested by digging? The answer really depends on how purist you want to be.

Most roots can be lifted simply by loosening the soil a little with a fork and gently pulling on the stalk or the top of the root. If a bit more disruption than this is caused it is not very different from the kind of digging that goes on in nature, like the little pits a badger digs when foraging for edible roots or making a toilet hole. The natural processes of the soil can live with this amount of disturbance. If the micro-organisms which inhabit that little patch of soil do not survive the disruption, they will soon be replaced by neighbours from the surrounding undisturbed soil. Growing the occasional roots here and there in a no-dig garden is by no means the same thing as digging the whole area each year and laying it bare to Sun, wind and rain.

All this applies to true root crops, that is plants with edible roots which are approximately conical. Plants of which we eat the tubers, like Jerusalem artichokes, cannot be harvested without more general disturbance to the soil, so perhaps there is more of a question mark over these crops in a forest garden.

Herbs, Vegetables, Flowers and Weeds

We do love to categorise things. In our desire to put everything neatly in its pigeon-hole we have made rather rigid distinctions between herbs and vegetables, and between crop plants and weeds. Although categories like this have their uses, accepting them too rigidly can be limiting. We get a fixed idea of what a particular plant is good for – or not good for – and that's that. We miss many opportunities that way.

The difference between herbs and vegetables is really one of quantity. We think of a herb as a plant used in small amounts either as a medicine or for flavouring food, and a vegetable as something we eat as food itself. But all plants we eat affect our health in one way or another, even if not dramatically; they all have their own taste, too, whether it is mild or strong; and they all help to sustain us. It is a difference of degree, not an absolute distinction.

There are a few plants which have a particularly strong medicinal principle and should only be taken in prescribed doses for a specific purpose.[2] But there is no reason why the majority of the plants we commonly call herbs cannot be eaten in belly-filling quantities.

Sometimes in the spring, when there was nothing else fresh to eat in the garden, I have eaten salads composed entirely of balm, mints, sweet cicely, fennel and a few wild leaves such as white and red dead-nettle. They were very good salads too – to my taste more pleasant than the rather blander concoctions we were brought up on. This mixture is just an example, and there are many other herbs which are equally good in a salad. The trick is not to put too much of any one kind in.

The greater the variety the better the taste.

The majority of so-called herbs are perennials while the majority of so-called vegetables are annuals, so it is not surprising that there are more herbs in leaf in the spring, before the annuals have had a chance to grow to pickable size. As perennials they are of course ideal for a forest garden, and many can stand some shade.

In fact it has almost become a convention to call a plant a herb simply *because* it is perennial. Good King Henry and Welsh onion are often found in seed catalogues under Herbs, while spinach and spring onions are listed under Vegetables. But the main difference between these vegetables is that two are perennials and two are annuals.

The boundary between flowers and vegetables is pretty arbitrary, too. Nasturtiums are perhaps the most obvious of the edible plants which are normally confined to the flower bed, though every part of the plant is edible; but there are many others.[3] Some of the plants which are grown primarily for food will produce attractive flowers if left in the ground to maturity, and the effect can be as pretty as many a flower border. This is of course necessary if the plants are going to self-seed.

In a forest garden the distinction between weeds and crop plants is another one which is relative rather than absolute.

Fat hen, bittercress, and dandelion are normally thought of as weeds, while mint, lamb's lettuce and winter purslane are normally thought of as edible garden plants. Yet all of them are edible, and all of them can get out of hand and become invasive. The truth is they are all useful plants when they are present in the quantity we can use, and weeds when they exceed that quantity and start competing with neighbouring plants.

Of course there are some plants for which we have no use at all, such as couch grass, and these are always weeds. They may have their uses. Couch, for example has certain medicinal properties, but the quantities we could use are minuscule compared to the enormous quantities of it which will grow if we let it.

A plant becomes a weed when it outgrows its usefulness to us. (What we mean by useful is up to us. It can include ornamental or wildlife value just as much as food value.) Harvesting becomes weeding when a plant grows faster than we can eat it, and becomes harvesting again when our appetite catches up with the plant's growth.

Light and Shade

Like the shrubs, most woodland herbs can happily produce leaves year after year under a closed canopy, but need more sunlight in order to flower. In the prehistoric wildwood we can assume that they waited

---

2   To the best of my knowledge, none of these is included in this book.

3   For a wide variety of flowers which can be eaten in salads see *The Salad Garden*, under Further Reading.

patiently with the shrubs for a gap to appear in the canopy. When a gap occurred there would be a year or two when the shrubs were still thin and drawn up from their long spell in the twilight. Then the herbs had their chance to flower and set seed, before the shrubs and young trees thickened up and took away the light.

In general the vegetables in a forest garden do not need to flower and set seed. We eat their leaves, or occasionally their stems and roots, not their fruit. As long as they get enough light to grow healthily most plants respond to shade by increasing the size of their leaves.

More light is needed for self-seeding. For the perennials this is relatively unimportant. They do not need to reproduce very often, and many reproduce vegetatively anyway. The annual and biennial vegetables need to self-seed each year, but only a few plants need do so in order to provide enough plants for next year's generation. They may need to be given a less shady spot than the perennials. But some of them, pink purslane for example, will happily self-seed in a wood with a closed canopy.

Mushrooms can be grown in the very darkest parts of a forest garden, because they do not manufacture their own food by means of the Sun's energy, as green plants do; they consume organic matter which has been manufactured by plants. The ones we can grow to eat in a forest garden consume dead plant material. The mushroom itself is only the fruiting body of the fungus, the fungal equivalent of a flowering shoot. The vegetative body is a mass of threads, hidden inside its growing medium, which may be dead wood or the soil. In the soil they seek out the organic matter and play an important part in its decay.

At the other end of the spectrum there are some useful perennial vegetables and herbs which do not tolerate much shade but which we may want to grow in the forest garden. The perennial onions and the aromatic herbs such as thyme and sage are examples. These light-demanding plants will grow best in the same situations as the shrubs: on edges, and in the early stages of the succession.

Succession

When a grassland regenerates to woodland, the coming of shrubs and trees is accompanied by changes at ground level. Most of the grassland plants, including the grasses themselves, are relatively intolerant of shade and soon die out once the shrubs and trees start to form a closed canopy. A few grassland herbs, such as sorrel, can stand shade and may survive into the woodland stage. Some shade-tolerant herbs will colonise the new woodland fairly quickly, but most take a very long time and a new wood usually has a low diversity of herbaceous plants.

When planting a forest garden it is possible to make the most of the changing light conditions and maintain a high diversity of plants throughout the succession. When the trees are still small and cast little shade a mixture of light-demanding and shade tolerant vegetables can be planted. Not many of the shade tolerant ones actually need shade in order to grow well, and most can be planted in full Sun, as long as they are kept reasonably moist. But as the level of shade increases they will tend to do better than the light-demanders, and the latter can be progressively weeded out as they weaken.

Edge

This need not be the end of light-demanding herbs and vegetables in the woodland garden, as they will do very well on the edges. In fact the edge areas, where herbaceous vegetation merges through shrubs into trees, are the most diverse and the most productive of food in both natural woods and forest gardens.

This productivity is in part due to the favourable microclimates created by the diversity of structure. The nearby trees and shrubs can make a sun trap for the herbs in the unshaded areas, buffer them against extremes of temperature, regulate the humidity and protect them from wind. Also, the leaf fall from the woody plants contributes to the soil fertility of the nearby open ground. From an ecological point of view the herbaceous edge is as much a part of the wood as a part of the open country.

So we may think of a forest garden not only as that part of the garden where all three layers grow one above the other, but also as including some edge areas and glades where the Sun reaches right down to the herb layer.

Chapter 3

PUTTING THINGS TOGETHER

The principles of forest garden design –
putting the components together so they work harmoniously
in relation to each other and their environment

THE LAND AND THE PEOPLE

The aim of good landscape design is to meet the needs of both the land and the people. Meeting the needs of the land is not a familiar concept in our culture. We are more familiar with the idea of using the land to meet the needs of the people, rather than considering both as equal partners in a joint venture. But that kind of thinking has led us to the ecological crisis we now face. Where better to start changing our attitude to the land than in our own back gardens?

The Needs of the Land

In most situations planting a forest garden is a benefit to the local ecology: it is much closer to the natural vegetation of this country than most other forms of land use, and fruit trees and perennial vegetables both make good habitat for wildlife. But occasionally the existing vegetation may have even greater value to wild plants and animals.

For example, in rural areas there are still a few remaining herb-rich meadows – semi-natural ecosystems of inestimable value, and quite irreplaceable. Land like this is certainly not a suitable site for any major changes in vegetation, even a forest garden.

Many ordinary gardens have features which are worth preserving. Old trees, for example, are particularly valuable to many kinds of wildlife, especially if they are native species. Hole-nesting birds find old knot-holes and dead branches useful places to excavate a nest; many insects only start to colonise trees when they are old and have a bit of decay about them; and, in areas of low air pollution, there may be lichens, some of which are becoming increasingly rare, which only live on old wood.

It takes many years for a young tree to mature into this ecological richness. Replacing a single old tree with several young ones will usually mean reducing the wildlife value of the garden for decades to come. It may do so permanently if there is no other old tree nearby to act as host while the young trees grow to maturity.

Poorly drained soil is one thing that fruit trees and shrubs cannot stand. If you only have one possible site for your forest garden and it is poorly drained, it may well be worth installing land drains. But if the site is really boggy it may be better to work with that characteristic rather than against it, and create a water garden rather than a forest one. Another factor to seriously consider before growing a forest garden is if there have been fruit trees growing there before (*see Replant Disease, page 26*). Most other kinds of adverse conditions, such as poor climate or exposure to salty coastal winds, can be countered by careful choice of plants and good design.

Having decided that a forest garden is right for the place, there are often choices to be made about the design of the garden which can affect the well-being of the land. It may be possible, for example, to plant the forest garden in such a way as to make it a wildlife corridor between woods, shrubberies or thick hedges on adjacent pieces of land.

Soil erosion is the ultimate degradation of the land, and the design of a garden can do much to keep it to a minimum. Steep slopes should always be covered in robust perennial vegetation to protect the soil from water erosion, and a forest garden is ideal. If annuals are to be grown on a steep slope the ground must be terraced first to prevent soil erosion. If the whole garden is steep a possible solution is to terrace the whole area and grow strips of forest garden along the risers, with annuals on the steps.

Paths which go across the slope rather than up and down it help to reduce soil erosion. Where access is needed up and down steep slopes, steps cause less erosion than a steep path.

It is all a matter of working with the land, of co-operating with it rather than imposing ourselves on it. Every situation is unique, and no hard-and-fast rules can be made. But as a general principle the question to ask is "What is this land offering me?" rather than "What can I do with this land?"

The Needs of the People

As we have seen, there are many different reasons for growing a forest garden, and it is important to be clear right from the start what things you and your family want from it, and what priority you place on each of these. This will have a big effect on the choice of plants and layout.

It is also important to be clear about how much time, energy and money you want to put into the garden. Although it takes little effort to maintain a forest garden, it does take a considerable effort, and some expense, to get one established.

It is easy to get carried away with enthusiasm and design a garden which will yield far more produce than the family can use; or one which contains exotic trees which may produce delicious fruit, but which need a great deal of care and attention if they are to yield reliably.

The best recipe for success is usually to start small, and with plants which are easy to grow. Success breeds success, and it is always possible to expand from a modest start in later years. Starting small also allows

Plate 3.1 Steps give access to the steep south-facing slope of the Naturewise forest garden. (Naturewise)

REPLANT DISEASE

If a young fruit tree is planted where an old tree of the same kind recently grew it very rarely thrives. It may exist in a chronically sick state, making little or no growth year after year, or be given the *coup de grâce* by a relatively mild disorder. This condition is known as replant disease. It is partly due to the buildup of disease organisms in the soil during the life of the old tree: a mature root system can handle a level of pathogens which a young one cannot. It is also caused by chemicals released by the roots of the old tree which inhibit the growth of its own kind (an allelopathic effect – *see pages 34-35*).

Avoiding replant disease is basically a matter of following good crop rotation. Replanting like with like is not recommended for at least 15 years, so if you have moved recently it is worthwhile to check the history of your garden. Replanting with trees from a different group is acceptable, and the relevant groups are:

* Pome fruits, including: apples, pears, medlars.
* Stone fruits, including: plums, cherries, peaches, apricots.

Vigorous rootstocks are no less susceptible, although there is one apple rootstock which is said to be somewhat resistant. This is EMLA7[1], which is moderately dwarfing, somewhere between M26 and MM106 in size (*see page 85*).

In a traditional orchard, on very wide spacings, it can be alright to plant between the previous or existing positions, but not with trees on normal garden spacings.

The last resorts are to grow trees in tubs or to swop the soil with an unaffected area. This should be done to two spits depth over the entire planting area! Commercial growers sterilise the soil with methyl bromide when replanting an orchard on the same site.

Young trees affected by replant disease usually do well if transplanted to a clean site.

---

[1]   Not to be confused with M7 or EMLA7A.
       It is not widely available.

you to use your early experience to make your later plantings even more successful. Although much can be learnt from books they are no substitute for actually doing it.

If you do decide to start small, the initial design must allow for future expansion. It is necessary to have at least some idea of where the rest of the forest garden will go if you decide to expand it later, and to be sure that the new will not interfere with the old, by taking its light for example.

Whole Garden Design

A forest garden cannot be designed in isolation from the rest of the garden. Some people may decide to put all the space available down to forest garden, but most will also want to include other elements, such as a lawn, flowerbeds, annual vegetables and so on. In deciding how much of the garden will be forest, and which part of it, a number of things need to be considered.

One is what you want from the garden. The main produce from a forest garden is fruit and perennial herbs and vegetables. There is obviously no point in growing more of these things than you can use. The amount of work you want to do is another. Once established, a forest garden needs less work than either a lawn or annual vegetables. (The average lawn in this country is mown some thirty times each year.) Aesthetics and space to play and relax are other considerations.

Aesthetics also plays a part in deciding where to put a forest garden. Light and shade is another factor: a forest garden can either cast shade on a lawn, an annual vegetable patch or the house; or it can cradle them in a suntrap. It is also handy to have the forest garden near the kitchen door, so you can easily nip out and pick a few leaves for a lunchtime salad. Other elements in the garden, such as the annual vegetables or ornamentals, may compete for this prime position, but a forest garden should never be tucked far away in an inaccessible corner. It does need attention.

LIGHT AND SHADE

A friend of mine showed me a gooseberry and a currant bush which she had planted under the almost closed canopy of some willow trees, by way of an experiment. They each had a miserable little crop of fruit on them. "Really we should be talking about 'woodland edge gardens' rather than woodland gardens or forest gardens," she said, pointing to a thicket of wild

---

blackthorn spreading out from the edge of a nearby wood, "Look at the production going on over there!"

She was right, of course. Light is the major limiting factor to forest gardening in our climate, and the more edge we can work into our designs the more productive our gardens are likely to be.

This does not mean that a forest garden must be composed entirely of edge, without any area of continuous canopy. But where there is a continuous canopy it must be composed of trees which cast only a light shade, and have some gaps between the crowns of the trees. The kind of fruit trees that are suitable for a forest garden do not cast as much shade as the willows my friend planted under. As for the gaps in the canopy, these will decrease as the trees approach maturity, but they can be maintained by pruning, at least with spur-bearing fruit trees.

Nevertheless, the edges are the most favoured growing position for shrubs, Sun-loving vegetables and tender trees. The direction the edge faces has an effect. Due south obviously gets a lot of light, but a south-westerly aspect gets almost as much, and also tends to be relatively hot as the Sun is warmer in the afternoon than in the morning. A south-easterly aspect should be avoided if there is any danger of frost damage, because a quick thaw in the morning is more damaging to frosted blossom than a slower thaw through the day. A north-facing edge can receive some direct sunlight morning and evening during spring and summer[2], as the Sun rises and sets to the north of the due east-west line during this period. It can also receive indirect light at any time, and is much lighter than places inside the forest garden unless it is overshadowed by other trees or buildings.

Patterns

There are a number of basic patterns for forest gardens which give plenty of edge. These are broad concepts, and they must be adapted to suit the unique conditions of individual sites. On some sites a hybrid of two or more patterns may be the best design. *Note: the illustrations which follow represent design concepts. They are not accurate plans of actual gardens.*

A. In this pattern areas of almost closed canopy alternate with areas with a very open canopy (*see Figure 3.1 Pattern A plan & elevation*).

This is very much the pattern of Robert Hart's forest garden. In the closed canopy areas the shrubs, mainly currants and gooseberries, tend to grow up tall and thin as they try to get to the light. Their yield is moderate. In the more open areas the shrubs tend to grow outwards and use up the available space more

---

2   From the spring equinox till the autumn equinox, 21st March to 21st September.

thoroughly. Here they yield more heavily. In both areas there are vegetables and herbs, some of which grow up to a comparable height to the bush fruit.

One advantage of this pattern is that it is possible to concentrate much of the soft fruit in certain parts of the garden, and where the bushes are grouped together netting them in summer is more of a practical proposition than where they are spread out one by one among the trees.

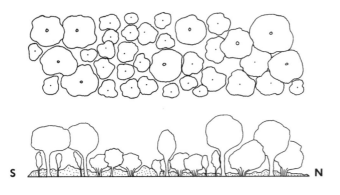

Figure 3.1 Pattern A plan & elevation

B. Robert Hart's garden is comparatively large, at 25m x 11m. Another option for forest gardens of this size or larger is to spread out the trees more evenly over the whole area to give a generally broken canopy.

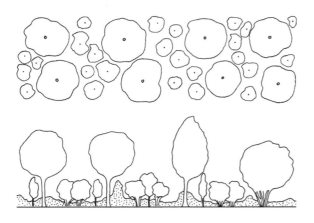

Figure 3.2 Pattern B plan & elevation

C. Many home gardens are long and thin. If the long axis runs approximately east-west the best option may be to plant the forest garden in a strip along the south-facing wall or fence, i.e. the north side of the garden. This leaves a narrow strip to the south for other elements, such as lawn and vegetable or flower beds.

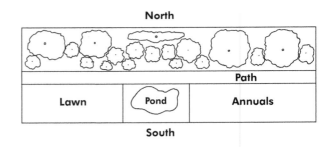

Figure 3.3 Pattern C plan

This pattern allows maximum light to penetrate to all parts of the forest garden, without any shading of the other elements of the garden. It also allows very good access to both the forest garden and vegetable beds, but it does make the lawn a rather impractical shape. When the trees are mature, they will cast some shade on the neighbouring garden to the north, so consultation with the neighbours may be called for before deciding on this kind of design. *See elevation 1:*

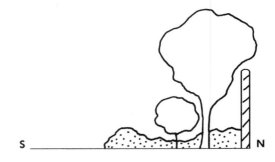

Figure 3.4 Pattern C elevation 1

It can also be used in gardens which are not long and narrow. Obviously this will mean a smaller forest garden, as it will still be thin, but not so long. It may be specially useful if there is a tall, south-facing wall which can be used for growing tender fruits in a fan or espalier form. *See elevation 2:*

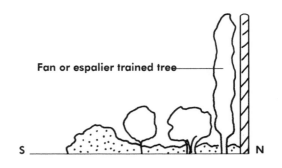

Figure 3.5 Pattern C elevation 2

D. Another option for a narrow garden is to plant a spine down the centre of the garden, with a path on either side and vertical plants by the fences, thus:

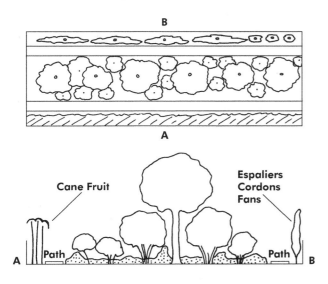

Figure 3.6 Pattern D plan & elevation

This can be used in a garden with any orientation, though if the long axis runs north-south both edges of the garden will benefit from direct sunlight for part of the day. It avoids the problem of shading the neighbours.

E. The woodland glade pattern is an option for gardens which are not so narrow. The tallest trees are planted round the outside of the garden, with the vegetation becoming progressively shorter towards the middle. The forest garden thus forms a suntrap, and the centre of the glade can be used for Sun-loving perennials, annuals, a lawn or even a pond and water garden.

This is another pattern which may shade neighbours' gardens when the trees are mature.

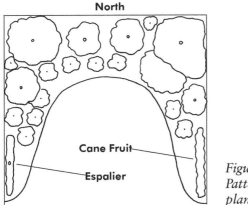

Figure 3.7 Pattern E plan

F. Where space is limited a forest garden can be created around a single tree.

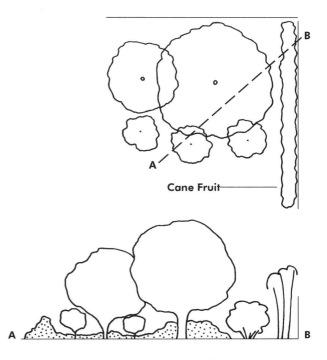

Figure 3.8 Pattern F plan & elevation

The illustration shows a large tree with a dwarf planted beside it, but in very small spaces there may only be space for a single dwarf tree and a couple of shrubs. It is even possible to grow a mini forest garden in a wooden tub, with a single tree, a single shrub and a few herbs. (Very dwarfing rootstocks are not suitable for this. The tub itself causes dwarfing, and a more vigorous stock is more tolerant of the water shortage experienced in a tub. MM106 is suitable for apples.)

G. The best solution for very small spaces is probably to make maximum use of the vertical dimension with cordons, espaliers and fans, leaving the centre open for shrubs and vegetables.

Restricted form trees are sensitive to competition, especially when young, and especially cordons. Vigorous shrubs and vegetables can be too competitive for them, both by root competition and by shading their lower parts. So with this pattern it may be a good idea to leave out the shrubs and any vigorous vegetables for a few years till the trees are well established, and in any case to avoid planting them too close to cordons.

Vertical space is a great asset wherever horizontal space is limited. Wherever you feel crowded by

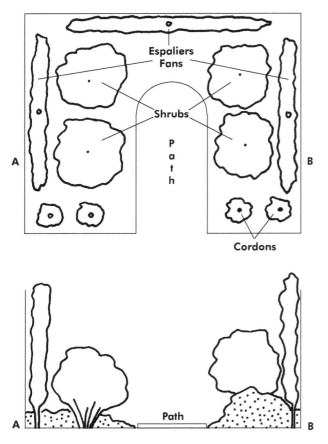

Figure 3.9 Pattern G plan & elevation

buildings, cast your eyes up and see how much wall space there is available for fruit growing. Even north-facing walls can grow fruit if the right kinds are selected.

In the above examples, restricted tree forms – cordons, fans and espaliers – are only shown in positions against walls or fences. But it is also possible to grow them in the open along specially constructed frameworks of vertical posts and horizontal wires. This can be worthwhile where space is limited, as more fruit can be grown on a smaller area. If the 'fences' of trees are aligned north-south, or nearly so, they cast much less shade, and successful shrub and vegetables layers can be grown beneath them.

This gives a very formal garden, far removed from the natural style we associate with forest gardening. It also involves a fair bit of construction work before you start, and more intensive pruning to keep the trees productive. But this style does have its place, particularly in urban settings, where space is often restricted and the formal, geometric appearance harmonises with the heavily built-up landscape.

❀   ❀   ❀

Whichever general pattern is chosen, it needs to be tailored to the conditions of the individual site. The thing most likely to modify the pattern is shade cast onto it by nearby buildings and trees. If possible a sunny site should be chosen for a forest garden. If there is no really sunny area available it may be necessary to cut the garden down from three layers to two, or at least to design a very open structure with plenty of edge, and choose shade-tolerant plants.

As well as shade from outside the garden, plants get shaded by their neighbours. This is pretty obvious with regard to the shrub and vegetable layers, but it also applies to the trees. A light-demanding tree will do better to the south of a big, vigorous neighbour than it will to the north.

ACCESS

Paths
Making use of existing paths saves a great deal of work: both in making new paths and in removing the old ones and rehabilitating the compacted soil under them.

Plate 3.2 A wide, bricked path gives wheelchair access to Simon Phelps' forest garden on his smallholding near Bristol. (Simon Phelps)

A path between the forest garden and a hedge or windbreak is a particularly good idea, because hedging plants are more competitive than food plants, and this strip will not be very productive.

A principle of no-dig gardening is that you never walk on the soil where plants are growing. Soil compaction is one of the things which makes digging necessary, and treading can cause soil compaction. A forest garden needs to be designed so that it is accessible without the need to step onto the growing area. Fortunately many of the patterns which let more sunlight into a garden also give more access to people. Access is really just another kind of edge.

Patterns C, D and E consist of fairly narrow belts of forest garden, much of which can be reached from outside without stepping on the soil of the forest garden itself. In most cases this boundary is a good place to have a major path, giving access both to the forest garden on one hand and whatever adjoins it on the other.

There will still be areas which are out of reach from the main paths, especially in E, the woodland glade pattern. These can be brought within reach by keyhole paths or stepping stones, or a mix of the two.

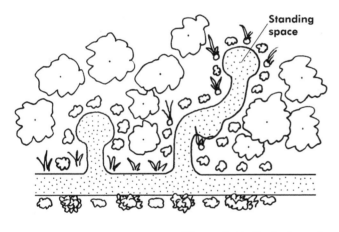

Figure 3.10 Keyhole paths

A keyhole path is a cul-de-sac, ending in a small, circular standing place. A short straight one is much the same shape as the keyhole of a mortice lock. They should be placed so that the plants which need the most frequent attention or harvesting can be reached from the path.

A series of paths which enables you to reach every bit of the garden would take up a high proportion of the total area, and paths can be supplemented with stepping stones. They take up less space than keyhole paths, but they are a bit less comfortable to work from. They are most useful for giving access to plants which need less frequent visits.

Pattern G, the very small garden, can perhaps be served by a single keyhole and a few stepping stones, while F, the single tree, may not need anything more than the occasional stone. In large forest gardens, such as patterns A and B, only a small proportion of the area can be reached from the edge, and these will need a whole network of paths and/or stepping stones.

Fertile topsoil is wasted on a path, so it is a good idea to remove it and add it to the adjacent growing area. This makes sunken paths, and they can fill with water in rainy weather. The design must allow for this water to drain away somewhere. In fact, on poorly drained soils this structure can be a useful aid to drainage. On well drained soils there will be less of a problem with paths filling with water.

Lightly used paths have an extra function on very well drained soils which are prone to drought: the surface of the path, whether slabs, gravel, woodchips or whatever will reduce evaporation from the soil directly beneath and thus make more moisture available to the trees during dry times.

Vertical Access

As well as laying out paths on the ground it is necessary to give some thought to vertical access. If you are planting standard or half standard trees you need to think about where you will place the ladders for picking and pruning. Shrubs must be placed so that you can reach the trees above without damaging the shrubs.

These three-dimensional problems can often be solved by working with the fourth dimension, time. The fruit bushes beneath the tree would be most susceptible to damage when they are in fruit. Since most soft fruits are earlier than most top fruits it should be easy to choose bush fruits which will have finished fruiting before the tree is ready for picking. On a longer timescale, one of years rather than months, a tree on a vigorous rootstock may not even start fruiting till the shrubs are near the end of their productive life.

CO-OPERATION AND COMPETITION

The two soft fruit bushes planted by my friend beneath the willows, as already mentioned, had more to contend with than the shade from the trees. They were also trying to compete with the roots of one of the most competitive of trees, the willow. It was not a good combination of plants.

There is no hard-and-fast distinction between plant combinations which co-operate with each other and those which compete. There is always some degree of competition when two or more plants are living close together and making use of the same resources. There is a continuum all the way from those which positively benefit each other, through those which co-exist quite happily, to those where one plant takes such a large share of the available resources that it kills the other.

The aim of forest garden design is to make the relationships as co-operative as possible, while acknowledging that very few of the plants will yield quite as much as they would if they were living alone. It is the cumulative yield of all the plants living on the same piece of land that makes forest gardens productive, not the high yield of individuals.

Neighbouring Trees

Existing trees on the edge of a forest garden will not only shade it, but the roots will compete for water and plant nutrients. Most other trees are more vigorous than fruit trees, and thus likely to out-compete them. The most competitive kinds are leyland cypress, willow, poplar, ash, garden privet and eucalyptus, and these will deplete the yield of a forest garden planted near them.

It is often assumed that the roots of a tree reach out about the same distance as the branches, but in fact they usually spread further. In a clay soil they may spread half as much again as the canopy, and in a loamy or sandy soil as much as three times as far. Established paths and roads may restrict the root area, because roots will not penetrate compacted soil.

A careful assessment must be made of existing trees. In some cases a choice will have to be made between making the forest garden a little smaller than was first planned, or removing an existing tree or hedge. It is not necessary to have soil totally devoid of other tree roots in order to plant fruit, but the more of them there are the more fertility they will take from the forest garden. If the adjacent trees are retained the most vigorous varieties of fruit trees should be planted nearest them. Extra manuring and watering is only a partial solution, as the non-fruit trees will take the lion's share of the water and plant nutrients – which is what is meant by saying they are more competitive.

Plant Spacing

The plants within the garden have similar relationships. Light and shade has already been considered as a topic on its own, but it is part of the co-operation/competition equation. The other factors to consider are space to grow, and the supply of water and nutrients. All these must be taken into account when deciding how far apart to place the various plants.

In the later chapters on Trees, Shrubs and Vegetables, the normally recommended planting distances for the various plants, or their expected size when mature, is given. These must be taken as a rough guide only. They are for plants grown in a monoculture, or at the very most for a mixture of plants of the same size and growth habit, such as a mixed orchard. The figures must be adapted to suit the very different conditions of a forest garden.

It is not possible to be precise about just how much normal planting distances should be modified in a forest garden. There are so many different possible permutations and combinations of trees, shrubs and vegetables that every forest garden is a one-off. Also there is not the same accumulated experience of forest gardens that there is of orchards and annual vegetables. Maybe in the future, when more forest gardens have grown to maturity, some reliable averages will emerge.

However it is possible to suggest the main ways in which we should modify the recommended spacings to suit conditions in a forest garden.

Trees and Shrubs

Where there is a continuous canopy of fruit trees they should be planted rather further apart than recommended, so as to allow more light to reach the lower layers, as in pattern B (*see page 28*). But note that traditional orchards of standard trees were planted at a wide enough spacing that the canopies of adjacent trees did not meet. This not only allowed plenty of light in for ripening, but reduced root competition between the trees when mature.

The shrubs will tend to grow taller and thinner under a continuous canopy than they would in full Sun. If they are planted at the normally recommended spacing this thinning of the shrub layer should allow enough light to reach the vegetable layer. Alternatively they could be planted closer than normal if no vegetable layer is required in that part of the garden.

It is doubtful whether shrubs should be planted right close under the trees, for three reasons. Firstly there may not be enough height for them unless the trees are grown in a standard or half standard form. Secondly there will be less light there than there will nearer the edge of the tree. Thirdly there is the question of root competition.

Mature fruit trees on vigorous rootstocks can stand a good deal of root competition, but not so young trees. It is normally recommended that they should have their root area kept totally free of other plants for the first four or five years. Very dwarf trees, cultivated hazels and soft fruits are normally grown in bare soil throughout their lives.

To some extent we can take these recommendations as erring on the side of caution, because they are made with a conventional growing system in mind. In an orchard or soft fruit cage the plants most likely to grow around the roots of the trees or shrubs are grasses, and grass is the worst competitor there is for young trees. A ground cover of broad-leaved herbs and vegetables is a much better companion to a young tree.

Nevertheless the most competitive vegetables should be kept away from the immediate root area of young trees, those on very dwarfing rootstocks and cordons.

Mints are the most competitive of the herbs. They are voracious feeders and should be kept well away from any plant which would suffer from excessive competition. Any vegetable which puts on a prestigious amount of growth each year, such as lovage should also be regarded as a keen competitor. Lovage would not fit under any but the tallest fruit trees anyway.

It would certainly be wise to keep soft fruit well away from young fruit trees, ideally by a distance equal to the diameter of the mature soft fruit bush (not the radius).

Plate 3.3 This currant bush has probably been planted too close to the young fruit tree, which is already starting to lean away. (Jane Powell)

Vegetable Layer

The initial spacing of plants in the vegetable layer is not nearly so critical as that of the shrubs and trees because it is much easier to change it in the light of experience. When the garden is mature the vegetables may need to be on a wider spacing than normal, as many of them respond to decreased light intensity by growing larger leaves. But in the early years of the garden they can be planted at their normal spacings.

Experience to date with growing polycultures of vegetables suggests that planting them in drifts is often more successful than mixing individual plants of many different kinds. A drift is a small patch of plants, anything from half a dozen to a hundred individuals, depending on the size of the plants.

Many plants grow in clumps of their own kind in the wild, and they tend to grow best that way. Some woodland herbs can be seen growing wild in almost pure stands (*see Plate 3.4*). Bluebells and ramsons are examples, and where these occur in the same wood they often map out the differences in moisture content in the woodland soil, with bluebells growing on the drier parts and ramsons on the wetter. Other herbaceous plants occur in smaller groups, and relatively few are found dotted around singly among other kinds.

In the garden it is easier to give plants the conditions they like if you can plant out a number of plants of the same size and shape together: if one plant needs 60cm of space and its neighbour needs 5cm, how far apart do you plant them in a mixture? In drifts you can give more of the plants their ideal spacing and only make compromises round the edges of each drift. Planting in drifts also makes it easier to match different plants with the conditions they like: moisture-loving ones in wet spots, Sun-lovers in sunny spots and so on.

Plate 3.4 A pure stand of wood anemones growing in a semi-natural wood in Hampshire.
(Tim Harland)

On the other hand, there are situations where mixtures are appropriate. Short plants growing among tall thin ones and small ones filling in the spaces between larger ones are two ways of making the maximum use of space. A mixture of early- and late-leafing vegetables is a way of making more complete use of time. And if a successful mixture starts to develop by self-seeding it is something to encourage, whether it fits any theory or not.

Roots

The plants in a forest garden are fitted together so that tall, medium and short plants combine to make maximum use of the available resources above ground. It would be ideal if we could do the same thing below ground. The roots could share space in the same way as the above-ground parts, with deep- medium- and shallow-rooted plants grouped together so they made use of the full depth of soil rather than all competing in the same part.

There are two problems with this. Firstly, as roots are so much more difficult to study than the above ground parts of plants, there is not so much information available about them. Secondly, what we do know is that the vast majority of plant roots are found in the same part of the soil, the topsoil. 85% of tree roots are found in the top 60cm of soil, where most of the soil micro-organisms, available nutrients and water are found.

Many plants do have deep roots, but these tend not to be so finely divided, so the total mass of roots in the deeper soil is much less. These roots are mainly for anchorage, though they do contribute to water supply, especially in drought conditions, and to the mining of fresh supplies of plant nutrients from the subsoil.

While all plants make maximum use of the topsoil, the shape and depth of their overall root system varies. So we can assume that a mixture of plants will make more thorough use of the soil than a monoculture. What we cannot assume is that the taller a plant is above ground the deeper its roots are. Herbaceous plants can have deeper roots than trees growing beside them in the same soil. This is especially true of perennials, which have had more time to grow deep roots than annuals. The beet family, many of which are suitable for forest gardening, often have roots which reach deeper than those of neighbouring trees.

Allelopathy

So far we have been looking at interactions between plants in terms of how they share resources, including light, water, plant nutrients and physical space. But there is another way in which plants interact, and that is by producing chemicals which have an effect on other plants.

Strictly speaking allelopathy is the term used to describe all biochemical interactions, both beneficial and detrimental, that occur between different plants. If a plant produces a chemical that has an effect on another plant, the first plant is called allelopathic, or an allelopath. But in practice most of the allelopathic interactions which can be easily recognised are detrimental ones, and the term is commonly used to imply a detrimental effect by the allelopath on its neighbour.

The advantages to a plant of reducing the vigour of its neighbours, which are potential competitors, is clear. Some plants produce allelochemicals which inhibit the growth of their own kind. This discourages recolonisation of the same ground by the same species in the short term, perhaps a natural form of crop rotation. Replant disease is an example of this (*see page 26*).

Walnuts, elders and sages are three forest garden plants which have negative allelopathic effects on other species. The details of these are described under the main entry for each plant, but two general points can be made. Firstly, plants vary greatly in their sensitivity to allelopathic chemicals, so the negative effects can be avoided by choosing suitable neighbours for allelopathic plants. Secondly, negative allelopathy can sometimes be useful in restricting the spread of an invasive plant.

Positive allelopathy, one plant producing a chemical which enhances the growth of another, is much less common. Some allelochemicals can be positive at low concentrations but negative at moderate or high concentrations. But completely beneficial allelochemicals are virtually unheard of.

Many gardeners have an intuitive belief that aromatic herbs are beneficial to the general health of the garden. The intuitions of experienced gardeners are to be respected, but they are hard to corroborate. Gardens, especially forest gardens, are complex places with many different interactions going on simultaneously. It is impossible to ascribe any effect, such as healthy fruit trees, to one specific cause. In theory it should be possible to grow two forest gardens which are identical in all respects except the presence or absence of aromatic herbs, and compare the health of the trees in each. But in practice it would be very hard to make an exact copy of something so intricate as a forest garden.

There is no doubt that many commonly grown herbs are allelopathic. Most of them belong to one of three families: the labiates (including mints, thyme and sage), the umbellifers (including fennel, angelica and lovage) and the daisy family (including chamomile and marigolds). All three families include plants with well known negative allelopathic effects, interfering with the germination or growth of other garden plants. It is quite possible that they also have positive allelopathic effects, but it is more likely that any positive effect is indirect rather than strictly allelopathic, i.e. plant to plant. For example, the chemicals involved in allelopathy are often the same as those which protect the plants from pests and diseases, and they may be able to afford some protection to nearby plants as well as to themselves.

Allelochemicals may be produced in various forms: root secretions, chemicals which are washed from the leaves of plants to the soil, products of decomposition of the dead plant, and volatile chemicals which are released into the atmosphere. The aromatic herbs produce volatile chemicals, and this means they can affect plants, and animals, which are not immediately adjacent to them. If their effects include positive ones as well as the more easily observed negative ones then they could have a significant effect on the health of the garden as a whole.

There are two possible drawbacks to this. Firstly, it may be necessary to plant aromatic herbs in large quantities in order to achieve a significant effect. This could mean planting far more of the herbs than you can consume, which is alright if you have more than enough space in the vegetable layer, but not if you want to grow as much edible produce as space allows. Secondly, aromatic herbs need plenty of sunshine in order to produce their volatile oils, and sunny spots are at a premium in a forest garden. The exceptions to this are the mints, which are happy in the shade, but these are really too competitive to grow in a polyculture.

We are at the very beginning of learning about allelopathic interactions. The amount of time and energy which has been put into studying allelopathy is minuscule compared to the effort that has gone into less subtle ways of helping plants to grow, such as poisoning weeds and pests. We have much to learn, and there are no doubt many beneficial interactions which can be used on a garden scale which are yet to be discovered.

Companion Planting

Positive allelopathy is not the same thing as companion planting. Companion planting is the practice of planting certain combinations of plants together because one or more of them do better when they are growing together than when growing alone. Positive allelopathy is one of the mechanisms by which companion planting may be presumed to work, but only one of them.

Another one is by attracting beneficial insects into the garden, and this is dealt with under Pest and Weed Control in the next chapter, Home-Grown Resources. But many good companions fit together simply because their shapes are complementary, such as when a tall thin plant like garlic is interplanted with a short bushy one

like lettuce. This is good companion planting, and there is nothing mysterious about it. In fact the whole of a forest garden is companion planted. The shapes, annual cycles, and shade tolerance or amount of shade cast by the plants are all carefully matched so that the plants will co-operate rather than compete.

There is a big gap between companion planting theory and practice. A number of books have been written on companion planting lore, but the combinations they recommend do not work reliably in practice. What works in one garden, for one gardener, in one season does not necessarily work in another time and place.

Robert Kourik has made a study of companion planting which is included in his book, *Edible Landscape*.[3] He collected together the results of all the trials which had been done on traditional companion planting combinations and looked at the results. Roughly speaking they were as follows:

- Companion planting reduced pests or increased yields: 8 combinations.

- Companion planting made no difference: 12 combinations.

- Companion planting increased pests or reduced yields: 20 combinations.

In some cases the reduced yield of the main food plant was due to competition from the companion plant. If all the plants in the garden are useful this is no loss to the gardener – the total produce of the garden is what we are interested in, not the yield of individual plants. But many of the companions in Kourik's study were plants which humans can only consume in very small quantities, like catnip and tansy, or not at all, like annual rye-grass and Dutch white clover.

Kourik also lists 67 non-traditional combinations which have been found by experiment to work in various parts of the world. But he makes the point that "this list is just a steppingstone for trial studies in your unique microclimate and ecology." Trials which have been successful in one climatic area have often shown no beneficial effect when repeated elsewhere.

Even this list should not be accepted uncritically. For example, he includes the carrot-onion combination, for controlling carrot root fly, which he says has succeeded in England. Indeed it has, but only when you grow four times as many onions as carrots. It is a possible combination, but only a useful one if you want onions and carrots in those proportions.

Companion planting is certainly a valid idea, but we have only just started to accumulate a usable store of knowledge about it. I am sure that to a great extent it will be recognised as something which each gardener

3   See Further Reading.

has to learn in the context of their own unique garden, rather than something which can be prescribed in books for whole countries or continents.

SUCCESSION

You could get the impression from the patterns on pages 27-30 that a forest garden is static in time, with all the plants reaching their maximum size at the same time and staying like that indefinitely. Of course it is not. Plants grow and develop at different rates. Some live for a hundred years, others for five. A forest garden is not three-dimensional, but four-dimensional, and the fourth dimension is time.

For example, a standard apple tree may not start to bear fruit for ten years after planting, and not reach its full size or yield for many years after that, whereas blackcurrants may be getting to the end of their productive lives after a dozen years. So blackcurrants may be planted close to standard fruit trees even though they would not get the light they need once the trees are mature, because by that time they will be at the end of their productive life anyway.

Most of us will not be planting anything so large and slow to mature as a standard apple, but in any forest garden there will be a variety of quick-and slow-maturing plants with shorter and longer lifespans. This means that the mix of produce from the garden will change from year to year. It also means that the structure of the garden will change, changing the internal microclimate, and this in turn will have an influence on which plants can be grown at different times.

A succession is a pattern in time, and there are three main patterns for the development of a forest garden:

1. **Planting all the layers at once.** This is the closest of the three to a natural succession, in which light-demanding herbs gradually give way to shrubs then to trees and shade-tolerant herbs, as the larger but slower-growing plants become dominant.[4]

   In the first year the edible produce is all herbaceous, mainly from the annual and biennial self-seeders since many perennial vegetables can only be picked lightly if at all in their first year. In the second year most perennial vegetables can be picked and some kinds of soft fruit start to bear. As the trees grow bigger and cast more shade the yield of the lower layers is reduced, and light-demanding vegetables and shrubs may need to be moved out of the heart of the garden onto an edge. How soon the trees start to bear fruit depends very much on which rootstocks have been chosen. So does how soon the

canopy closes. Standard trees planted far apart will take much longer to block out the Sun than dwarf bushes planted closer together, even though they grow at the same rate.

2. **Planting in stages.** Trees first, with shrubs and vegetables a few years later; or trees and shrubs first, followed by vegetables. This is appropriate if you want to defer your full-blown forest garden for a number of years.

   An example is the market gardener who planted apple trees among his annual vegetables with a view to having an orchard for his retirement. When it comes to it he could equally well make it a forest garden, by replacing the annual vegetables with shrubs and perennial vegetables rather than grass and sheep.

   In some cases low maintenance in the early years may be a priority, for example if you don't have much time to spend in it at present but hope to in the future. In that case the space between the trees can be put down to a perennial green manure crop, which can simply be mown a couple of times a year and left as a mulch. The other layers can be introduced at any time that suits you.

3. **Underplanting existing fruit trees.** This will suit a person who wants an instant forest garden and is fortunate enough already to have either an orchard or one or two fruit trees in the back garden. But it would be a mistake to assume that a forest garden established in this way will be static and not change its structure through time.

   Old trees may die or lose branches, letting in more light and so giving opportunities for heavier yields in the lower layers or for growing more light-demanding shrubs and vegetables. Dead trees, or old ones which no longer yield very much, may take on a second career as a ready-made trellis for climbers. In other parts of the garden the amount of shading may increase as trees continue to grow, or shrubs which were planted more recently grow thicker at the expense of the vegetables beneath them.

   The disadvantage of developing a forest garden by underplanting existing trees is that you inherit the existing perennial weeds along with the trees. It is impossible to extract weed roots from the interstices of living tree roots. Couch grass in particular can regenerate from small pieces and in time become a real problem. Starting the garden with a clean sweep of perennial weeds is a great advantage.

---

4   In semi-natural successions the trees usually appear much later than the shrubs. But this is more often because they have been concealed by the faster-growing shrubs than because they have seeded themselves later.

MICROCLIMATE

A microclimate is the climate of a small area. This can mean the climate of an individual garden as opposed to the general climate of that region, or it can mean the climate of a specific part of the garden as opposed to the whole.

The different microclimates within the garden can be used in two ways. The first is to increase the range of plants grown. For example, in many gardens it may not be worthwhile trying to grow a peach in the open, but against a sheltered south-facing wall it may do quite well. The second is to increase the overall yield. Hardy varieties of apple and plum, for example, will yield almost as well in a relatively exposed position as in a sheltered, sunny spot, whereas a more tender pear or gage may handsomely repay you for giving it the most favoured place in the garden.

There are various factors which go to make up a microclimate, and we have already had a detailed look at one of them, light. This is of such importance to forest garden design that it warrants a whole section on its own (*see Light and Shade, page 27*). The other micro-climate factors to consider are:

- wind;
- frost;
- warm south-facing walls;
- water.

Wind

Wind protection is important for fruit production, especially at blossom time. In an exposed site a forest garden may need an overall windbreak. In built up areas strong winds can be expected in a passage between two buildings, and downwind of it. This is because the wind gets funnelled into a narrow gap and has to speed up just as a river does where its bed narrows (*see Figure 3.11*). A small windbreak covering a gap like this can be very valuable.

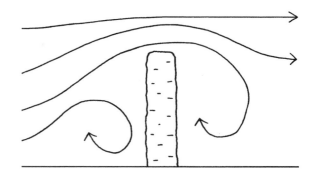

Figure 3.12

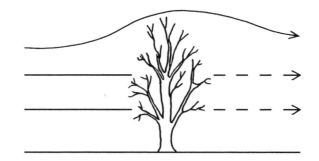

Figure 3.13

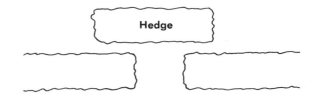

Figure 3.14

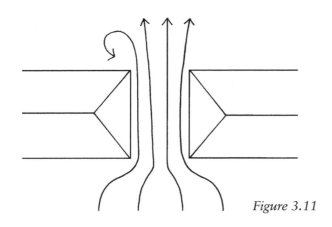

Figure 3.11

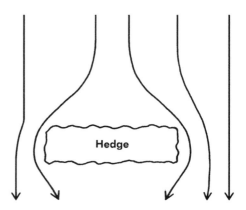

Figure 3.15

A windbreak should always allow some of the wind to pass through it. If it does not it causes eddies which can be more destructive than the unchecked wind would have been in the first place (*see Figure 3.12*).

The ideal windbreak deflects 60% of the wind upwards and allows 40% to pass through (*see Figure 3.13*). If you are planting a living windbreak it is not possible to be this accurate, but the figures give something to aim for. Deciduous hedges and trees, open paling fences, and wire or plastic meshes make good windbreaks. Walls, evergreen hedges or tree belts, and closed paling fences make bad ones.

It can be worthwhile to put up a temporary mesh windbreak while a hedge is growing in its lee. Otherwise you may be faced with the choice between waiting for the hedge to grow up before planting the rest of the garden or exposing the tender young plants to the wind. No plant which is subjected to stress when young will ever give its full potential.

Any gap in a windbreak will speed up the wind, just like the gap between two buildings (*see Figure 3.11*).

Entrance ways must either have a gate or a baffle (*see Figure 3.14*). The wind also speeds up round the end of a windbreak, so it must be longer than the area it is protecting, or surround it completely (*see Figure 3.15*).

The effect of a windbreak steadily decreases as you go away from it. At a distance of five times the height of the windbreak it reduces the wind speed by something like half. There is still a worthwhile effect at a distance of ten times the height, and a measurable one at twenty times.

Windbreaks can have their negative effects too. They can shade the garden, and the roots of windbreak trees can compete with the garden plants. These problems can be minimised where there is enough space to set the windbreak back from the forest garden, with perhaps a wide path or a strip of grass intervening.

Even the windbreak itself takes up space, and in a small garden you may not want to use any space for plants which do not produce food. Here an edible windbreak can be a good idea, as long as the site is not subject to severe winds. The plants in the windbreak will

PLANTS FOR WINDBREAKS

Native Shrubs and Trees
A thick hedge of mixed native species makes a good windbreak for all but the tallest fruit trees. Hawthorn in particular makes a good dense hedge when clipped, and leafs early, so it offers more than twigs to the wind at blossom time. Young plants of 40-60cm size take quickly and grow well. They should be planted in two rows, 60cm apart both between and within the rows with the plants staggered opposite each other.

Beech has the advantage of keeping its leaves through the winter if the hedge is kept clipped to a height of around 2m or less. For very exposed sites the two toughest natives for a windbreak are rowan and birch.

Edible Windbreak Plants
Damson is a good tree to use, tough and twiggy, and so is crab apple. Elder is also wind-hardy, but it can take over a hedge if allowed to grow unchecked. The Siberian pea shrub is doubtfully edible, but certainly a good windbreak plant, even on very exposed sites, and much the same could be said of rowan. The various kinds of *Elaeagnus* are also hardy.

Wind-pollinated trees and shrubs like mulberry and hazel do not need the same protection at flowering time as do most insect-pollinated ones, but they are only marginally more tolerant of wind than insect-pollinated kinds.

As a hedge or windbreak grows it often gets thin and gappy at the base. If this happens the wind will rush through the gaps at the bottom and speed up just as it does when it blows between two buildings. Worcesterberry and ramanas rose are a couple of fruiting shrubs which can be used to thicken up the bottom, and possibly gooseberry where only moderate winds are expected. They should be planted at the same time as the taller plants. When used in a windbreak fruiting plants should be planted closer together than normally, perhaps at half the normal spacing. Blackberry is a fruiting shrub which can fill out the top as well as the bottom of a windbreak.

Coastal Sites
These have the special problem of salt-laden winds, which make it difficult to grow most kinds of fruit. But a good windbreak can make a lot of difference, and one combination which can do well in salty winds is a mixture of elder, hawthorn and ivy. Beach plum, saltbush, *Elaeagnus* and Siberian pea are some edible plants which may be suitable, and gorse is especially useful on nutrient-poor sandy soils. Sea buckthorn (*Hippophae rhamnoides*) is sometimes suggested as an edible windbreak plant for coastal sites, but the fruit is only just edible, and the plant is really too invasive to use safely.

yield less than if they were themselves protected from the wind. But they will yield something, especially in years when the weather is not too rough, so the total food yield of the garden will be greater. On the other hand the plants will almost certainly cost more than ordinary non-fruiting hedge plants, so a fruiting windbreak is probably only worthwhile where space is a limiting factor.

On the majority of sites no overall windbreak is necessary, though the problem of a gap between houses is common. If only gentle winds are experienced, the forest garden itself may act as a windbreak to other elements in the garden. This is especially so if the garden is laid out in the woodland glade or horseshoe pattern.

As well as protecting all or part of the garden with a windbreak, it may be worthwhile to position individual plants within the garden with an eye to the wind. More tender trees like pears and gages can be placed on the lee side of tougher ones like apples. This must be balanced with the plants' needs for sunlight, and the trees which need most shelter from the wind also need most sunlight. As the prevailing wind in this country comes from the south-west, there may be a conflict between the two.

Although the south-west wind is the most frequent, it is relatively warm and not usually the most damaging to plants. The north-east wind, though less frequent, can be bitterly cold. One day of a cold north-easter can do more damage to trees and shrubs than a whole year of south-westerly winds. Which direction the most damaging wind comes from on any particular site is very much a matter of the local topography and nearby buildings and trees.

Frost

The damaging frosts are the spring ones. In the depths of winter the plants are well prepared for frost. But in the spring, when there is every reason to believe that the frosts are over, the trees and shrubs come into blossom. Then even a light frost can be devastating, as most kinds of fruit blossom are killed by it. The tree or shrub rarely suffers permanent damage, but the flowers die and so there is no fruit that year.

The frosts of midwinter are often heavy ones, and every part of the landscape gets frozen. But the spring ones are usually light, and light frosts do not occur uniformly over the landscape. Cold air sinks, so it flows downhill and tends to collect where there is a basin with no way out, just as water ponds up behind a dam. Places where cold air collects can suffer sharp frosts when nearby land which stands a little higher remains frost-free. These places are known as frost pockets.

They can be very small scale, often as little as a couple of metres across and a few centimetres deep, or large scale, covering whole valleys. They also tend to be

remarkably constant, covering exactly the same area each time there is a frost which is not cold enough to freeze up the entire landscape. When there is an overall frost it will be even colder in the frost pocket than elsewhere.

Frost pockets can form where the lie of the land leaves no way out for the frost, such as in a natural basin or narrow valley, or where some obstruction like a wall or thick evergreen hedge runs across the slope. Where a frost pocket is caused by an obstruction across the slope, it can often be enough to make a gap in it, or if it is a hedge simply to thin out the lower branches, to allow the frost to drain away (*see below*).

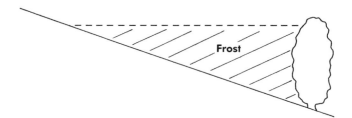

Figure 3.16

Alternatively, frost pockets can be prevented by stopping the downward flow of cold air from above. A single hedge or wall across the slope may be enough to do this if it is tall and impermeable enough (though this is exactly the sort of barrier which is least suitable as a windbreak). A number of cross-slope hedges or other barriers is more likely to be effective, but not many of us have control over that much of the adjacent land.

If neither of these remedies is possible, the frost problem can be avoided by growing taller trees at the bottom of the slope, and keeping dwarf trees and shrubs further uphill. But this does rather limit the possibilities of multi-layer growing.

Wall-trained trees can be covered with an insulating layer of hessian or straw on spring nights when frost is expected. But it is questionable whether this kind of thing is appropriate in a low-maintenance forest garden. Sometimes the heat lost from a poorly insulated house is enough to ward off the first autumn frosts and the last ones in the spring. Frost-tender plants like nasturtiums and lemon balm growing against a house wall often stay green a few weeks longer in autumn than their fellows a couple of metres away. It is sometimes possible to make use of this effect – but it's not sufficient reason for keeping a house badly insulated!

Where all structural means fail, the only option is to grow frost-tolerant fruits, or varieties which are frost-tolerant or late-flowering. In fact this is probably a good idea in any garden which is prone to late frosts, even if something can be done to mitigate the problem by altering the structures. The key to reliable crops and a low maintenance requirement is to match the plants to the existing microclimate.

On the whole the vegetables are less susceptible to frost damage than the trees and shrubs, as they do not need to blossom in order to produce food. But some tender kinds, such as chard, can be killed by hard frosts, so they are more likely to survive the winter outside a frost pocket than within it. Plants which die down in the winter at the onset of the first frost, such as mints, will have a shorter season if growing in a frost pocket.

The structure of the forest garden itself will have some influence on keeping frost off the vegetables. The network of twigs on the trees and shrubs acts somewhat like a blanket; so a spot underneath the canopy may remain frost free on a night when a spot just outside it is frozen.

Warm Walls

Tender plants need to be protected from wind and frost, and given the sunniest positions in the garden. A position on a south-facing wall will give them the additional benefits of heat storage and reflection. Tender fruits may be trained up the wall, and Sun-loving aromatic herbs can be grown at its foot.

The wall need not face due south. Somewhere between south-south-east and west-south-west is suitable for most tender fruits. For the very tenderest plants, such as figs in the south of England or pears in the north of Scotland, a south-facing corner or niche is an ideal place, as the tree gains some benefit from both walls (*see below*).

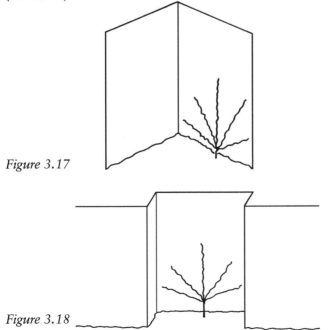

Figure 3.17

Figure 3.18

When the Sun is shining the wall warms up the tree by reflecting light onto it. The wall also stores heat as it warms up during the day and releases it at night or during cool spells, so keeping the tree at a more even temperature.

The reflection of light is greater if the wall is light coloured, whereas the storage of heat is more if it is dark. It can be painted white or black according to which characteristic you want to enhance most. Where late frosts are likely black may be the best bet, especially if you want to save yourself the trouble of covering the trees on spring nights. In other situations white is usually most popular.

If the wall is on a house there is the added benefit of the heat loss from inside – if, like most British houses, it is poorly insulated. But any wall can store heat by virtue of its mass. Broadly speaking, the greater the mass of the wall the more heat it can store, but the longer it will take to heat up. Retaining walls, which have tons of soil and rock at their backs, come at one end of the scale and flimsy garden palings at the other. But the paling will reflect light just as well as the retaining wall, even though its heat storage capacity is negligible.

The soil at the base of a wall is usually drier than in other parts of the garden (*see Water, next page*). This is beneficial to tender plants in the winter. Many of them cannot stand prolonged wet at the roots, especially if a long wet spell follows a hard frost. On the other hand it means more work in the summer, as fruiting plants are most likely to need watering, in addition to heavy mulching.

As well as extra watering, wall-trained trees need more regular and conscientious pruning than free-

---

TREES AND HOUSE FOUNDATIONS

Some people are concerned that planting trees near walls may interfere with the foundations of the building. Fortunately this is not a problem with any of the fruit trees we may be likely to plant in a forest garden. Only big, competitive trees can harm buildings, and then only if they are on a clay soil.

They do the damage by pumping water out of the subsoil so that the clay shrinks. This leaves the foundations unsupported, and they can crack. If an existing tree dies the foundations can be damaged by the clay swelling up with the unaccustomed water. Trees which use a lot of water, like willows and eucalyptus, can be particularly damaging, but fruit trees should pose no problem.

standing ones. If you stop pruning a tree which is trained in a restricted form its yield falls sharply, much more so than with an open-grown tree. A framework of wires must be attached to the wall to train them on, and this will need some regular maintenance. All this extra work must be balanced against the advantages of growing trees up walls: higher yields, the chance to grow more tender fruits, and more intensive use of space.

A similar effect to a south-facing wall can be had off paths, patios and driveways. They too can absorb heat and release it, and reflect light onto trees and shrubs. This is especially so if the tree or shrub is to the north of the paved area, as sunlight will be reflected directly onto it. In this situation it may be worthwhile to paint the tree trunk white to avoid Sun scald. A water based paint rather than an oil-based one should be used (*see below*):

Figure 3.19

Water

The microclimate of the garden can affect the moisture content of both the air and the soil.

Shelter increases air humidity. A sheltered garden is likely to be more humid than an exposed one, and within the garden the forest part is likely to be more humid than other parts. This is beneficial to most of the plants which grow there. The woodland herbs have evolved to grow in relatively humid conditions, and leafy greens, such as the spinaches, may be less prone to running to seed in a humid microclimate. So the woodland structure can reduce the need for watering.

Humidity is actually more important than shade to most woodland herbs. They can tolerate shade, and are therefore able to out-compete light-demanding herbs in a wood, but they don't need it. They do need humidity, though. A good example of this is bluebells, which can be found growing happily in the open in the wetter west of Britain, while in the drier east they are confined to woods.

High air humidity does have its disadvantages too, mainly an increased risk of fungus diseases. This can be a problem in a forest garden where a combination of a sheltered site and dense planting means there is very little air circulation. A combination of good layout and selection of resistant plants and varieties can keep this problem to a minimum.

Variations in the moisture content of the soil from one part of the garden to another are something to take account of when choosing the position of a forest garden or of individual plants. The variations can be due to differences in the soil itself or to impeded drainage. But they are also influenced by microclimate factors, such as the position of buildings and other walls.

The masonry of a wall acts as a wick, which draws water up from the soil and allows it to evaporate into the air. The presence of a damp course does not seem to seriously hinder this process. Even walls which face south-west, directly into the direction where most of the rain comes from, tend to have drier soil at their foot than adjacent open ground. Although they get the most rain they also get the most Sun, so they lose the water more quickly than walls facing in other directions. The soil at the base of north- and east-facing walls hardly receives any rain at all because it is shielded from most of the rain by the wall itself, but it doesn't dry out so quickly if it is watered.

SOIL

Four important characteristics of the soil are:

- its water relations;
- its structure;
- how rich it is in plant nutrients, and how well it can hold onto them;
- how acid or alkaline it is.

Soil Water

A constant supply of water is essential to plant growth, but too much means that air is excluded and roots suffer from lack of oxygen. As well as being a matter of climate and microclimate, the water content is very much influenced by the nature of the soil itself.

A soil with a high proportion of clay in it holds more water than one with a high proportion of sand. Broadly speaking a clay soil is more prone to poor drainage and a sandy one more prone to drought. Loam soils, which have a mixture of clay and sand, are less troubled by either problem, which is why they are ideal for fruit and other crops.

Poor drainage can also occur because of some obstruction to the passage of water through the soil, such as a layer of impervious clay below a loam. In urban areas impeded drainage may be due to a former path, patio or floor, now buried by a depth of soil. This kind of layer in the soil, or one of compacted clay, is a barrier to root penetration as well as drainage, and must be removed or broken up before planting fruit trees.

Fruit trees are particularly sensitive to poor drainage. There is a small range of fruits which can tolerate less than perfect drainage, but only a couple which thrive where it is really poor (*see list on page 75*). On really badly drained land there are only two options: drain it, or grow something else. Underground pipe drains are the most effective, but a network of ditches can do the job. So can a series of mounds with the fruit growing on them, and the vegetables, many of which tolerate wet soil, on the low ground between.

Soils which are too dry are usually easier to deal with. These include light sandy soils and any soil at the base of a wall. If plenty of organic matter is incorporated before planting, good thick mulches are regularly used, and the garden is watered in long dry spells virtually all fruit can be grown. Only the very dwarfing apple rootstocks, M9 and smaller, should be avoided.

Often the driest spot in a garden is a hot, south-facing slope, especially if it is on a freely-draining soil. This would be an ideal spot for tender fruits like peaches, figs, apricots and grapes as regards temperature, but too dry – and probably not a good site at all for a forest garden composed of less heat-loving plants. But there is something which can be done in addition to digging in organic matter and using mulch, and that is to install swales. A swale is a furrow in the ground which does the opposite to a ditch (*see Figure 3.20*). A ditch is deep and narrow, with a fall on it, and is designed to take water away (*see Figure 3.21*). A swale is broad and shallow, running exactly on the contour so that water does not flow in it. It is designed to stop water flowing away and give it a chance to infiltrate the ground.

A series of swales can be dug across the slope so that whatever rain does fall is absorbed into the soil rather than running off. This also prevents soil erosion. The swales need to be big enough to take the heaviest rain that is likely to fall on the site without overflowing. If a swale does overflow, a gully will form at the point of overflow, and this can carry away more soil than would have been eroded if the swales had not been dug in the first place.

Once the forest garden is mature the swales can be allowed to fill up gently by the natural process of siltation, because the dense vegetation of the established garden will do the job instead. But they will continue to be the moistest part of the garden for many years to come, the ideal place to plant things which appreciate extra moisture, such as pears, gages and the annual spinaches.

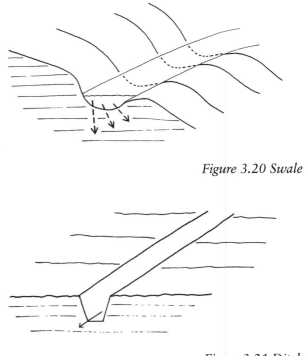

Figure 3.20 Swale

Figure 3.21 Ditch

Structure

Clay soils need good structure more than sandy ones. The clay particles must be aggregated together into crumbs, with pore space between, if a clay soil is to stay sufficiently open to allow the free passage of air, water and plant roots. The opposite to this condition is compaction, where the soil is pressed together in a homogenous mass, and clay soils are much more prone to this than more sandy ones are. A soil may be generally compacted or it may be compacted at a certain depth only, for example where the constant use of a plough or rotovator has smeared the top of the subsoil into what is called a pan.

The best way to improve and maintain soil structure is to add as much organic matter as possible. Ways of relieving soil compaction are discussed in Chapter 5, Preparation, Planting and Maintenance.

Plant Nutrients

Clay soils have more plant nutrients in them than sands, and more capacity to hold on to any plant nutrients which are added in manures. Nutrients can be quickly lost from a sandy soil, especially in wet weather, when the water which flows freely through a sand takes them away. But sandy soils can be improved. Organic matter has at least twice the capacity of clay to hold onto nutrients, so adding plenty of it to a sandy soil can make a real difference.

Excess Lime

Very high alkalinity is a problem for almost all fruits. It can cause chlorosis, which is a yellowing of the shoot tips and the space between veins on the leaves, due to the lockup of iron and manganese by the lime in the soil. This is usually only a problem on thin soils over chalk or limestone. Where there is a good spade's depth of soil or more, chlorosis is much less likely.

Another kind of soil which may be excessively alkaline is one overlying rubble from the demolition of old buildings which were built with lime-wash mortar. Modern builders' rubble is not highly alkaline because modern cement is not soluble once it has set. If in doubt it is worth getting professional advice before planting fruit on thin soils over chalk, limestone or demolished buildings.

Various things can be done to lessen the effect:

- If there is any choice, choose another soil.
- In mild cases, apply masses of organic matter – especially shredded conifers, laurel and rhododendron which are all acid, but any organic matter will help.
- Grow plants which can tolerate high alkalinity (*see page 75*).
- Lower the pH by chemical means – flowers of sulphur or sequestrene. These will need to be applied regularly throughout the life of the forest garden.
- Consider growing another kind of garden.

Soil, Summary

As a general rule, the soils to avoid are extreme ones: loams are better than sands or clays, soils around pH 6.5-6.7 are better than those which are more acid or alkaline, and places prone to waterlogging or excessive drying out are best avoided. Much can be done to improve a soil which is less than ideal, and plants can be chosen which tolerate extreme soil conditions. But where there is a choice between two or more soil types it is a good idea to fit the forest garden to the most suitable soil. This is not necessarily the most fertile soil: a high yield of annual vegetables may be more of a priority for you than a high yield from the forest garden.

Fortunately, most soils are loams, and unless a drainage problem is suspected the relative proportions of sand and clay in the soil need not be of too much concern to a forest garden designer. A high level of organic matter is always beneficial, and it goes a long way towards improving the weaknesses of both clay and sandy soils. It improves the structure of clays, allowing better penetration of air and roots and better drainage, while it improves the water and nutrient holding capacity of sands. Excessive alkalinity is rare, and in relatively mild cases organic matter can help to alleviate this problem too.

MODELS

Designing a forest garden is not a precise art. One day, no doubt, we will have accumulated enough experience to work out some average recommendations for plant spacing, the amount of shade each plant can cope with and so on. But that day is far off.

Trying to calculate how to arrange the plants in a garden on the basis of theoretical knowledge of light levels and requirements is futile. There are too many variables, from the vagaries of the weather, to the ever-changing shade patterns from year to year as the garden grows and matures.

What can be helpful is to observe existing plant communities, not in order to copy them directly but to get a feel for what will work and what will not. As I write, there is only one mature forest garden in Britain, Robert Hart's forest garden in Shropshire. Two-layer plantings – trees over soft fruit or vegetables – are a bit more common, but they are still rare, and not quite the same thing as a full forest garden. The closest model we have in any quantity is probably to be found in semi-natural vegetation – woods and hedgerows – and there is much we can learn from them.

The woods and hedges that can teach you most are ones in the same area as your forest garden site, where climatic conditions are similar. They are also the old, semi-natural ones rather than more recent plantations. Distinguishing between the two is not difficult. Semi-natural woods and hedges tend to have more variety of different trees, shrubs and herbs. The woods usually have trees of all different ages, in contrast to the uniformity of a plantation, and a more complex structure, usually including trees which have been coppiced in the past.

Old hedges which have not been cut for a number of years are very much like woodland edges. It is important to note which direction they face, as this has a big effect on the vegetation. Comparing different hedges and hedgebanks facing different ways can be very revealing.

We cannot hope for precise answers from woods and hedges. They are different from a forest garden in both scale and function, and contain only a few of the edible plants we are interested in growing. But familiarity with woodland can give us a feel for what will work and what will not. It is an intuitive process. Getting to know a number of different woods is useful for comparing the effect of different kinds of woodland structure on the growth of the plants, while observing a single wood through all the seasons, or even better over a number of years, gives a good idea of how woodland changes through time.

Observations made in summer, when the leaves on the canopy trees are fully expanded, are perhaps the most important. In winter or spring it is easy to assume that the sketchy network of twigs overhead will let in at least some light during summer. A visit later in the year can often reveal a surprisingly dense canopy. In order to manufacture food, plants need a greater intensity of light shining on their leaves than we need in order to see clearly, so most of us tend to overestimate the amount of usable light which penetrates a dappled canopy. It is important to bear this in mind when looking at light penetration in a wood.

In fact the best way to find out how much light is penetrating a wood is to see how well the shrubs there are actually flowering and fruiting. Compare the blossom or fruit on shrubs of the same kind growing in both sunny and shady spots. The difference is often much greater than the contrast between light and shade that we can perceive with our eyes.

The vegetable, or herb, layer is not so dependent on the intensity of light reaching it as the shrub layer, because production is not dependent on fruiting. But there can be great contrasts between different times of the year. You may visit a wood in winter which appears to have no herb layer but a carpet of golden saxifrage hugging the ground. Come back in spring and you may find nettles erupting through this carpet. Come back in midsummer and you may be hard put to see any golden saxifrage beneath a chest-high sea of nettles.

Not all woods change this much through the seasons. But becoming familiar with the kind of annual dynamics that are possible in woodland vegetation can help to give a feel of what may go on in a woodland garden.

Another thing to bear in mind is that wild plants can vary greatly from one individual to another. I have picked wild hazels from a hedge which had the same conditions of light, soil and moisture along its length, but ninety-five percent of the nuts came from one bush. They also vary greatly from year to year. The previous season I didn't get a single nut from that hedge, and the year before that there was a moderate crop all along its length.

Although most of the knowledge we can learn from observing woods and hedges is intuitive, it is possible to get some quantifiable information too. My own observations have given me some useful pointers to how much direct and indirect light hazels and elders need in order to yield well (*see pages 99-100 and 106*). But these observations should be used with care. Wild hazels and elders do not necessarily have the same requirements as the cultivated varieties, and oaks and ashes are definitely not the same things as apples and pears.

Nevertheless I am sure that people who spend time in woods and carefully observe what is around them are likely to develop more flair for designing a forest garden than those who do not, whether they learn any specific facts in the woods or not.

Chapter 4

HOME-GROWN RESOURCES

Some extra components to consider at the design stage

By its very nature a forest garden needs less inputs from outside than most other kinds of garden.

Different plants have different nutritional needs, so the diversity of plants in a forest garden makes it less likely that any single plant nutrient will be in short supply. Different plants also specialise in extracting different nutrients from the soil, and their neighbours can benefit from this when they shed their leaves. Leaf fall also helps to supply the soil with the organic matter it needs. Water is used more frugally by a wide diversity of plants than it is by plants which all have a similar growth habit and annual cycle. The microclimate created by the garden reduces evaporation and increases the efficiency of water use. Many pest and disease problems are reduced or eliminated because of the diversity of plants.

If the low-maintenance aspect of forest gardening is more important to you than high production, then the garden can get by with very little in the way of inputs. But production is potentially very high, and if this potential is to be realised some inputs will be necessary to balance what is coming out.

One of the principles of forest gardening is to produce as many of the inputs as possible at home. But this is an ideal, and it is not always possible, or even desirable, to be totally self-sufficient. In the early stages of development, it will probably be necessary to bring in bulk manures, mulch materials and, of course, plants. If you want to get a high level of production from a small garden, it may be necessary to go on importing some of these things when the garden is mature.

This is not necessarily unsustainable. Throughout history intensively cultivated areas have usually been net importers of fertility from the wider landscape. The point is to use home-grown resources as a first choice, local ones second, and things brought from far off only as a last resort. This contrasts with most present day gardening and farming, where materials are brought from the other side of the Earth as routine.

Using coir-based compost, produced from coconut trees which grow on Pacific islands, may be an improvement on destroying peat bogs, but only just.

As well as being local, home-grown resources are usually biological resources. This means we are using a plant or animal to fulfil a need, in preference to a chemical or mechanical resource. Biological resources tend to be most efficient if we use a living plant or animal rather than a dead one.

For example, growing a hedge for a windbreak rather than erecting a plastic mesh saves the energy and pollution cost of producing the plastic. But the hedge also has a lower ecological cost than a wooden paling, brought from afar at a high cost in energy and treated with chemical preservatives. Living biological resources, like a hedge, usually replace themselves free of charge. This makes them cheaper in the long run, though they sometimes cost more to set up in the first place.

Four kinds of resource needed by a forest garden which may be produced at home are:

* plant nutrients;
* organic matter;
* water;
* means of controlling pests and weeds.

PLANT NUTRIENTS

Nitrogen, phosphorous and potassium are the three mineral nutrients needed in greatest quantity by plants. There are another fifteen elements which are needed in varying quantities, and all are essential for healthy plant growth. They can be brought into the garden in manures, but they can also be accumulated within the garden by growing certain plants.

Nitrogen is unique in that it is stored in the air, and needs to be constantly reintroduced to the soil, while the others are stored in the soil.[1] This means that the biological mechanisms for making nitrogen available to plants is different from that for other nutrients. We talk of 'fixing' nitrogen and 'accumulating' the others.

Nitrogen Fixers

Certain soil-living bacteria have the ability to take nitrogen from the air and incorporate it in their bodies. Some of these bacteria are free-living in the soil. Others live in a close relationship with certain plants, in which the plant provides the bacteria with energy and the bacteria supply the plant with nitrogen. The bacteria live in little nodules on the plant roots. When the bacteria die the nodules become detached from the plant and decompose in the soil, right beside the roots, which can then absorb the nitrogen.

Most members of the legume family have this relationship with nitrogen-fixing bacteria. The legumes include clovers, peas, beans, a number of shrubs and many trees – though none of the trees is native to Britain. Very few of the legumes, herbaceous or woody, tolerate shade, and they usually die out as succession proceeds. Non-legumes which fix nitrogen include the alder tree and *Elaeagnus*.

Other plants can benefit from the nitrogen fixed by these plants in two ways:

- By absorbing the nitrogen directly from the nodules in the soil. This only happens on a significant scale when some of the legume's roots die, otherwise the legume itself gets the lion's share of the nitrogen. Roots may die when the plant suffers some trauma, such as defoliation by a grazing animal or an increase in shading.

- By benefiting from the extra nitrogen in the legume's body when it dies or when it sheds its leaves, and these are decomposed in the soil. The neighbouring plants stand to gain most if the legume is prevented from setting seed, because by the end of the growing season 90% of the nitrogen fixed in its root nodules ends up in the seed. Only 10% of the total is left in either the plant body or the soil.

Thus a legume which lives out its life without a setback and produces a good crop of seed each year will only provide a little nitrogen for its neighbours. In order to benefit them significantly its growth must be checked in some way. This is what happens when sheep or cattle graze a pasture of mixed grass and clover, or when a gardener digs in a green manure crop.

Each kind of legume only plays host to certain strains of bacteria, and if none of the right strains are present in the soil no nitrogen will be fixed as a result of planting a legume there. If a species of legume has not been grown in the garden for a number of years its particular strains of bacteria may not be there. Inoculants can be bought for most of the commonly grown legumes, and these can be used to make sure the right bacteria are in the soil. For native plants, a little soil taken from a place where they are already growing will do as well. Exotic legumes, such as Siberian pea, usually have native counterparts which play host to the same strains of bacteria, and soil from these native plants can be used as an inoculant (*see box on opposite page*).

To test whether a legume is actively fixing nitrogen, a small portion of root can be dug up and examined for nodules. These are tiny round blobs, not much bigger than a pin head, and if they are there then the bacteria are there.

The non-leguminous nitrogen-fixers have a different kind of bacteria in their root nodules. These bacteria are not so choosy, and each strain will associate with a much wider range of plants including natives and non-natives. Inoculation is not really necessary, but to be absolutely sure a little soil from a place where alder trees grow should be an adequate inoculant for any of these plants.

There are really three options for using nitrogen-fixing plants in a forest garden:

1. **Trees and shrubs growing in the forest garden.**
   The first option is best for big forest gardens where there is plenty of space, and the fruit trees are mainly longer-lived ones on vigorous rootstocks. Nitrogen-fixing trees and shrubs can be planted in the gaps between the young fruit trees, coppiced for a few years, then removed as the fruit trees grow and take up the space available for them.

   In the first few years the nitrogen-fixers will contribute nitrogen mainly from leaf fall. As their roots grow and intermingle with those of the edible plants there will be some nitrogen supplied directly from the nodules, but this will only become substantial once coppicing starts, perhaps three to five years after planting.

   In smaller gardens, with trees on more dwarfing rootstocks planted closer together, there may not be enough space for legume trees between the young fruit trees. The difference between the size of the fruit trees at planting and their mature size is less, so the gaps between them are smaller. In a small garden there is also more incentive to make every plant a food

---

[1]   This is true in temperate parts of the world, but in tropical parts most of the nutrients are held in the biomass, the bodies of plants and animals.

NITROGEN FIXERS FOR FOREST GARDENS

Trees

Alder (*Alnus glutinosa*) is a native, non-leguminous tree. It is hardy in all areas, tolerates a wide range of soils, grows quickly when young and regrows well when coppiced. The leaves are rich in nutrients, though the wood is not very useful, being neither durable nor very good firewood. It is a late leafer and does not start to cast shade till the second half of May, which is an advantage in a forest garden. It prefers a moist soil, and in really dry soils the Italian alder (*A. cordata*) is more suitable.

The amount of space needed for each plant is variable, since they can be coppiced more or less often to control the size. Coppicing should be done in winter, at an interval of anything from one to five years according to the size wanted and the condition of the plant. The stools may need to be grubbed up when the time comes to remove them, although intensive cutting plus the shade of the surrounding trees may be enough to kill them off.

The black locust or false acacia (*Robinia pseudoacacia*) is a legume from North America which has long been grown here as an ornamental tree. It grows well on dry sandy soils, and produces durable timber and bee forage, but it has the disadvantage of producing suckers (*see Figure 4.1*) This means that if you tried to coppice it it would throw up a whole lot of new shoots from the roots. These could come up all over the place and be a real pest in the garden. It is host to the same strains of bacteria as broom, and possibly gorse.

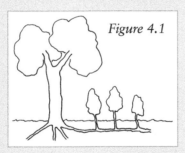

Figure 4.1

The honey locust (*Gleditsia triacanthos*) is a legume which will grow in Britain, but it is one which does not fix nitrogen. It deserves mention simply because it has sometimes been planted under the misapprehension that it does.

The Siberian pea tree (*Caragana arborescens*) is a multi-purpose plant: ornamental, edible and hardy enough to be used in a windbreak. Fixing nitrogen may be seen as a bonus on top of its other outputs. The appropriate inoculant is not available in this country at present, though it is in North America. It is host to the same bacteria as the clovers (*see also page 94*).

Shrubs

Elaeagnus spp. are a group of non-leguminous nitrogen fixing shrubs. They also have edible fruit and most are shade tolerant (*see also page 110*).

Gorse (*Ulex europaeus*) and broom (*Cytisus scoparius*) are found throughout Britain and much of Europe. Both need well drained soils. Broom is acid-loving and will not tolerate a pH over 6.5, but gorse is not fussy about pH. Gorse is spiny and extremely tough. It can be used as a hedging plant in windy situations, including coastal areas. Broom is not spiny and can be killed by very extreme frosts, but it regenerates easily from seed. Neither stands much shade and as the forest garden matures they will naturally weaken and give place to the growing fruit trees.

They are both very decorative shrubs. There is no month in the year when gorse is not flowering, and there are cultivated varieties of broom with delightful fiery-coloured flowers, as well as the natural bright yellow. They are good wildlife plants, and like all legumes they provide fodder for bees. A good wine can also be made from the flowers of gorse.

Herbaceous Legumes

Perennial clovers (*Trifolium* spp.) can be grown in the vegetable layer of a newly established forest garden. White clover (*T. repens*) is a good choice. It is a short, mat-forming plant, which means it can suppress emerging weeds without competing too strongly with the established vegetables. Even so it will need cutting back occasionally until the light level decreases as the trees and shrubs grow up. Alsike (*T. hybridum*) is an alternative for cold sites with wet or acid soils.

Lucerne or alfalfa (*Medicago sativa*) is the most productive of the herbaceous legumes. It is most suitable for growing outside the forest garden in a fertility patch. It is a vigorous and long-lived perennial, with extremely deep roots, which make it resistant to drought and enable it to forage for mineral nutrients in a great volume of soil. It does not like very wet conditions, especially on a heavy soil. It is usually inoculated when grown in a garden for the first time.

Clover and lucerne seeds are listed under Green Manures in garden seed catalogues. They are normally established by sowing direct into the ground, but if there is any difficulty with establishment they can be raised in pots and planted out.

plant. It may be more worthwhile to plant short-lived food plants in any temporary gaps between immature trees than to put nitrogen-fixers there.

2. **Herbaceous legumes growing in the forest garden.** Much the same can be done with herbaceous legumes. They can be planted as part of the initial vegetable layer, and allowed to die out as shade levels increase. The legumes must be regularly cut in the early years, or they will crowd out the other herbaceous plants. If some legumes survive into the later, shadier years they will continue to provide a little nitrogen. They may not need to be cut in order to release nitrogen: the increase in shade as the mature canopy leafs up each year will cause some dieback in the above-ground parts of the legumes, and some of the roots will die back to balance the plant.

Both these options yield more nitrogen in the early years than later on. As leafy vegetables need more nitrogen than fruits, this fits well with a succession in which the vegetable layer gives way to shrubs and trees as the level of shade increases. Young trees need a good supply of nitrogen for growth, but too much can delay cropping.

3. **Herbaceous legumes growing nearby in a fertility patch.** Once a forest garden is mature, the best way to supply it with home-grown nitrogen is to grow herbaceous legumes nearby and cut them for use as mulch in the garden. Even in the early stages this is probably the most productive way to grow legumes, but it is more labour intensive than growing them in situ (*see box, this page*).

Dynamic Accumulators

Most soils contain enough plant nutrients, apart from nitrogen, to grow heavy crops for thousands of years, but the nutrients are held in forms which are relatively unavailable to plants. There are some plants which are particularly good at extracting nutrients in less available forms from the soil. When they die and decompose the nutrients contained in them become available to other plants.

They are known as dynamic accumulators, and different ones specialise in different nutrients.

Comfrey is the foremost of dynamic accumulators. It has a long tap root which can forage in the subsoil for new supplies of its favourite nutrient, potassium, which it accumulates in large quantities. It also accumulates other nutrients and has a very high nitrogen content – with a correspondingly high appetite for nitrogen in the soil (*see page 121*).

Some of the best accumulators of phosphorous are the legumes. So a mixed planting of comfrey and a perennial legume can make the basis of a good nutritious mulch or compost, containing high levels of the three major nutrients. If the two plants are grown close together and cut regularly the legume can also contribute towards the comfrey's high nitrogen requirements. Legumes, especially lucerne, also accumulate calcium, which is important particularly on acid soils.

Many other nutrients are needed as well as these three, and there are plants which specialise in accumulating them. But it is probably not worth including specific plants in the mix to provide the minor nutrients. As long

---

GROWING A FERTILITY PATCH [2]

A fertility patch of comfrey and lucerne can be laid out in rows, with one row of comfrey to every three rows of lucerne. 25cm should be left between the rows of lucerne and 30cm either side of the comfrey, with the comfrey at 45cm apart within the row. The lucerne should be sown thinly at any time after the first of May. It is slow to establish, and the comfrey should be planted a little later to give the lucerne a head start. Grass is the main competitor, and it must be controlled during the first year when the plants are getting established; the first cut gives an opportunity to hoe between the rows, alternatively a mulch can be used.

The first cut, in both the first and subsequent years, is best taken when the lucerne is at the quarter-flower stage – an obvious scattering of blue across the stand – normally in June. Once the plants are well established, usually from their second year, they can be cut three times a year, or four in a good season in the south of England. No cuts should be taken in the autumn, so the plants can build up their roots for the winter. The last cut can be in the third week in August in the south, but earlier further north.

On a light soil it is possible to rotate the fertility patch around the garden, because the comfrey can be dug out, albeit with great labour. On a heavier clay soil this is pretty well impossible, and the lucerne will eventually die out as it is not as long-lived as comfrey. It should be replaced with a non-legume, such as chicory or cocksfoot grass for a couple of years, as legumes do not do well after other legumes. Then lucerne can be re-established.

---

2   This description is based on the work of Nic Pawson of Exmouth, who has pioneered the technique on his allotment.

as a wide variety of other plants are included there should be no deficiency problems. As a general rule wild plants are better accumulators than cultivated ones, and deep-rooted plants are often particularly good. Chicory, dandelion, nettles and yarrow are useful, but there are many others.

Comfrey can be grown inside a forest garden in the early stages of succession just as legumes can, and it can survive a moderate shade, though it prefers full Sun. Another alternative is to grow a fertility patch of comfrey and legume outside the forest garden, and cut it for compost or mulch. This may sound a bit laborious, but regular mulching is a normal part of forest garden maintenance and having some of that mulch material growing nearby will save work, not increase it.

In most gardens the space required for a fertility patch is likely to be more limiting than the labour. On a poor sandy soil the comfrey and legume patch will need to be something like one third the area of the forest garden it is manuring, i.e. one square metre of fertility patch to three of forest garden. (If it is used to manure annual vegetables it may need to be half the area of the vegetable patch, i.e. one to two.) On a rich clay soil half this area would be more than enough.

Whether you choose to devote some land to this will depend on a number of factors, including:

- how keen you are to get a high yield from the garden;
- whether the soil is inherently high in nutrients or not, i.e. clay or sand;
- how much land you have overall, and what other elements you want to fit in;
- whether you have another source of nutrients nearby;
- whether you actually mind bringing in nutrients from far away.

Compost Toilets

The other main source of plant nutrients available at home is what we flush down the toilet. This is not just a terrible waste of resources, it turns those resources into a pollutant.

Many of us feel a bit uneasy about the idea of using human manure on the garden. But a great deal of work has been done on compost toilets, by the Centre for Alternative Technology among others. Their booklet, *Fertile Waste*[3] tells you all you need to know about constructing and managing a compost toilet. The whole process can be perfectly safe if you follow the instructions.

The risk of any disease-causing organisms surviving the composting process is negligible. Nevertheless it is

usually recommended that the compost should not be used on vegetables which are to be eaten raw. This could make it difficult to use it at all in a forest garden with an extensive and diverse vegetable layer. An alternative would be to use it to manure a fertility patch – applied as a mulch 8cm thick – or on a plot of bulk mulch material, and thus keep it at one remove from the edible plants.

A well-designed compost toilet is completely smell-free, and the privy can be placed near the house or built onto it.

MULCH MATERIAL

Comfrey and lucerne both produce large quantities of organic matter compared to most other plants, but they both decompose quite rapidly, especially comfrey. This is an advantage for feeding the soil, but not for a mulch whose main function is to suppress weeds, reduce evaporation and protect the soil: the longer such a mulch lasts the better, so materials which decompose more slowly are needed.

A thick mulch of this kind, covering all the ground between the individual plants, may be needed in a garden where there are perennial weeds to be suppressed. This can take a lot of material. If straw is used, as much as half a tonne a year may have to be bought in to mulch a garden of 10 x 25m.

This would be an extreme case, but even light mulching will require more organic matter than most gardens can provide. So an area of the garden devoted to the bulk production of organic matter, regardless of its nutrient content, is worthwhile if space allows.

The most productive ecosystems on Earth in terms of organic dry matter produced per square metre are kelp 'forests' in certain shallow seas. Second only to these are semi-aquatic ecosystems. In tropical climates this means mangrove swamps; here it means reedbeds. Growing a mini-reedbed in your back garden can give you a greater supply of mulch material per square metre than any other kind of planting.

Of course these semi-aquatic plants will only yield to the full if they get plenty of water. Fortunately we all have a supply of suitable water in our houses, one which we presently pour down the drain. It's called grey water, and it includes all water which has been used in the house, other than that which has been used to flush the toilet. It can be diverted into a suitably designed reedbed in the garden, where it will be purified by the bacteria living on the roots of the reeds, and give you a bigger yield of mulch material than you could get by any other means.

Various aquatic plants can be used, but the most productive is probably the common reed (*Phragmites australis* or *communis*). This is like a huge grass, over

---

[3]   See Further Reading.

2m tall when fully grown, with a large, feather-like flower at the top. It spreads by underground rhizomes, so it is a good idea to contain a reedbed within a low underground wall. This will also prevent the grey water from spreading where it may not be wanted.

Professional advice should be taken before designing a reedbed, especially where space is restricted. It is necessary to calculate the likely yield of grey water, the space available for the reedbed, the probable yield of reeds and so on. Soil type, plumbing and other structures also need to be taken into account. It is by no means a forgone conclusion that a reedbed is the best solution for every site.

Where plenty of space is available, as in a large rural garden or smallholding, it may be possible simply to drain the grey water away to a suitable low-lying area, plant the reeds, and see what happens. But they should not be planted near any existing aquatic or semi-aquatic vegetation of any value because they may invade it and take over completely.

Producing mulch from grey water is turning a problem into a solution. What was a burden on the local sewage works has been transformed into an abundant supply of organic material.

WATER

Grey Water

In addition to using it to produce mulch material, grey water can be used to water the food plants themselves. It is best not to apply it direct to vegetables, especially salads, because of the risk of infection – though this risk is small. It can be applied underground through a series of perforated pipes, and this is successful in annual gardens, but in a forest garden the pipes would probably get clogged in time by the roots of the perennials. It can be applied to the base of fruit trees and shrubs where there is no vegetable layer, or at least where there are no salad vegetables.

Wherever grey water is used, it must not contain chemicals which could harm the soil life or the plants themselves. Only natural, biodegradable cleaning and washing products can be used. Bleach in particular must be avoided.

Grey water should not be used as the sole water supply, especially on clay soils, because detergents contain sodium, which causes clay to deflocculate. This weakens the structure of the soil, eventually reducing crumbs and pore space into a homogenous mass like plasticine. It should be used to supplement rainfall and other irrigation water. On a heavy clay soil it should be not more than a third of the total water received by the soil. On sandier soils it can be a much larger proportion of the total. On a reedbed it can be used in any quantity, as reeds can cope with structureless soils.

Rain Water

Rainwater from the roof can also be collected. Indeed if it is not collected it is another potential asset going down the drain, where it becomes a nuisance to be got rid of. Some sewage systems get overloaded after heavy rain, then raw sewage gets put straight into the rivers. Thus a potential supply of clean water becomes a cause of pollution.

At present saving rain water does not save you any money – although it is much better for plants than mains. But it is only a matter of time before water will have to be metered. In the meantime hosepipe bans are becoming the norm rather than the exception in some parts of the

Plate 4.1 Simon Phelps beside his rainwater harvesting system. Note that the tank is raised off the ground so that all the water in it can be used by gravity. (Steve Easton)

country. Now is a good time to install a rain harvesting system – while second hand tanks are still available at bargain prices. It doesn't matter what the tank was used for before, as long as you wash it out well.

Your house roof will probably collect much more water during the course of a year than the garden will ever need. The limiting factor is storing enough to be really useful during a long dry spell. Most predictions for climate change over the next few decades suggest that summers will get drier, so the best rule of thumb for choosing the size of a rainwater storage tank is to get the biggest you have room for and can afford.

The best place for it is usually the darkest, dingiest part of the garden, where you couldn't grow anything if you tried. If possible raise it up off the ground, so you can use the water with a hosepipe rather than having to bucket it. This may require a pretty hefty construction, because water is heavy, but the investment will save you a lifetime of bucketing, and you may be able to use the space below for storage.

To fill the tank there are gadgets on the market which will divert rainwater from the downpipe into the tank till it is full, and then send it back to the downpipe. They are advertised in gardening magazines.

PEST AND WEED CONTROL

The diversity of a forest garden goes a long way towards preventing pests and diseases becoming a problem. But there is also a specific design feature which can help to protect plants from pests, and that is to introduce pest predators into the garden. These may be relatively large animals which we can bring into the garden to eat slugs and snails; or insects which prey on plant pests, which we can attract by growing certain plants.

Slug-Eaters and Other Animals

Slugs can be a problem in a forest garden. The moist environment, dense perennial vegetation and copious mulch are just the conditions they like. Most of the plants recommended in this book are to a greater or lesser extent resistant to slugs, but when they get really numerous they will eat anything. I have even seen them climb shrubs and young trees to eat the leaves.

There is some evidence to suggest that slugs and other pests become less of a problem as a forest garden matures. Robert Hart is able to grow small patches of lettuce in the sunnier parts of his garden, though all around is thick perennial vegetation and deep mulch – ideal slug habitat. He does use garlic as a slug repellent, popping a clove into the ground with each lettuce he plants. But my experience tells me that this would not be effective in a *really* sluggy garden. I suspect that the slug population there is low because a population of beetles and other slug predators has built up over the years. They like very similar conditions to slugs, but are slower to colonise a new habitat. In any succession the predators are usually the last members of the community to build up their population.

It is in the early years of a forest garden, before a diverse and stable fauna has had time to develop, that slugs and snails are likely to be a really serious problem. This is when it is most useful to deliberately introduce animals into the garden as predators on slugs.

Two candidates for the job are ducks and frogs. The advantages of ducks are that they give you a multiple yield – eggs as well as slug control – and can be much more effective than frogs. The advantage of frogs is that they need no looking after once you have got them established. You have to choose one or the other, because ducks also eat frogs.

Ducks

You should not think of keeping ducks unless you are prepared to take on the commitment involved in keeping domestic animals. You need to be there every morning and evening to let them out of their house and shut them away again, otherwise the fox will have them, whether you live in town or country. You also need enough space to give them a run of their own, with a little pond or bath in it, where they can stay when not on slug patrol. Two or three ducks are quite enough for all but the biggest garden. Keeping a single duck on her own is cruel.

Plate 4.2 Khaki Campbell ducks on slug patrol in a Devon garden. (PW)

It is important to get ducks of the right breed. Khaki Campbells and Indian runners are the most carnivorous breeds. The others actually prefer vegetables to slugs. Even so you can't let them free range over the whole garden all the time, because they will eat the vegetables as soon as they have finished the slugs. The best thing to do is to let them into the garden when you are working there yourself and can keep an eye on them. When they finish the slug course and start on your vegetables it's time to put them back in their run. Their favourite plants, which include strawberries and young cabbages, must be protected with some kind of netting.

Frogs

A healthy frog population in the garden won't totally get rid of slugs, as no wild predator ever eliminates its prey. But it can make the difference between hardly being able to grow a thing, and just having to take some sensible precautions with the more susceptible plants.

First you need a pond. The adults lay in it and the young live in it for the first few months of their lives as eggs and tadpoles. The pond should be sited in a sunny place, near dense ground vegetation, but if possible away from trees, as too many leaves in the water cause problems.

In most gardens a pond liner will be necessary, and flexible ones can be bought quite cheaply from garden centres. An old sink dug into the ground will do, but a few stones will have to be placed near the edge to allow the frogs to hop out. Frogs like to lay their eggs in shallow water, so the pond should be around 30 cm deep. It can be as small as 1m x 1.5m if space is short (*see Figure 4.2*).

The best water for the pond is some from an existing pond, as this will contain the microscopic spores and eggs of the tadpoles' food plants and prey. Above all make sure the water is not polluted, as frogs are very sensitive to pollution. Some water plants should be added too. These will both feed the animals on which the older tadpoles prey, and give cover for the tadpoles against predators which may want to eat *them*.

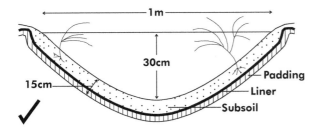

Figure 4.2 The right and the wrong way of constructing a frog pond

Adult frogs may find your pond and lay in it of their own accord. But if you want to be sure of getting frogs in the first year it is best to find some spawn and put it in. Most spawn is laid during March and April, though in mild years, and especially in mild areas such as Cornwall, it may be found as early as February. The best source is probably from a friend or neighbour who has frogs in their own garden pond, or from the county wildlife trust.

Collecting from the wild should be done with caution, because frog numbers in the wild have fallen catastrophically in recent years. Spawn can be taken from ponds with an obvious excess – so much that the little bit needed to stock a garden pond will not make a noticeable difference – or from a shallow puddle which is likely to dry up before the tadpoles mature. A single mass of spawn is the right amount for a pond of the minimum size.

The tadpoles become frogs some time during June, July or early August. Once they are out of the water they need plenty of dense, shady, low-level vegetation to hide them from predators and keep their skin moist. In fact they like just the sort of habitat that slugs do! The pond can then be allowed to dry out. Many natural ponds are seasonal, so frogs, and other aquatic life, are adapted to this cycle.

In the first year of their life they will not grow big enough to eat slugs, but since it is the smallest slugs that do the most damage to plants the frogs should start to earn their keep by the end of their second summer.

Moving adult frogs into a garden in the hope that they will stay there and kill the slugs is not a good idea. You are unlikely to build up a significant frog population this way. It is also cruel because it causes stress – and it's illegal.

There are many predators on frogs. Unfortunately one of the most effective is the domestic cat. If you keep a cat, or if cats frequent your garden, you will have to accept that they will take some of the frogs. It will still be worthwhile to breed frogs for slug control, but somewhat less so.

Other Animals

Toads rarely if ever eat slugs. Their favourite food is beetles, which do eat slugs, so they will tend to increase the population of slugs rather than decrease it. They do eat snails, so they are a help where snails rather than slugs are the main problem, which is often the case in gardens with a drystone wall or other masonry with crevices in it. It is very easy to distinguish toad spawn from frog spawn, as it is laid in long thin strips like strings of beads, rather than in masses like frogspawn. They like to lay their spawn in deeper water than frogs, 60cm deep or more. So if you want to attract frogs but not toads, keep the pond shallow.

Hedgehogs also eat slugs and snails, but it does not seem possible to increase hedgehog populations enough to make a significant impact on the local slug population. Nevertheless, they are part of the wildlife of many gardens, and it is important to encourage all kinds of wildlife – not just because they help us by keeping pests in balance and contributing to nutrient cycling, but because they have as much right to be here as we have. (The best hedgehog attractant is said to be a permanent water supply – such as a pond.)

A forest garden is always good for wildlife, but there should also be at least a corner which is kept primarily for the benefit of wild plants and animals. A pile of rotting logs is a good thing to have in a wild corner. In a small garden it may be all there is room for, and it will make good use of the space. Dead wood supports ten times as much animal life as live wood. It is a storehouse of food for decomposer insects and other creepy-crawlies, and these provide food for birds, small mammals and reptiles.

A pond dug for breeding frogs will soon attract other wildlife – some of which will eat the tadpoles, but never mind, there's enough for all. If you want dragonflies to breed in the pond you must have at least one tall emergent plant, like a reed or reedmace, for the young to crawl up when they are ready to transform to adults and leave the water for the air. A bed of nettles is another good wildlife attractant. Many butterflies and other creatures feed on them in the larval stage.

Chickens are not a good idea in a forest garden, although they can play a part in the initial preparation of the ground (*see page 61*). It's not so much a matter of what they eat, but of the mess they make of plants and mulch as they scratch for insects. Geese have their place in orchards, keeping the grass down, but young trees must be protected because they can debark them. Geese are vegetarians and in a forest garden they would make short work of the vegetable and shrub layers.

BEES

Bees have nothing much to do with pest control, but they are animals which it is well worthwhile having in a forest garden. The beauty of bees is that keeping them is a win-win situation. Usually adding another productive plant to the garden makes use of some resources which were previously unused, but also takes some which were previously used by other plants – so although the total yield of the garden goes up, there is a price to pay in reduced yield of something that was already there. But when you keep bees, not only do they produce honey entirely from resources that were previously unharvested – the nectar and pollen – they also increase production of fruit by improving pollination. Nothing is lost. All is gain.

Bees do need regular attention, but it is nothing like as much as poultry. People very rarely get stung unless they walk through the bees' flight path. In a very large garden this can be avoided by placing the hive well out of the way. In smaller gardens the hive should be placed high up, over people's heads. A flat roof or the top of a steep bank are good situations, as long as they are reasonably sheltered. The hive should be sited in a warm microclimate, but not too warm, as that could encourage the bees to come out when the general temperature is still too cold for them.

Bees are ideal animals to keep in towns and suburbs. There are more flowers there than in the country; there is usually a safe, sheltered niche for the hive, over a porch or even on a high rooftop; and the bees appreciate the warm urban microclimate. Unlike poultry, they do not make a noise which can lead to disputes with neighbours.

If you don't want to keep bees but would like to get some of the advantages of pollination from them, there are certain plants which will attract them into the garden. These include almost anything with a blue flower, such as borage or rosemary. Comfrey can become a buzzing mass of bees when it flowers in June.

Plate 4.3 Glen Finn tends his bees, in a corner of Permanent Publications' forest garden in Hampshire. (Tim Harland)

Pest Predator Plants

Two kinds of insects which are particularly worth encouraging into the garden are hoverflies and parasitic wasps. Hoverflies are those flies which mimic wasps with a yellow and black colour scheme to frighten off any creature which might want to prey on them. The wasps are tiny insignificant ones, not the big yellow and black bruisers which we all know and see each year in the season of rotting fruit.

It is the larvae of the hoverflies which eat aphids, and the eggs of the wasps which parasitise various pests. The adults of these beneficial insects feed on flowers, and as they have very short mouth parts they need tiny flowers to feed from. Therefore the plants which they need for their food supply are those with composite flowers, that is flowers made up of many little florets instead of one big bloom. Most of these plants belong to one of two families: the umbellifers or cow parsley family, and the daisy family, which includes many composite flowers such as thistles and dandelions.

In fact cow parsley and dandelions are two plants which are particularly valuable in attracting insects, because they flower early. Some pests can build up their populations quite early in the spring, so it is good to have a population of predators there as soon as possible to start eating them. Most gardens already have an abundant supply of dandelions, and it may be worthwhile allowing some of them to flower in the spring. Cow parsley may need to be introduced, and is best planted in a sunny position if you want it to flower early. Alexanders and sweet cicely are two more umbellifers which flower early.

Another useful plant which may be allowed to stay where it already grows is the stinging nettle. Nettles have two functions in pest control. Firstly they play host to their own species of aphid in the spring, an aphid which does not feed on any other plant. This allows populations of aphid predators to build up early in the year, so by the time other plants are being troubled by aphids there will be a good population of predators around. Secondly, dry nettle stalks are just the kind of thing which ladybirds like to overwinter in, and ladybirds are redoubtable killers of aphids. So as well as allowing the nettles to grow, it helps not to tidy them up too much when they die down in winter.

Quite a number of edible forest garden plants are also pest predator attractant plants, many of them members of the umbellifer and daisy families. Indeed, dandelions, cow parsley, alexanders, sweet cicely and nettles are all edible. But often designing for pest predators can be more a matter of allowing things to continue growing than of bringing in special plants. Robert Kourik's list of 67 successful companion planting combinations is illuminating (*see page 35*). Most of the companions are for annual crop plants, and so not very relevant to forest gardening. But apples and walnuts appear in the list, and in both cases pests have been reduced by having a 'weedy ground cover'.

Weed Control

The kind of 'weeds' which were so beneficial to the orchard trees were probably much the same plants as the edible wild ones which we grow in the vegetable layer of a forest garden. But there are some weeds which are not welcome at all, especially the creeping perennial ones.

If at all possible these weeds should be eradicated from the garden before planting. But sometimes it is not possible to eradicate them from an adjacent piece of ground, and then there is an excellent home-grown resource which can be used to prevent them from creeping back in – comfrey.

A belt of comfrey plants can act as an effective barrier to creeping weeds. It grows vigorously and casts such a heavy shade that no weeds can establish themselves underneath it, yet it does not spread itself, either by seed or by root. (This applies to Russian comfrey, not the common native kind. *See page 121*.) Plants should be spaced 60cm apart each way, and two or three rows may be needed according to the virulence of the weeds. This space, 120 or 180cm wide, must be allowed for in the design of the garden.

It will not be possible to pick very much of this comfrey. Since it prevents the growth of weeds by shading them out, it becomes less effective as a weed barrier if its leaves are removed. If comfrey is wanted for soil fertility purposes a separate planting must be made.

Chapter 5

PREPARATION, PLANTING & MAINTENANCE

MULCHING

Mulching is such an important technique in forest gardening that a whole section of this chapter is devoted to it. In the separate sections on Preparation, Planting and Maintenance, reference is made to the various kinds of mulch described in this section.

A mulch is any material laid on the surface of the soil. The functions of a mulch can include one or more of the following:

- to kill weeds by denying them light;
- to conserve water by reducing evaporation from the soil;
- to protect the soil surface from Sun, wind and rain;
- to add plant nutrients and organic matter to the soil.

There are three kinds of mulch:

1. **Clearance mulch** – used to clear the ground of weeds prior to planting.
2. **Grow-through mulch** – similar to a clearance mulch, but with crop plants growing through holes made in it.
3. **Maintenance mulch** – used in an already established garden.

Clearance Mulch

This occupies the ground for a period of time before planting, and is removed before planting starts. It is suitable for ground which has a serious problem with perennial weeds.

Mulch kills the plants beneath it by denying them light. The plants try to grow, but they need sunlight in order to manufacture food, so they use up all their food reserves and die. This means that mulching is only effective when the plants are actively growing. A mulch from autumn to spring will kill some plants, but not the strong perennials, which have considerable stores of food in them. To kill them you need to mulch from spring to autumn.

A completely light-excluding mulch kept down through the whole growing season will eradicate most perennial weeds. Some of the tougher ones, like couch, will survive in patches, but you can expect a 90% kill. You may then need to do a little digging to finish the job off, but it is much easier now all the other plants are gone, and will only disturb a fraction of the garden's soil.

Bindweed is the main exception. It is hardly affected unless you mulch an enormous area at once, because a well-established plant can send out roots for several

---

MATERIALS FOR CLEARANCE MULCH

Black plastic sheeting is ideal. It is energy intensive to produce and non-biodegradable, so buying it new is questionable on ecological grounds. But using it second hand means getting another use out of something that would otherwise go straight to landfill. In country areas it is readily available from farmers in the form of broken silage bags or silage clamp covers. It can be dug in round the edges and weighted down with a few planks, bricks etc. across the middle.

Old carpets can usually be found in skips. They should either be totally artificial fibre, or totally natural (which is rare these days). If they are half and half the natural part may rot away leaving thousands of little tufts of nylon in the soil. They are not suitable for severe infestations of couch, which can grow straight through a carpet.

Large sheets of cardboard can be used, but they need a lot of weighing down and can rot before the weeds do.

metres before they reach light without exhausting its food reserves. At the edge of the mulch they put out masses of leaves and thrive. When you pull back the mulch at the end of the year the soil surface can look like a plate of spaghetti. At least you can scoop the majority of the roots up, rather than having to dig them out, but a few will always remain underground to start again next year.

Simply knock down any tall weeds – there's no need to cut them. Lay the mulch material over the whole area and weight it down. A layer of manure can be put under it. This gives the worms a head start at incorporating the manure into the soil, but is not essential to the purpose of the mulch, which is to kill weeds.

Grow-Through Mulch

This is suitable for land with rather less persistent perennial weeds in it, as some weeds can grow up through the holes left for the crop plants. Its advantage over a clearance mulch is that you do not have to wait a whole growing season before starting to plant.

A simple grow-through can be made by using the same materials as for a clearance mulch and cutting holes in it for the plants.

The classic grow-through mulch combines the weed control job with a heavy dressing of manure. It is completely biodegradable, and usually does not last long enough to completely kill the most persistent weeds. Long-term weed control depends on the vegetable plants growing strongly and suppressing any weeds which survive. This is the kind of mulch described here.

Method

1. Plant the trees and shrubs.

2. Cover the ground between with a layer of cardboard, newspaper or any other biodegradable sheet material. Use the largest sheets you can get, and wherever two sheets meet, overlap them by about 20cm. Newspaper should be 15-20 sheets thick.

3. Add a layer of manure, or other material which is both heavy enough to hold the first layer in place and contains plant nutrients.

4. Where you want to plant a vegetable, make a hole in the mulch with a spike, such as an old knife. Scrape the manure away from the spike, and replace it with a double handful of topsoil or very well rotted compost. Plant the vegetable into this. Don't try to plant it in the soil beneath – the roots will find their own way down through the little hole (*see Figure 5.1*).

Figure 5.1

5. A top layer of loose material is optional. It looks good, and helps prevent the manure from drying out in summer. On the other hand, in wet weather it may harbour slugs and encourage rotting in vegetables which are not actively growing.

Plate 5.1

Plate 5.2

A grow-through mulch placed around existing trees for the addition of shrubs and vegetables, Michael and Julia Guerra's front garden, Welham Green, Hertfordshire. Bottom layer – newspaper; middle layer – well-rotted compost; top layer – plastic to stop the compost blowing away (Plate 5.1). The same plot planted up (Plate 5.2). (Michael Guerra)

Some of the original vegetation will survive the mulching, and you can choose which of these volunteer plants to leave and which to remove. A proportion of the yarrow or dandelions which come through, and perhaps the odd plant of hogweed, may be useful additions to the garden ecosystem, and can be left to grow. Little bits of couch and creeping buttercup can easily be removed with finger and thumb from the friable, organic topsoil you have created.

Paths should be mulched at the same time as the growing area. Grassy paths are a constant source of work; the grass and other plants in them are forever creeping into the growing area, and have to be weeded out.

MATERIALS FOR GROW-THROUGH MULCH

The largest sheets of cardboard are the ones bicycles, fridges and televisions come in. Cardboard or paper with too much coloured printing on it should be avoided. Some coloured inks are made with organic pigments, others, especially reds and yellows, may contain heavy metals which are poisonous in high concentrations. If your cardboard and paper come from a variety of sources and don't have too much coloured ink on them, there should be no problem. Black ink is harmless.

Manure can be used partly rotted, as long as the heap has heated up well enough to kill weed seeds. But if it has wood chippings in it it should be well rotted, which can take a couple of years as wood is slow to decompose. Most urban areas are ringed by riding stables only too pleased to get rid of their manure. Manure from intensive animal rearing, especially pigs, should not be used because of the residue of copper and other substances added to the feed as medicines and growth promoters.

Fresh seaweed is an alternative to manure if you live near the coast, but it needs to have the salt washed out of it before use. If you cannot get a material which both contains plant nutrients and is heavy enough to keep the cardboard down, you can apply a layer of concentrated organic manure, such as blood fish and bone meal, and one of something heavy, like leaf mould or sand. Avoid anything with too many viable weed seeds in it, which includes most home-made compost.

For the top layer any of the materials used for regular maintenance mulching are suitable (*see box on next page*).

If a path is mulched with a loose material, such as wood chippings, gravel or straw, weeds constantly sprout up in it and have to be removed. A sheet mulch is needed. Black plastic, cardboard and paper are all a bit vulnerable to damage from feet. Strips of old carpet are much the best. It looks quite inoffensive when turned upside down, and a sprinkling of one of the loose materials on top helps it to look much more pleasant. But only a thin layer of loose material should be used, or weeds will start growing in it, especially if it collects some soil off muddy boots.

Maintenance Mulch

Clearance and grow-through mulches are one-off operations for clearing new ground. But a maintenance mulch is one which is used regularly as part of the gardening round. Its main function is weed control, but it has many other beneficial effects. On the other hand it has its disadvantages.

Advantages
- Controls weeds without the need for digging or hoeing.
- Decreases evaporation from the soil, reducing the need for watering.
- Protects the soil surface from Sun, wind and rain; prevents capping on soils which are prone to it.
- Keeps the soil warm in winter, and encourages early growth of perennial vegetables.
- Provides habitat for beneficial creatures, such as frogs and beetles.
- Supplies the soil with organic matter and plant nutrients.
- Reduces the need for making compost – material can simply be laid on the surface.

Disadvantages
- Collecting mulch material can be a lot of work.
- Prevents light summer rain penetrating the soil.
- Can cause rotting of perennial vegetable crowns in winter, and on stems of trees and shrubs if it is allowed to touch them.
- Slows the warming up of the soil in spring. Can increase frosts by preventing radiation of heat from the soil.
- Can harbour slugs, and prevents birds from eating slug eggs and overwintering pests in the soil.

The advantages of mulch are considerable, and it is possible to keep the disadvantages to a minimum by wise management:

Reducing the quantity needed
Three ways to do this are:

1. *Use green manures or perennial ground covers as an alternative in some parts of the garden.* A green manure crop is one which is grown mainly in order to protect the soil, to add organic matter and plant nutrients to the soil, and to hold plant nutrients which would otherwise be leached away by the rain. They are usually short-lived annuals, and are most important over winter, when the soil is vulnerable and there are least crops in the ground.

   In a forest garden some of the self-seeding winter salad plants, such as lamb's lettuce, winter purslane and land cress can act as green manures if they seed in sufficient quantity. In spring, if there are more of them than you can eat, they can be chopped off at ground level and left to lie on the surface, or gently incorporated into the top few centimetres of soil with a hoe. If they are incorporated it is best done before they flower, as they become more fibrous then. In either case they will decompose rapidly, and other plants can be planted or allowed to self-seed in their place.

Perennial ground cover plants, such as *Rubus tricolor* and white clover can effectively suppress weeds and protect the soil.

2. *Start with a weed-free soil and discourage recolonisation.* If perennial weeds are not eradicated when the garden is established, or if they creep back in, it may be necessary to cover the entire surface of the soil between the crop plants with as much as 10-15cm of compact mulch material. This needs replacing at least once a year as it rots down (*see pages 60-61 for means of removing perennial weeds*).

   Many soils contain masses of annual weed seeds in a viable but dormant state. They only germinate when they are brought to the surface by disturbance. Anything which disturbs the surface, such as hoeing, should be avoided if at all possible. If you are tempted to hoe or dig remember that as well as killing the present generation you are bringing forth the next one. So the more you use mulch instead of the hoe, the less weeds you have to control, and the less mulch you need to use each time.

MATERIALS FOR MAINTENANCE MULCH

Whatever you use, try to be sure it has no weed seeds in it, or you could end up causing more weed problems than you solve.

Straw is usually free of weed seeds. Some cereal crops are sprayed with hormones which shorten and stiffen the straw. Straw from these crops should not be used because the chemical can have an adverse effect on the plants grown in it. It is safe to use after it has been composted for at least a year, but most of its volume will have rotted away by then. Fortunately, with the introduction of more short-strawed varieties, these chemicals are used less often these days.

Beware of *hay*. It is usually full of grass seed, and maybe seed of weeds like docks. Only use it if it has rotted enough to kill them, when it is known as 'spoiled hay'. Riding stables may be only too pleased for you to take it away, as it will no longer be fit for consumption by horses. If in doubt, let it rot a bit longer before use, but then you will lose some of the bulk.

Bracken is excellent, slow to rot down and slightly allelopathic – enough to inhibit the germination of weeds beneath it, but not to harm the strong perennial food plants it surrounds. Do not cut it in July and August when it is producing spores, which is what ferns have instead of seeds, because these can be carcinogenic. It is perfectly safe at other times of the year.

Reeds etc. These are the home-grown alternatives, if you have the space for them (*see pages 49-50*).

Commercial mulches, such as composted forestry bark tend to be prohibitively expensive.

Dry leaves tend to blow about and not stay where you want them. If they are wet or slightly decomposed they will stay put better. Otherwise they can be mixed with something that holds them together, like grass mowings. In urban areas the council may be only too pleased to deliver leaves to you in autumn at no charge.

Grass mowings. If used alone in anything more than a thin layer they heat up and rot down to a slimy mess which is generally offensive to plants, soil and people. But if applied thinly, or mixed with something that keeps them open, like dry leaves, they are fine. They are a good source of nitrogen.

Wood chippings. Anything containing wood is probably best avoided, unless very well composted. Composting takes much longer with wood chippings than other organic materials. If uncomposted wood gets incorporated into the soil it can cause lockup of nitrogen.

Compost, manure, comfrey etc. These are used more for their nutrient content than for covering the soil surface overall.

3. *Slip a layer of newspaper under the mulch.* The effectiveness of any loose mulch material can be greatly increased by this. You may need as little as a third or a quarter the amount of material to get the same degree of weed control.

Light Rain

Light summer rain can be absorbed by mulch and re-evaporated before it reaches the soil. This is only a problem if the mulch is applied to a dry soil. If the soil is thoroughly moist beneath the mulch at the start of the growing season, the amount of water retained in the soil due to decreased evaporation is much greater than the amount kept out by the mulch. Heavy winter rain easily penetrates mulch, so every forest garden soil should be thoroughly moist at the beginning of the growing season.

Rotting

The crowns of overwintering perennial vegetables are only likely to rot under a layer of mulch in mild, wet weather. The mulch can be drawn back a little to let the plants breathe in this kind of weather, but should be replaced in cold, dry weather if you want the plants to sprout early for spring. If you don't want to be bothered with changing the mulch every time the weather changes it is probably best to leave it drawn back from plants' crowns through the whole winter, at least in the wetter parts of the country.

Whatever kind of mulch is being used, no mulch materials should ever touch the stem of a tree or shrub, as this can cause rotting. In the case of a grafted tree it can also cause the scion to take root if the mulch reaches that high.

Temperature

The overall effect of mulch on the temperature of the soil is to even it out over the year. The warmer temperatures over winter are counterbalanced by slower warming up in the spring. But on the whole plants like stable conditions, so the evening out of temperature fluctuations is generally beneficial to plant growth.

The possible increase in frosts due to mulch is marginal, and should only affect particularly frost-sensitive plants, like peaches.

Pests

It is hard to say whether the net effect of mulch on pest populations is positive or negative. Pests have a hiding place, but so do predators. The answer is probably that it varies from place to place and from season to season. The experience of the Henry Doubleday Research Association is interesting in this respect. Their members have done trials in their own gardens all over Britain comparing potatoes grown on the no-dig, mulched system and on the conventional system. Slug damage

was one of the observations they made, and there was little difference in damage between the two methods. Sometimes the mulched potatoes had more slug damage, sometimes those that had been dug.

This is a surprising result, as we always think of slugs as the inevitable down-side of using mulch. It may be because the mulch provides cover for the larger kinds of beetles which all eat slugs. They also account for a good many codlin-moth and apple sawfly larvae, as they drop off the trees in autumn, heading for their winter home in the soil.

Since predators build up their populations more slowly than pests, problems are likely to decrease as the garden matures.

If there are problems with pests which overwinter in the soil, it is always possible to draw back the mulch for a time during winter or early spring to let the birds have a go at them. The soil surface could even be lightly hoed to expose the pests a bit.

PREPARATION

To Dig or Not to Dig?

That is the big question. A forest garden is essentially a no-dig garden. Accepting the gifts of a natural, undisturbed soil rather than imposing our will on it by digging is very much part of the whole forest garden approach. The specific advantages of not digging have already been noted in Chapter 1 (*see pages 7-8*).

On the other hand there are a few things which can be done by digging which may be worthwhile to do just once in a forest garden, to get it off to a good start. They are:

- relieving soil compaction;
- weeding;
- manuring.

Digging is not the only way to do these things, and whether we choose to dig or not depends on a number of factors. The first of them is how long the soil has been undisturbed up to now. The benefits of an undisturbed soil develop over time, as a healthy and diverse soil fauna and flora and the natural structure slowly build up. If the forest garden site has lain undug or unploughed for a number of years it would be a shame to disrupt it and start again without very good reason.

Of course you cannot plant a tree or shrub without digging. If the design is for a small number of large trees and shrubs this will not disturb much of the ground. But if it calls for a larger number of smaller trees and shrubs it may seem that virtually the whole area will be dug by the time they are all in. In fact, even where smaller plants are grown the great majority of the soil remains

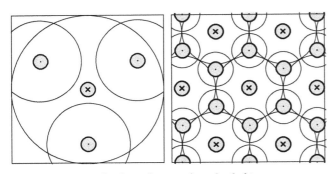

Figure 5.2 Standard apple over hazels (left).
Dwarf apples (M26) over currants and gooseberries (right).

undisturbed (*see above*). The vegetables do not figure in the calculation, because most of them can be slipped in without any real disturbance to the soil.

So let us look at the main reasons for digging, and what alternatives there are.

Soil Compaction

A soil which has been much walked upon, driven over, used as a dumping ground by builders, or even farmed or gardened badly, is likely to be compacted. The only way to do much about severely compacted soil by hand is to double-dig the whole area. This is an enormous amount of work, and will, of course, thoroughly disturb the soil. It is not something to be undertaken unless you are quite sure it is necessary, but nor should it be avoided where it is necessary. The whole volume of the soil must be well enough structured to allow tree roots to penetrate, otherwise they may never extend beyond their original planting holes and the trees will never thrive.

If you are developing a rural site where it is possible to get a tractor into the garden, you can open up the subsoil without disturbing the surface by means of an implement called a subsoiler (*see Figure 5.3*). This consists of one or more heavy tines which penetrate deep into the soil. At the base of each tine is a triangular shoe which lifts the soil and cracks it, enhancing the natural structure rather than chopping the soil up or turning it.

The job must be done when the soil has the right moisture content. If it is too wet it will smear instead

Figure 5.3
A subsoiler

of cracking. Late summer and early autumn are usually the best time for subsoiling.

Regardless of the condition of the subsoil, it is usually worth loosening the topsoil before planting, unless the soil is a very open sandy one. This can be done without disturbing the surface by using a tarmac fork. This looks just like a garden fork except that it has a metal handle. You push it into the ground as deep as it will go and then lean on the handle to gently open up the soil. This is why you need the metal handle – a wooden one snaps sooner or later under this treatment. It is not a laborious job, and the fork is a useful tool to have around permanently for no-dig gardening.

Weeds

There are weeds and weeds. Some are useful plants, like mints and dandelions, which become weeds when they outgrow the gardener's need for them. Here we are concerned with the ones which are not wanted in the garden at all.

In a garden of perennial plants the most troublesome weeds are perennial ones. In an annual garden you get a chance to eradicate them at least once a year when the soil is free of crops. But with perennial crops you do not get that chance: it is impossible to extract all the roots of perennial weeds from the roots of a tree or shrub without actually digging up the tree or shrub, or using poison.

Couch grass, bindweed, creeping buttercup and ground elder are among the most troublesome perennial weeds. They have amazing powers of regeneration – a single piece of couch rhizome one centimetre long can grow in time to infest a whole garden. So it is an extremely good idea to start with as clean a sheet as possible.

The boundary of the garden is as important as the garden itself. If there are invasive weeds growing happily in the hedgerow, it will only be a matter of time before they creep in. If you want to keep the hedgerow – and are not prepared to kill the weeds with poisons – you may just have to accept that your weed-free garden will not remain weed-free for long. This is not a complete disaster, as you will give the garden plants a good start, and they should be mature and well-established before they suffer any competition from invading weeds.

But perennial weeds can be kept out with a barrier of comfrey, as described on page 54. Comfrey does not compete well when it is young, so the ground must be weed-free to start with. Alternatively the comfrey can be planted through holes in a black plastic sheet without removing the weeds first (a grow-through mulch). The sheet should be left down for a couple of years, or however long it takes for the comfrey to form a complete barrier.

The main ways of getting rid of weeds are: digging; ploughing; rotovating; poisoning; mulching; biological methods.

Digging. In theory it is possible to dig the soil and remove every single bit of perennial weed root. In my experience, on a loamy soil it takes about ten times as much work as mulching, and on a clay soil it is more or less impossible.

In fact digging can make the weed problem worse, as new seeds are brought to the surface and dormancy is broken.

Ploughing. If you are able to get a tractor onto your forest garden site and have a friendly farmer neighbour, you may be tempted to have it ploughed. Ploughing does as much harm to the natural life of the soil as digging, but has very little effect on perennial weeds. The plough simply buries them, and they shoot straight up again. It can have the same effect on weed seeds as digging.

Rotovating. This actually multiplies perennial weeds by cutting their roots and rhizomes into many little bits, each of which can form a new plant. It can only kill them if it is done repeatedly as the successive waves of new plants start to grow. It is also a harsh, violent way to treat the soil structure, can cause compaction, and chops up earthworms as readily as weeds. If annual weeds are the main problem a very shallow rotovating can kill them without bringing too many new seeds to the surface.

Poisoning. Overall use of poisons as a first resort is utterly irresponsible and unnecessary. Spot treatment of one or two plants which have survived all other attempts to kill them is another matter. Bindweed in particular is hard to eradicate by any other means, and when it gets its long white roots into the crevices of a wall, almost the only alternative to poisoning it is to demolish the wall. Whether you think the pros outweigh the cons is up to you.

There are a few weedkillers which are deadly to weeds, but soon degrade to harmless substances in the soil. They should be painted carefully onto the leaves of the weed in question. Lawrence D. Hills used to recommend ammonium sulphamate, which degrades to ammonium sulphate (an ingredient of fertilisers) in about two months, or three if the soil is dry. Glyphosate is a more modern alternative, and more effective against many weeds, including couch.

Clearance Mulching. This method takes the least work, does least damage to a healthy, uncompacted soil, and is the most effective. The only real disadvantage is the time it takes. But it can be very beneficial to spend a year getting to know your garden and refining your design, rather than rushing into planting trees which will last a lifetime or more, so the enforced wait may be beneficial in the long run (*see Chapter 10*).

Biological methods. There are allelopathic plants which can kill perennial weeds. The best known are members of the *Tagetes* family, especially the Mexican marigold,

T. minuta. But they are annuals which have to be raised under cover and planted out at 30cm each way all over the plot, preferably after you have already dug out all the roots you can find. So they are very laborious, and more a way of making up for the deficiencies of digging than a cure on their own.

Animals can be more effective. Chickens, kept at a high enough density or for a long enough time on a piece of ground will remove all herbaceous vegetation. If you want to clear enough ground for your forest garden all at once you will need a large number of chickens, and you may not have either the space or the need for so many once the job is done. A temporary flock of broilers for sale would fit the situation. If you want to plant up your garden over a number of years, you could rotate a small domestic flock of layers around the site. Chickens do slightly compact the surface soil, but this can easily be loosened before planting with a light forking, without any need to invert the soil.

The one weed that chickens least like to eat is bindweed. Pigs love it, but they don't eat couch, which chickens do. If you have access to a pig or two, or would like to fatten a couple of weaners over the summer, you could alternate them with chickens to cover all the weeds. But pigs do spoil the structure of the soil, and churn it about a great deal. They may also damage any trees or shrubs you want to leave within their run. In common with chickens they need expensive fencing – not the same fencing though – and they can be very destructive if they get out.

Manuring

This is your last chance to incorporate organic matter into the soil. Once the garden is planted organic matter can only be added to the soil surface. In a natural woodland most of the organic matter in the soil comes from the surface litter, which is taken down into the soil by earthworms. This means that in a woodland soil most of the organic matter is concentrated near the surface. This is not a problem, and woodland plants have evolved to live in this kind of soil. All the same it can be useful to thoroughly mix organic matter throughout the rooting depth of the soil.

Manuring is most worthwhile in extreme soils, ones which are very sandy or heavy clay. Well-rotted organic matter acts like a sponge in a sandy soil, increasing its ability to retain both water and plant nutrients. (Though it is debatable whether it is better to dig it in or simply apply it to the surface. The downward movement of materials, including humus, is so fast in sandy soils that it may be better to start off with the organic matter above rather than at root level.) Dug into a clay, it will help to improve the structure, and thus aeration, drainage and root penetration.

Unrotted organic matter should never be dug into any soil. The organic matter must be thoroughly mixed in with the soil, ideally to a depth of 45-60cm. Simply dumping it in the bottom of the digging trench is a waste of time.

Where the soil is a well-structured loam, with moderate proportions of both sand and clay, there is much less to be gained from incorporating organic matter. It can all be applied as a surface mulch.

PLANTING

Late autumn is the best time to plant trees and shrubs. Perennial vegetables can be planted then too, but if they are to be planted with a grow-through mulch it is best to leave them till the spring. If a grow-through mulch is put down in autumn it will start to rot at a time when the weeds are dormant, and so it will not be so effective at killing them. So the planting sequence may often be determined by how weedy the site is, and thus whether a clearance or grow-through mulch is used.

	Weedy Site	Less Weedy Site
Summer	Clearance mulch	
Autumn	Plant all, with maintenance mulch	Plant trees and shrubs, leaving existing vegetation between them
Spring		Plant vegetables with grow-through mulch

Table 5.1

All the vegetable plants must be ready to go at planting time, so they can grow and cover the ground quickly. If there are not enough vegetables to cover the whole area, extra ground cover plants should be used. Trailing nasturtiums are useful, as they can cover a lot of ground quickly and are not persistent (*see Plate 5.3*). Clovers can be used where longer-term cover is required, and they will improve the soil.

It is essential to make sure there are enough plants to cover the ground completely at the recommended spacing. The weed-free ground afforded by a clearance or grow-through mulch will only stay weed-free if the vegetable layer grows quickly to cover all the ground. If there are gaps between widely-spaced vegetable and herb plants, or areas of the garden without any herbaceous plants,

Plate 5.3 Vigorous nasturtiums cover the ground in Paul Benham's forest garden on his farm near Brecon. (Paul Benham)

Plate 5.4 The result of an incomplete ground cover: extra work and masses of mulch are needed to get the weeds under control. (Paul Benham)

weeds will rush in to fill the vacuum. It is hard to get back on top of a situation like this; the forest garden can become a source of endless work rather than the low-maintenance garden it was intended to be (*see Plate 5.4*). This is the commonest problem with new forest gardens, and it is hard to over-emphasise the importance of this point.

Where a maintenance mulch is applied to the garden in its first autumn there may be a problem with slugs. If a mild winter follows they may eat those vegetables which stay in leaf over winter; if the spring is wet they will catch the others as they come up. It may be necessary to balance the need to protect the soil over winter with the need to keep the vegetables alive. This is only a problem with young vegetables, once they are well established they are much less vulnerable to slugs.

Vegetables

On the whole it is better to raise the vegetables in a seedbed and plant them out than to sow seed directly into the garden. It is much easier to create ideal conditions for them in a nursery bed or cold frame than out in the garden itself.

Self-seeders benefit from this treatment as much as perennials. Self-sown seedlings often survive when hand-sown ones of the same kind are demolished by slugs and other pests. The fact that something can survive by self-seeding does not necessarily mean it can easily be established in the open from seed.

A nursery or cold frame should be sited as close to the back door as possible. The young plants will benefit greatly from the extra attention they will get there. Choose a sheltered, sunny microclimate. A cold frame not only provides extra warmth, it also keeps out most of the slugs, and you can easily pick off the one or two that get in.

Seed should be sown according to the instructions on the packet. But the following points give a general guide for the vegetables mentioned in this book:

Sowing in a cold frame:
- Sow from early April to the middle of May, according to the local climate. It can be tempting to get the seeds in as early as possible, but a good start is of more value than an early one. It is better to wait for some reliably warm weather so that the seeds can get away to a good start without a check.

- Sow in seed trays. They can be filled with home made compost if it is free of weed seeds. Otherwise use John Innes No 1. Do not sow too deep; as a rough guide, cover seeds with soil only as deep as the diameter of the seeds themselves. Keep moist, but not wet, and well ventilated.

- When the seedlings are big enough to handle – say 2cm tall – transplant them from the seed tray into small pots. If you have compost with weed seeds in it, you can half-fill the pots with this, and top them off with weed-free commercial compost. Larger seeds, such as beets, can be sown directly into pots.

- When they are big enough to plant out, harden them off by placing them outside in the daytime and inside at night for three days.

Sowing in a nursery bed:
- Sow about two weeks later than in a cold frame, but pay more attention to the weather than to the calendar date.

- The ideal soil is a crumbly, dark, humus-rich loam. It an be worth bringing soil from another part of the garden to make a nursery bed in a favoured spot.

If you have good, weed-free compost, mix some into the topsoil. Otherwise give a light dressing of organic fertiliser.

- Sow thinly in drills about 10cm apart. Thin the seedlings progressively to about 5cm apart within the rows. Plant out when the seedlings meet within the rows.

Planting out:
- Half a cupful of seaweed solution in each planting hole will get the plants off to a good start. Plants which look poorly, either before planting out or after, can be sprayed with seaweed solution as a tonic.

- If slugs are a problem, or if there is a spell of cold weather at planting-out time, cover each seedling with a bottle cloche. This is easily made by cutting the bottom off a clear plastic bottle. It should be pushed well into the soil around the plant, and left there till the plant outgrows it.

Wild Vegetables

The way we introduce wild plants into our gardens can have an effect on the local ecology. There are three main options:

1. Buying commercial seed from a wild plant specialist.
2. Collecting seed from the wild.
3. Collecting plants from the wild.

Most of the wild plants listed in this book are common, and it might seem absurd to suggest that by taking them from the wild we are depleting the natural populations. Well, people used to think that about many wild plants. Cowslips, for example, were once so common that they were picked in their thousands to make cowslip wine. Now they are rare, and though most of their decline is due to changes in farming practice, the extra pressure of picking has made a difference.

Although fat hen and chickweed may be able to survive any assault we can mount on them, you could not say the same of ramsons or golden saxifrage. Unless you are quite sure that the plant you want is very common it is best to get the seed from a commercial supplier. They will have built up their stock from seed carefully collected from wild populations which can spare it.

On the other hand there is a good reason for using seed collected locally. It's not just that the local strain will be best adapted to the local climate and soils, but also that plants grown from seed introduced from another area can often interbreed with the local wild plants and dilute the unique genetic character of the local variety. In time this can significantly reduce the total genetic variability of the species, and this makes it more vulnerable to extinction.

This only really applies in the country. In urban areas exotic plants are the norm. In fact many of the native plants growing there are not native varieties, but ones which have been accidentally introduced from overseas. Here the odd few ramsons plants from another part of the country are not going to make any difference – not so if your garden is right beside an ancient woodland in the heart of the country.

If you do decide to collect from the wild, let seed be your first choice. The wild population can spare some seeds much more easily than whole plants. In fact it is illegal to dig up any wild plant without the permission of the landowner.

Always collect seed from areas where the plants are abundant, allowing for the fact that some plants are more gregarious than others. Where many plants grow together conditions for that species are favourable, so the plants should be healthy and so should the seed. As a rule of thumb if you take a hundredth of the seed which is there you are not likely to do any harm, and that should be plenty for the garden.

Wild annual and biennial plants tend to be easy to reproduce by seed. Simply find a stalk with mature or nearly mature seed on it, break it off and leave it lying on a patch of bare or lightly mulched soil. You will soon have lots of little plants springing up. Perennials, which do not have to rely on reproducing by seed each year, can be a little more reluctant to germinate, and may need to be carefully nurtured in seed trays (*see box below*).

If you really want to take plants, the proportion should be nearer one in a thousand. Many perennial plants have parts which can be detached from them which are capable of growing into a whole new plant without damage to the parent plant. In some plants, such as sea beet, these are in the form of offsets, little daughter plants which grow round the edge of the parent.

MAINTENANCE

Feeding the Soil

Since a forest garden is no-dig, nutrients are always added to it as a surface mulch. The best way to apply nutrient-rich materials to the soil is to lay them under the maintenance mulch.

The best time for this is in the spring, when the plants are starting to grow and can make immediate use of the nutrients. If they are put on in autumn much of the nutrient content can be leached away by the rain during winter, when there are few actively growing roots to take it up.

GROWING WILD PLANTS FROM SEED [1]

Not every plant has the same needs for germination, but the following method is worth trying on most kinds of wild perennials which are reluctant to germinate:

- Collect the seed when it is nearing maturity, but before it starts to be shed. Pick entire seeding heads, and hang them up in a cool, dry, well-ventilated place, with a paper bag around them to catch any seeds which fall (*see Figure 5.4*).

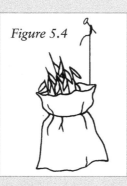

Figure 5.4

- The seed is ready to sow when it is completely dry. Some plants will indicate this by shedding their seed, others will hang on to it even though it is mature. This will be in late summer or autumn with most plants.

- Fill a seed tray with John Innes No 1 potting compost. Make sure it is thoroughly moist but not wet. This can be done by standing the tray in water for a few minutes and then allowing it to drain for an hour.

- Scatter the seed thinly on the surface. Scatter sharp sand over it until it is barely covered. As a rule of thumb the sand layer should be the same thickness as the diameter of the seeds.

- Cover the tray with a sheet of newspaper and a pane of glass. Put it in a sheltered outside spot or an unheated shed. Some kinds, such as ramsons, need to go through the cold of a winter before they will germinate.

- Have a look every week or so through the winter. When the seedlings emerge move the tray into the light (if necessary) and remove the newspaper.

---

[1]   A leaflet giving detailed instructions for sowing seed of wild plants and herbs is supplied by Suffolk Herbs with their seeds.

Composting

The question arises whether nutrient-rich materials should be composted before putting them on the soil surface or not. When we make compost all we are doing is decomposing organic material in a heap or bin rather than on the soil surface, which is the natural place for decomposition to happen. In theory the composting process is quicker than natural decomposition, and generates heat. But in practice most compost heaps are cold and slow. The main reasons for making compost rather than putting the materials straight on the soil surface, are:

- so it can be dug into the soil;
- to kill weeds seeds etc.;
- to make potting compost;
- to mellow concentrated manures;
- for lack of space to put bulky organic materials;
- for fear of slugs.

If undecomposed organic matter is dug into the soil the soil bacteria immediately start breaking it down, and in order to do this they need nitrogen. A young, sappy green manure crop has enough nitrogen in it, but for most organic matter the bacteria must draw on the soil's supply of that nutrient. They are more efficient at extracting nitrogen from the soil than plants are, so the plants suffer a temporary deficiency of nitrogen. Eventually, when the decomposition is complete and the bacteria die back to their previous population, the nitrogen becomes available to plants. But for a season you get stunted little plants with yellow leaves.

If the organic matter is simply placed on the surface of the soil, it is taken down bit by bit by earthworms. There is never so much organic matter actually in the soil at one time that the nitrogen gets seriously depleted.

The heat generated by the composting process can be enough to kill weed seeds, and disease organisms. In practice very few compost heaps reach the required temperature to kill seeds. Composting is an art, and even the most experienced composters have their failures.

Animal manures, on the other hand, heat up very readily, especially if they are mixed with straw or wood shavings rather than composted neat. Bought-in manure may have all sorts of weed seeds in it, and it is a good idea to compost it.

Home-made compost can be used for potting, as long as it is free of viable weed seeds.

Animal manures, especially poultry manure, contain soluble nutrients which can burn plant roots and cause rapid, sappy growth, which leaves plants weak and prone to disease. They must be composted, at least partly, before being used, whether on the surface or dug in. The same applies to human urine, which is best used as a compost heap activator, though limited amounts may be used as a liquid manure.

If a large amount of material becomes available at a time when you do not want to lay mulch – perhaps when there are many young plants which are vulnerable to slugs – you will need somewhere to put it for a while. Similarly, if you are weeding in wet weather there is no point in leaving the weeds to lie on the surface, because they will re-root themselves immediately.

Where there is a serious slug problem it may not be possible to mulch with anything other than compost for fear of harbouring slugs. But remember the Henry Doubleday Research Association and their experience with mulched potatoes (*see page 59*). And as Bill Mollison, one of the founders of permaculture, once said, "You haven't got an excess of slugs. You've got a deficiency of ducks."

How relevant are these reasons for composting in the specific conditions of a forest garden?
Since no digging goes on in a forest garden, the first reason for making compost does not apply. The second reason, killing weed seeds and disease organisms, is easier said than done. On the other hand, there is no doubt that even partial composting is good for general garden hygiene.

If you keep poultry or buy in unrotted manure you will need to do some composting. There is one plant, however, which can take fresh manure, even chicken manure, and thrive on it, and that is comfrey.

Urine is a valuable concentrated manure. It is best kept out of the compost toilet, but can be collected separately for use in the garden. Only small quantities can be used directly as a liquid manure (*see page 66*), but it can be combined with something which is dry and has a high carbon content. This will soak it up and the carbon will combine with the nitrogen in the urine which would otherwise be lost to the atmosphere. A bale of straw, a heap of sawdust, or a pile of autumn leaves kept together in a ring of chicken wire are all suitable. They should be covered to keep the rain off, and have urine poured into them whenever they look like drying out. Eventually they will rot to a rich, mellow manure.

Kitchen scraps and lawn mowings are both wet and quite high in nitrogen, and are not suitable for absorbing urine. The best thing to do with kitchen scraps is to slip them under a bit of more aesthetically appealing mulch, such as straw or bracken. If they are spread thinly they will not stink.

Finally, if you accumulate a lot of organic material when there is no suitable place for fresh mulch on the garden, what you need is a temporary dump heap, not a compost heap. The material will rot down a bit while it is waiting, but you do not need to compost it.

Liquid Manures

The basis of organic plant nutrition is to feed the soil, not the plants. A healthy soil will support healthy plants, whereas plants which are fed directly with highly soluble nutrients are sappy and vulnerable. What is more, a high level of soluble nutrients in the soil is actually harmful to the soil microbes which are the power-house of natural fertility. Liquid manures contain highly soluble nutrients, so their place in forest gardening is rather limited.

The plus side of being highly soluble is that they are quick-acting, so they can be useful as a tonic for sickly plants. If the weather is very wet, vegetables can get seriously short of nitrogen and other soluble nutrients, especially if they are growing on a sandy soil. Urine, diluted two to one, can bring back their colour and vigour and get them growing again. If used when the soil is dry it should be diluted more, down to ten to one in soil so dry that the plants need watering anyway. It should be used sparingly on clay soils, as its salt content can harm the soil structure.

Comfrey leaves or nettles both make useful liquid manures if soaked in water for a couple of weeks, as can weeds which are too seedy to be used as mulch. Their main use is to feed plants grown in containers, which only have a small volume of soil to forage in.

Pests and Diseases

These are really not much of a problem in a forest garden. The general level of diversity, the specific design features discussed in the last chapter, and choosing resistant plants and varieties are usually enough to make any further measures unnecessary.

These are some of the strands in an approach to plant health sometimes known as integrated pest management. It is based on two fundamental principles:

- growing healthy plants which have good natural resistance to pests and diseases;
- maintaining a low but stable population of pests.

Healthy Plants

A plant which has had a check to its growth during its early life is unlikely to be healthy in later life. So it is important to give plants the conditions they need for steady growth throughout their lives.

It starts with the soil: good drainage, enough water, a thriving soil life fed by plenty of organic matter, and a healthy level of nutrients. Careful planting is especially important for trees and shrubs, and so is careful pruning. Planting at the appropriate spacing, and thinning out herbaceous plants before they get too crowded are important too. Crowded plants compete and weaken each other. Good air circulation helps prevent fungus diseases, which are always a possibility in the sheltered environment of a forest garden. The appropriate micro-climate for the plant, with a minimum of sudden changes, especially of temperature, helps to ensure steady growth without checks.

Spraying plants with seaweed solution helps them to develop the strength to shrug off pests and diseases. Seaweed is definitely not a home-grown resource. Indeed in some areas it is a resource that is being exploited faster than it can replace itself, in order to supply the seaweed fertiliser industry. But only tiny amounts are needed for spraying compared to what is used for solid fertilisers, and if every gardener on this island used seaweed spray it could probably be done on a sustainable yield.

Seaweed contains all the nutrients plants need, including those which are only needed in minute quantities but can sometimes be deficient, plus vitamins and other growth substances. The solution can be absorbed directly through the leaves, which means much smaller quantities can be used than if it were watered onto the ground and absorbed through the roots.

The best results are had from spraying everything once a month from March to September. Spraying just once a year is less effective but worthwhile. It is best done in May, when everything is growing fast. Prevention is better than cure, but if you want to limit your use of seaweed solution as much as possible you can keep it in reserve and just use it on plants which already have a problem. This can be surprisingly effective.

Healthy Pests

It can come as a surprise to hear that a healthy garden needs a population of pests, but it's true. If there are no pests in the garden there will be no pest predators either. When the pests reappear, as they surely will, the natural controls will not be there, and the pests will multiply rapidly to a level where they can do real damage. A low level of pests does not do significant damage, but it does support a steady population of predators, and that helps to ensure that the pest population never gets out of control.

Spraying with poisons at the first sign of pests is not a good idea. As well as killing pests, most poisons kill the predators too. By and large the predators take longer to build up their numbers again than the pests do, so spraying often makes the problem worse. Spraying once makes it more likely that you will have to spray again, and again, and again. It can be a vicious spiral.

This applies to organically approved pesticides as much as to chemical ones. The main difference between the two is that the organic pesticides are made from plant extracts, whereas the chemicals are designed by humans and made from petroleum. The former are biodegradable, because the decomposing organisms have evolved with the plants that they come from. The latter are often very persistent, because they are substances which the decomposers have not evolved to deal with. Organic pesticides are usually less persistent than chemical ones, but they are not necessarily more specific.

It is particularly difficult to use poisons in a forest garden simply because of its diversity: you may want to spray the top fruit when you are harvesting the vegetables and soft fruit, which would be contaminated by the poison.

When it comes down to it, a poison is a poison.[2] They should not be necessary at all in a forest garden. If they are it is only as a last resort.

The first resort should always be a biological one, and if the garden has been well designed the biological checks and balances should prevent any problem becoming serious. If they do not, a physical intervention, such as picking off caterpillars, is always better than a chemical one, such as spraying them.

Getting to know the life-cycles of pests and their predators often reveals ways of controlling pests with a minimum of effort. Raspberry cane midge, for example, is one of those pests which overwinters in the soil. If you rake back the mulch around the canes during winter and lightly hoe the soil, the birds should get them for you. Ladybirds, those formidable killers of aphids, like to overwinter in the dried-out stalks of plants like nettles. So resisting the urge to tidy up in autumn may mean there is a resident population of ladybirds the following spring, ready to breed and build up their numbers along with their prey.

The Vegetable Layer

Ecologically, a forest garden falls somewhere between an annual vegetable garden and a wild plant community.

In an annual garden a number of highly-bred vegetables are planted and all other plants rigorously excluded. The aim – if not always the result – is total control by the gardener.

The plants which grow in a wild community are ones which have succeeded over time in out-competing other plants which have tried to grow there. This does not mean that they are the only plants which *can* grow

there, but that each one has a competitive edge over any other plant which could otherwise occupy its ecological niche. Sometimes this edge is very slight, but given enough time a plant which is only marginally better suited to its niche than its neighbour will survive and the other will die out.

The plants in a forest garden have been chosen to fit their niches as perfectly as possible, with the added proviso that they are edible or otherwise useful to humans. There will almost always be other plants which are more perfectly suited to the niches, and given time these will find their way in and take over, even if the difference in suitability is tiny.

The aim of the forest gardener is to make up for that difference just sufficiently to encourage the desired plants and discourage the unwanted ones so that the garden remains productive from a human point of view.

In the tree and shrub layers any invasion by unwanted plants would be a very long-term affair, but in the vegetable layer it happens year by year and month by month. If the gardener did nothing it would only be a matter of time before the vegetable layer lost most of its edible plants and became populated by a community of wild plants which are just that bit better suited to the conditions there.

Keeping the garden going in the desired direction does not take a great deal of work, but it does take attention. It's more like steering a boat than rowing one.

Self-Seeders

Three things are needed for successful self-seeding to happen:

1. **A supply of viable seed.** The best way to get good, healthy seed is to keep one or more plants apart as seed parents. They should not be picked for food, but allowed to put all their strength into seed production. Leaves are the food factories of plants, and a plant which tries to produce seed with only a few leaves will most likely produce weak seed.

    The seed parents should be strong, healthy specimens. If possible they should be growing in a relatively sunny position to help the ripening of seed. How many plants to leave depends on how prolific a self-seeder the plant in question is, and how much of it you want in the garden. Experience will tell how well a particular plant self-seeds in your garden, and results will be variable from year to year according to the weather.

    Self-seeders can be moved from one part of the garden to another by uprooting the seed parents once they have had time to mature the seed, and laying them on the ground in the area where they are wanted.

---

2   For a clear-headed discussion of pests and pesticides, see Robert Kourik's *Edible Landscape*, pp 19-21.

2. **An area of suitable soil surface.** A suitable soil surface is one that is not too heavily mulched. On the whole self-seeders do not need totally bare ground in order to get established. Most can germinate through a light mulch, but clearly a mulch designed to suppress all annual weeds will suppress self-seeders as well. Totally bare soil should be avoided as it may lose its crumb structure and present an inhospitable, compacted surface to the seeds.

3. **Not too much competition from other germinating seeds or established plants.** Competition can come from other self-seeders, perennial vegetables and weeds.

Some thinning is usually necessary, though it is not always possible to thin self-seeders to the regular spacings of hand-sown plants. But the overall plant density is much more important than regularity. If self-seeders come up thickly an alternative way to harvest them is as a seedling crop, or cut-and-come-again.

Neighbouring perennials can quickly crowd out self-seeders as they expand to their full summer size. What looked like a large enough space for a drift of self-seeders in early spring may rapidly shrink as the perennials grow, and it may be necessary to prune them back if the self-seeders are to survive.

Some weeding is usually necessary as the young

CUT-AND-COME AGAIN

This is like the mustard and cress we used to grow in the airing cupboard as children. The seedlings are not thinned, but cut overall with scissors when they reach about 3 to 7cm high. This can be repeated anything from two to five times, depending on the kind of plants, time of year and weather conditions. It is generally more successful in spring and autumn than in high summer, when the weather is drier and the plants tend to go to seed. A patch first cut in the autumn can sometimes overwinter and be cut again in spring.

Most of the self-seeding plants described in this book are suitable for cut-and-come-again if they seed themselves thickly enough. It is one of the most productive ways to grow leafy vegetables, as they cover the ground completely almost from the start and grow fast. The nutritional value of the seedlings is also higher than that of older plants – they can have twice the vitamin content.

---

plants get established, but self-seeding should not be tried in a really weedy garden. The biggest potential source of new weeds is the store of dormant seeds from previous years which is stored in the soil. The total number of seeds can be enormous. The old saying "one year's weeds, seven years' seeds" is an understatement if anything. Land which has previously been a garden is more likely to have a big store of garden weed seeds than land which was, say, lawn or pasture. But the only way to find out is to start gardening. Most of the seeds will remain dormant if the soil is not dug, but those which do germinate may be enough to cause trouble.

To prevent the build-up of unwanted seeds in the soil, flowering plants which can self-seed should be dead-headed before the seed matures, i.e. the dead flowers should be removed from the plant. The flowers most likely to self-seed are wild ones. These unfortunately tend to have many small blooms, compared to the few large ones of cultivated flowers, which makes dead-heading rather impractical. It may be necessary to choose between growing self-seeding vegetables and allowing the occasional wildflower which finds its way into the garden to bloom.

Wind-blown weed seeds are less of a problem, but worth keeping out if you want to grow self-seeders. There will be less wind-blown weed seeds near the middle of a garden surrounded by trees and shrubs on all sides (*see Figure 5.5*). The wind will be partly deflected over the garden and partly slowed down by the trees and shrubs near the edge, dropping its load of weed seeds before it gets to the centre. While the trees are still young a non-living windbreak can be used to filter out the weed seeds.

Self-seeders: Thin mulch   Perennials: Thick mulch

Figure 5.5

If the level of weeds in the garden, both annual and perennial, builds up as time goes by it may be best to stop growing self-seeders and move towards perennials only, with an overall mulch.

This does not mean an end to self seeding altogether. Many perennial vegetables reproduce themselves by self-seeding, and most have a productive life of only a few years. So we can let them self-seed in order to keep the garden well stocked with healthy and productive young plants. But the number of new plants needed each year is very small compared with annual and biennial self-seeders. It should be easy to get enough, even in a fairly heavily mulched garden.

Perennials

Most perennial vegetables need to be picked very lightly if at all in the first year of their lives. A plant which is picked too soon or too heavily is not likely to grow up strong and healthy, able to give good yields throughout its life. It is tempting to start picking as soon as possible, but the biggest total yield over the plant's lifetime will be had from holding back at first. In extreme cases, severely overpicked plants can die in their first winter.

Some kinds need to be left longer than others. For example seakale (*Crambe maritima*) grown from seed should be left for two years before forcing and picking, while perennial kale (*Brassica oleracea*) can be picked within months of planting strong cuttings. Details are given in Chapter 9 for each plant. Conditions vary from year to year and from place to place, and strong, well-grown plants may be able to stand picking when weaker ones of the same kind could not.

While leaves produce energy for the plant, flowers take energy from it to make seed and thus new plants. Flower buds should be removed from perennial vegetables during their first year so that all their energy can go towards building up their own strength. The flower buds themselves are often edible.

Once the plants are well established, regular picking of the leaves encourages more growth, and there is no benefit in leaving the plant unpicked. Regular picking will also help to keep the leaves young and tender, as the plants may not bother to produce any new ones if you do not remove the old. But this does depend to some extent on the time of year. Most plants produce new leaves early in the growing season and shift their energies into flowering as the season wears on.

Flower buds should be removed from established plants if you want to get maximum leaf yield, or to prevent too much self-seeding. But few perennials self-seed prolifically enough to cause a problem, and many of them have flowers which are beautiful and attract beneficial insects.

It is a good idea not to pick too heavily in the autumn, so as to allow the plants to build up strength for the winter. Once again this depends on the kind of vegetable, the condition of the plants, the local climate and so on. A combination of experience and a feel for plants is the best guide.

Plate 5.5 Working in the Naturewise forest garden, North London. (Naturewise)

The Yearly Round

Once a forest garden is established there is little work to do, and the seasons gently succeed one another with few major landmarks.

In a garden with a heavy burden of perennial weeds it may be necessary to mulch heavily in spring as soon as the perennial vegetables show their heads above the surface. On the other hand if there is a serious slug problem mulch may be withheld in spring until the plants have grown past the tender, vulnerable stage. But well-established perennial plants should be able to grow away from all but the worst of slug attacks.

Young plants which are particular favourites with the slugs, like lovage and skirret, may be eaten faster than they can grow. They can be protected with a mini-cloche for each plant made from a clear plastic bottle with the top and bottom cut off. This should keep off enough of the slugs to let the plants grow away from them.

Spring is the time to apply mulches containing plant nutrients, and to divide perennial vegetables, such as Welsh onions and comfrey, in order to increase their number. The main harvest of perennial vegetables is also in spring, and it can be hard to keep up with them if many things come ready at once.

Mulch can be added during the summer as it is needed. As self-seeders grow and are thinned it can be laid between them.

The fruit season starts with the first gooseberry thinnings at the end of May, and there should be something to pick from then right through to the major apple harvest in autumn, some of which can be stored through to the next spring. Most of the earlier fruit is soft fruit, and if the structure of the garden allows, it is probably worth netting it against birds. Some summer pruning may be necessary, including stone fruit, restricted forms of apples and pears, and some soft fruit.

Late summer is a fairly lean time as far as the vegetable layer is concerned. Some perennials are past their best now as the larger, tender leaves have given way to smaller, tougher ones and more energy goes into producing seed. Many self-seeding annuals also react to hot weather by going to seed, though they do last longer in the cooler conditions of a forest garden than in the open.

After the autumn harvests are gathered in it is time to put the garden to bed. Mulch applied now will protect the soil from the impact of heavy winter raindrops, and keep some of summer's warmth in it. Any plants which are to be forced or blanched for the spring, such as seakale, rhubarb and Good King Henry, can have extra mulch heaped on them now or later in the winter.

Some of the self-seeding salad plants come into their own in winter. Things like winter purslane, lamb's lettuce and land cress shun the high temperatures of summer, but they germinate and grow happily in autumn, and provide fresh salad greens through the winter and into spring till the hand-sown annuals like lettuces and radishes are ready. Some perennials, like salad burnet, welsh onion and sorrel, will stay green for all or most of the winter in milder areas. Winter salad plants can also be protected and encouraged to start growing early in spring with cloches.

Late autumn and winter is also the main time for pruning apples, pears and most kinds of soft fruit. Pruning can be a pleasant, meditative job for the quiet time of year. On the whole it is best to decide on a level of pruning, whether intensive, minimal or somewhere between the two, and stick to it. This is better for the trees than alternating regimes of hard and light pruning. At the very least any branches which are diseased, damaged or crossing over each other should be removed. When it comes down to deciding whether to cut out a particular twig or not, the golden rule of pruning is 'when in doubt, don't'.

The Daily Round

Robert Hart has a gardening kit composed of a bag of mulch material, a sickle, a pair of shears, a little bucket to pick produce into, and a wheelbarrow to carry the other things in. That is all he needs in his forest garden.

His weeding is mainly a matter of cutting back any plants which are crowding out their more desirable neighbours. Hence the sickle and shears. Whether the weed is an edible plant like a mint or something inedible like couch makes little difference: if a plant is growing in a larger quantity than it is wanted it is cut back; if it is growing in just the right quantity it is harvested; and if there is not enough of it it is encouraged to grow by cutting back its neighbours.

It is not necessary to remove all perennial weeds. Deep rooted ones can bring up nutrients from the subsoil. Cutting them at ground level rather than pulling them up is a way of harvesting this fertility for the topsoil, while leaving the root in place as a permanent pump. Creeping weeds are less useful and more invasive. They can be pulled out by the roots when the soil is soft after rain. Little bits of root may be left in the soil and will regenerate to a new plant, but the crop plants will have had a chance to grow big and strong by then, and will be in a position to compete successfully with the weeds.

Where self-seeders are crowded some thinning may be needed. This is not the same as cutting things back, as whole plants are removed. It is best done progressively, in two or three stages. Since thinnings are edible it can be tempting to wait until you actually need to eat them before thinning. This can be done up to a point, but if it means that the plants start to suffer from overcrowding it is a false economy. If the plants feel the stress of crowding they will most likely go to seed prematurely.

It is always a good idea to be on the lookout for new plants which have come up. These may be self-sown plants from outside the garden, or offspring of existing garden plants, either self-sown or rooted from runners. They may even be a resurgence of something you thought was dead a season ago. These plants can be either encouraged or discouraged as you see fit.

Apart from that, all is harvesting!

Chapter 6

CHOOSING PLANTS

How to select plants and varieties to suit you and your garden

As many species [and varieties] as possible should be planted. Such an approach will provide more information on suitability than all the published information on the subject. From this experimentation, certain species and varieties will be found to be of great value, while some will fail completely. The planning of more extensive permaculture in later years will then involve closer selection, based on first-hand information.
Bill Mollison & David Holmgren, *Permaculture One*

There is a lot of sense in this statement. Although the authors were thinking more in terms of a garden which is a forerunner of a larger planted area, the approach they recommend could equally be applied to a forest garden.

Plants are very variable things, much influenced both by local conditions and by the person who is growing them. Any statement made about a plant in a book is something of a generalisation, influenced by the writer's personal experience. Such information is best seen as a jumping-off point from which you can go ahead and find out what works for you in your own unique situation.

Growing a wide range of plants to see how well they do could be called the experimental approach to plant selection. At the other end of the spectrum is the not-reinventing-the-wheel approach: taking whatever knowledge is available and using it to make the selection of plants which is most likely to succeed. There is a lot of sense in this approach too. Despite its imperfections, the store of knowledge in books and in the memories of experienced local gardeners is a valuable resource, one that can save us from heartbreaking disappointments if we use it wisely.

In practice most people's approach falls somewhere between the two. In a forest garden it is a good idea to take different approaches to selecting the longer-lived plants and the shorter-lived.

If you are planting standard fruit trees, which may take ten years to come into bearing and have a productive life of well over a century, there is little room for experiment. You can't plant a dozen different varieties and choose which ones do best overall, because you won't live that long. But you can afford to make mistakes with perennial vegetables which complete their life cycles in five or six years, and which only occupy a small area of ground.

The size of the garden must also have a bearing on the approach to selecting plants. If you have enough space for 20 trees you may feel like taking a gamble on the odd peach or apricot. But if you only have space for four you probably will not.

A third factor to consider is just how experimental you want your garden to be. Is food production your first priority, or do you place a higher value on having fun and gaining knowledge about this new way of growing a garden?

Even if experiment is your priority, it may be wise to choose plants which are tried and tested. The multilayer food garden is a new idea in this part of the world, still at the experimental stage. If both the structure and the plants are experimental, and the garden is less than a complete success, it may be very hard to decide whether it was the structure or the choice of plants which was responsible.

CLIMATE, MICROCLIMATE AND SOIL

The Maritime Climate

The range of plants which will grow successfully in a cool temperate climate like ours is always less than the range that can be grown in the tropics. This is true whether we are growing a forest garden, a conventional garden of annual vegetables, or farm-scale crops.

The fact that a tree can survive here is not enough

to warrant its inclusion in an edible garden. It must grow sufficiently well to produce fruit or nuts and ripen them. It must be able to do so consistently, not just in an exceptional year.

We are surrounded by sea, and since water heats up and cools down more slowly than land this means we get mild winters and cool summers. The prevailing wind off the Atlantic gives us moist, cloudy skies, even in summer. In these conditions there are many exotic trees and shrubs which can easily survive, but rarely produce fruit.

This not only applies to trees from much warmer parts of the Earth, but also to those from more continental climates. There the average temperature may be the same as here, but with colder winters and hotter, sunnier summers. For example, some of the North American nut trees, such as the pecan, can survive much colder winters than anything they will encounter in Britain, but will not produce a crop in a British summer. In fact some species actually need the chilling of a really cold winter in order to fruit the next summer, and we do not get that every year.

Many of these plants also need a reasonably hot summer in order to ripen the wood of their new growth. If this does not happen the new twigs can be damaged even by a relatively mild winter.

The lack of contrast between the summer and winter temperatures in the maritime climate can cause problems at flowering time for some continental species, such as grapes and kiwis. Where winters are very cold and summers very hot, spring is a time of rapid and constant increase in temperature. But in a British spring an early mild spell is often followed by a late frost, and plants may be induced to flower early, only to have their flowers destroyed. Plants which flower in response to temperature as well as to increasing day length, such as walnuts, are particularly vulnerable.

This is not to say that our traditional apples and pears never have trouble with late frosts. It's all a matter of degree – how much of a risk do you want to take?

Our mild winters do have their advantages, though. Some perennial vegetables which would not survive a winter in, say, Germany can do so here, and others which would die down in the cold season stay green for all or most of the winter. This not only lengthens the picking season, but enables them to make better use of early spring sunshine when the leaves are off the trees and shrubs, as their own leaves will be bigger at that time if they have not had to grow from scratch.

Biennial self-seeders also benefit. They do not produce seed till their second year, so they must survive their first winter as plants. Tender ones, such as chard, cannot survive a really hard frost. Some annual self-seeders which would have to overwinter as seed in a colder winter can overwinter as plants here, which means we can eat their leaves through the winter and in the early spring.

Any plant which is actively growing during the winter can make use of plant nutrients in the soil which would otherwise be leached out by winter rains, thus conserving the fertility of the garden.

Regional Climates

The moderating effect of the sea on winter temperatures is much greater in the west of the country than the east. The further you go from the ocean and the nearer to the great continent of Eurasia, the colder the winters get. There are more frosts on the plain of East Anglia than there are on the Isle of Lewis – which has similar winter temperatures to the Isle of Wight. In the summer the picture is different. Broadly speaking, summer temperatures get cooler the further north you go, and the growing season gets shorter.

Height above sea level can have a dramatic effect on temperature and length of growing season. A hundred metres (330ft) of altitude makes the same difference to average temperatures as a hundred miles further north at sea level. In addition, increasing altitude generally brings higher winds, which intensify the effect of lower temperatures, and damper air, which increases rainfall and fungus diseases. In springtime it is possible to travel for hours by car and find things just about at the same stage as they were at home, but take a short walk up a nearby hill and find them weeks behind.

In most of Britain fruit growing starts to get difficult above 120m (400ft). Dessert apples, pears, plums and other more tender fruits are less likely to be successful at higher altitudes. Soft fruit, cooking apples and early dessert apples are a more reliable choice. Above 180m (600ft) you need a favourable microclimate to grow any fruit at all.

The likely date of the last spring frost is greatly modified by microclimate, so too much reliance should not be placed on regional averages for this important factor. There is no substitute for local knowledge, gained over a number of years. But the next best thing is to examine the local landform closely and try to predict where the frost pockets will be.

Rainfall also has an effect on what can be grown. In general, the climate gets wetter as you go west in Britain, though topography plays a part too. High hills and mountains have a higher rainfall, whereas western areas which are in the lee of higher ground, such as the plains of Cheshire and Somerset, have a relatively low rainfall.

High rainfall increases the likelihood of diseases such as canker and scab on apples and pears. Susceptible varieties, like Cox's Orange Pippin and Conference pear should not be grown in wet areas. On the other hand some of the spinaches are particularly liable to bolt in dry conditions, and mildew on apples and gooseberries is worse on a dry soil.

A good nursery should be able to advise you on what is suitable for your area, especially if it is a local one, or at least situated in the same region.

Cities

One thing which can modify a regional climate to a great extent is the presence of a city or large town. The most noticeable effect is on temperature. The average temperature in the centre of a large town can be 0.5-1.5°C greater than in the nearby countryside, and the growing season may be two to three weeks longer. City centres are usually warmer on four nights out of five, which means fewer frosts and less severe ones when they do happen.

The heart of London gets an average of ten more frost-free weeks in the year than the nearest rural areas. Unfortunately for urban fruit growers most of this extra frost-free time is in the autumn, rather than in the spring when it would be more useful. But the extra heat is enough to allow the most northerly olive tree (*Olea europea*) in the world to thrive in the Chelsea Physic Garden. Not only is it over 120 years old and 10m high, but it even occasionally ripens a few fruit!

Of course London is the largest conurbation in Britain, and the heat island effect may be expected to be greatest there. But there is a significant effect in any large or medium sized urban area, and it is good to know that not all the advantages lie with rural gardeners.[1]

Coasts

Gardening very near the coast has its advantages and disadvantages.

On the plus side the winters are milder than they are inland. Figs need a frost-free winter, and the old adage is that you should only grow them within sight of the sea.

On the minus side the summers are cooler, it is usually windy, and the wind is laden with salt. Most plants are very sensitive to salty winds, but those listed in the box are all to some degree tolerant. Figs are not tolerant of wind, but they deserve to have the most sheltered microclimate in a coastal garden in exchange for their delicious fruit.

---

[1]   This information on urban temperatures is taken from *The Ecology of Urban Habitats*, O.L.Gilbert, Chapman & Hall, 1989, pp 25-30. A brilliant book, highly recommended to anyone with an interest in ecology.

PLANTS FOR COASTAL SITES

Trees and Shrubs	Vegetables
Fig	Sea kale
Elders	Sea beet
Salt bush	Chard
Beach plum	Alexanders
Ramanas rose	Perennial kale
Elaeagnus	Lovage
Hawthorns	Fennel
Whitebeam	Buck's horn plantain
Wild service	

This list is not exhaustive, and experiment will show that many other plants can be grown in coastal forest gardens, especially those with favoured microclimates. Establishing a good windbreak before planting the productive trees and shrubs can make a big difference.

Microclimate

The three microclimate factors most likely to affect the choice of plants and their positioning within the garden are:

1. **Light and Shade**
    Where a forest garden is shaded from outside by trees or buildings, shade tolerance is needed in the trees as well as the shrubs and vegetables. Most fruits prefer full Sun, but some need it more than others. On the whole soft fruit need less Sun than top fruit, so in a very shaded garden, or part of a garden, it is worth considering a garden of two layers only, shrubs and vegetables. This will give an opportunity to grow some of the taller shrubs, which may not fit under the trees in a three-layer garden.

Trees
*   Tender exotics, including peaches, apricots, figs and almonds really need full Sun.

*   Pears and mulberries also need as much Sun as they can get, but are not quite so demanding.

*   Dessert fruits need more Sun than cookers. Cooking apples and cooking plums can be grown in positions where they receive direct Sun for less than half the day during the growing season, though they must have good indirect light in that case.

*   Sour cherries, medlars, elders and hazels are the most shade-tolerant of the tree fruits. They can produce a

crop with only indirect light. (Note: Elders and hazels are normally grown in a shrub form.)

Shrubs
- Autumn fruiting raspberries need full Sun.

- Most soft fruit needs direct Sun for at least half the day.

- Other cane fruit, gooseberries, and red and white currants can do with less than half a day's full Sun.

- Loganberries and elders can give a crop with only indirect light.

Vegetables
- The most shade tolerant of the forest garden vegetables are: Jerusalem artichokes, ramsons, mints, pink purslane, golden saxifrage, stinging nettles and ground elder (not recommended).

- The least shade tolerant are: Nine Star broccoli, sea kale, rock samphire, red valerian, nasturtium and those listed under the 'Sun-loving' sections of Herbs, Onions and Roots in Chapter 9.

- Perennials which leaf early or remain green through the winter tolerate shade cast by deciduous trees and shrubs better than ones which leaf later, when the trees and shrubs are leafing.

- The same goes for annuals which grow during autumn, winter and spring rather than summer.

- Plants with broad leaves are usually more shade tolerant than those with narrow leaves.

- There are exceptions to these general principles.

A note of its shade-bearing qualities is included under the main entry for each plant. These are based on my own observations and those of other gardeners, plus whatever published information is available. This is sometimes contradictory, one and the same plant being described as 'tolerates partial shade' and 'needs full sun' in different books or seed catalogues. As multi-layer planting has been greatly neglected in our culture, not much is known about the shade tolerance of vegetables. It is a prime subject for experiment in our own gardens.

Any forest garden can be a source of information about shade tolerance, whether precise experiments are carried out in it or not. If all three layers are planted simultaneously the shade level will gradually increase as the years go by. If a mixture of vegetables is planted to start with, the more shade tolerant ones will reveal themselves by succeeding at the expense of the more light-demanding ones as the level of shade increases.

2. Walls
- South, south-east and south-west walls are suitable for all fruit, but they are best reserved for the kinds that really need the heat and light: figs, apricots, peaches, dessert pears, dessert plums, gages, grapes and New Zealand kiwis. Mulberries and quinces also like this kind of microclimate, but they are lower value fruits. These walls are ideal sites for aromatic herbs, especially those of Mediterranean origin which like a hot, dry summer.

- West walls are the next warmest, as the afternoon Sun is warmer than the morning. They are suitable for all the above, plus: cooking pears and plums, all apples, sweet and sour cherries and soft fruit.

- An east wall is cooler, especially if it is exposed to easterly winds. It can grow early and mid-season pears, apples, plums, sweet and sour cherries and soft fruit.

- North-east and north-west walls are suitable for cooking apples and early season cooking plums. Moisture-loving vegetables and herbs should not be planted by a wall with a more southerly aspect than this. (If possible they should not be grown near a wall at all.)

- North walls, and very shady walls of other aspects, can grow: sour cherries, early season cooking apples, red and white currants, gooseberries, summer-fruiting raspberries, blackberries, Japanese wineberries, some hybrid berries, including loganberries, and the pear variety, Williams Bon Chretien.

Of course the aspect of the wall is not the whole story, and other microclimate factors must be taken into account, including shading and shelter. Remember that all plants grown on or by a wall will need extra watering and mulching.

3. Frost
The least favourable microclimate for a forest garden is one which is prone to late frosts. If the only land available is in a frost pocket, and nothing can be done to make it less of one by altering structures, hedges and so on, the only option is to choose fruits which are tolerant of late frosts.

These either flower late or have flowers which are resistant to frost. The plants listed here are not all equally tolerant of frost. Some flower later than others, and some can stand harder frosts than others. Reference should be made to the descriptions of the plants in the relevant chapters.

There is also a variation in frost tolerance between different varieties of the same fruit. Apples in particular have a wide range of blossoming times, and late ones can be chosen for sites where frost may be a problem.

FROST TOLERANT FRUITS AND NUTS

Cherry plum	Hawthorn	Blueberries
Asian pear	Elder	Manchurian kiwi
Mulberry	Blackberry	Oregon grape
Quince	Hybrid berries	Chinese dogwood
Medlar	Roses	Siberian pea
Hazel	Thimbleberry	

Note: Mulberries are susceptible to early autumn frost.

There are also varieties of most of the commonly grown fruits with blossom which can stand light frosts.

Soil

Most forest garden plants will grow well in a wide range of soils. The only kinds of soil which seriously limit the range of plants that can be grown are very alkaline ones (*see page 43*) and poorly drained ones.

Few of the forest garden vegetables are troubled by high alkalinity, but most fruits are. The most susceptible of all are raspberries and blueberries, and they should certainly be avoided on thin soils over chalk, limestone or old demolished buildings. The kinds most likely to succeed are listed in the box below:

FRUIT FOR THIN CHALKY SOILS

Apricot	Blackberry
Elders	Fig
Hawthorns	Hazels
Walnuts	Whitebeam
Rowan	Siberian pea

Some varieties of apple are less susceptible to high alkalinity than others.[2]

On the whole vegetables are less sensitive to poor drainage than fruits, and a wide range of cresses and spinaches may do well on soil which would be too wet for fruit growing. The vegetables listed here are very tolerant of poor drainage. Of the fruits, only quinces, guelder rose and possibly blackcurrant are tolerant of a really wet soil. The others may grow adequately with imperfect drainage, but would prefer it to be better.

PLANTS FOR POORLY DRAINED SOILS

Fruit	*Vegetables*
Quince	Ramsons
Guelder rose	Watercress
Cooking apples	Land cress
Crab apples	Golden saxifrage
Blackcurrants	Pink purslane
Blackberries	Hairy bittercress
Elder	Nettles
Hawthorn	Mints, especially water mint
Rowan	

Other fruits, including pears, plums, damsons and most soft fruit, will tolerate some impeded drainage in the subsoil, below 45 cm deep, but not above that. Raspberries, sweet cherries and peaches will not tolerate any imperfections in drainage.

CHOOSING VEGETABLES

For 'as many species as possible' in the quotation at the head of this chapter, perhaps we should substitute 'as many as practicable'. This is after all a kitchen garden, not a research establishment, and most of us want enough of each plant to make a decent meal. Anyway it would not be possible to base a useful assessment on one or two plants, and some kinds could die out by chance accident rather than because they were unsuitable.

There is also a limit to the amount of time and effort each of us wants to put into observing and recording plants. If it is done in too impressionistic and vague a way it becomes pretty pointless. It is probably more use to get to know a moderate number of plants well than to have a nodding acquaintance with many.

Nevertheless, the vegetable layer is the ideal part of the garden to experiment with, not just because the plants have a shorter life-span than the trees and shrubs, but also because less is known about them. Perennial vegetables are a neglected group of plants, an area of deep mystery compared to fruit-growing. This goes to make the vegetable layer the most interesting part of a forest garden to my mind.

Shade Tolerance

There are two kinds of shade: the permanent shade cast by buildings and evergreens, and the seasonal shade cast by deciduous trees and shrubs. In the descriptions of plants in Chapter 9, 'shade-tolerance' means the plant's

---

2   They are listed in the *Directory of Apple Cultivars*. See Further Reading.

tolerance for seasonal shade. Plants which can grow well under a closed canopy of deciduous trees will not necessarily do well in positions which get no winter Sun.

The shade-tolerance of many perennial vegetables is indirectly affected by the winter microclimate. Where it is mild they are able to start growth early, and complete much of their annual growing cycle before the trees and shrubs leaf up. As well as extending the picking season for these vegetables, this means they can be grown under a more complete cover of trees and shrubs than would be possible in areas with a cooler winter.

Sea beet, for example, can be found growing well under a closed canopy of deciduous shrubs within a stone's throw of the sea in south west England. But it would not do well under the same cover in an inland situation or on more easterly coasts.

Wild Food Plants

Many of the vegetables we can grow in a forest garden are wild ones. Since they grow in this country without any help from us they are likely to do well with a minimum of care and attention.

They have a greater natural resistance to diseases and pests, including slugs and snails, than cultivated kinds. They may not be immune, but they can usually live with the level of pests and diseases they are likely to find in a polyculture. They are also more likely to be able to propagate themselves year after year in the garden, more so than cultivated perennials and self-seeders.

Wild vegetables are almost always more nutritious than cultivated ones. They tend to be higher in protein, vitamins and minerals. As every other desirable characteristic has been bred for in cultivated varieties over the centuries, this one has gone by default. Until very recently it was not possible to measure nutritional content, so it could not be bred for, and there is no commercial advantage in breeding for it today.

One drawback of wild food is that the edible parts, whether these are leaves, roots, seeds or whatever, tend to be smaller than those of cultivated plants. This means that they take longer to pick than conventional vegetables, which have been bred over the generations to have large edible parts. But there is very little work involved in growing them other than the picking, so the total amount of time spent in getting them to the table is less. However the time it does take is concentrated at picking time, and this may be inconvenient.

Another possible drawback is the taste of wild food, which some people find less attractive than the food they are used to. Whether this is simply a matter of familiarity or because cultivated plants really do taste better is hard to say. No doubt it is a bit of both. But there are some wild plants which actually taste better than their cultivated equivalents. Fat hen and chickweed, for example, have a better taste than spinach and lettuce respectively. Most people don't know this simply because they haven't tried them.

Those wild plants which do have a strong or unfamiliar taste are usually most pleasant to eat in springtime, when the plants are young and tender. This is also the time when green food from a forest garden is most in demand, the hungry gap in the annual vegetable garden.

Invasiveness

Most of the plants which are suitable for the vegetable layer of a forest garden, whether wild or cultivated, are often described as invasive. What this means is that they are tough, self-reliant plants which can maintain themselves and reproduce without much help from us. In the conditions of a forest garden they can hold their own, but when they are presented with a garden of annual plants, with lots of bare soil between the plants, there is nothing much to stop them and they rapidly expand to fill the space.

Even so, some plants are more invasive than others. Some perennials which spread vegetatively, such as the mints, can expand at the expense of others in a forest garden and will eventually take over if allowed to. The most prolific self-seeders, like fat hen and shepherd's purse can be invasive while there is bare soil about, but as the garden matures the perennials take over and the self-seeders die out unless they are deliberately cultivated. The main problem with invasive self-seeders comes if they spread into an adjacent garden of annuals.

So any description of a plant as invasive must be taken in context. If it is in a conventional gardening book it probably means the plant is suitable for forest gardening. If it is in Chapter 9 of this book it means the plant is more than usually invasive. But much also depends on environment. A plant which is very competitive in one garden may be unable to maintain itself without help in another.

CHOOSING FRUIT VARIETIES

Summer apples are crisp and juicy, with plenty of refreshing acidity and are best eaten straight from the tree. Typical varieties are Beauty of Bath and the tiny Jenetting that since the sixteenth century has opened the apple season. More complex flavours generally appear later, beginning to show in mid-season varieties that, once picked, will keep for weeks rather than days. September brings the scarlet Worcester Pearmain with the densely sweet flavour of strawberries that it has

passed on to its commercially popular modern seedling Discovery. Then comes the rich and almost pear-like taste of the russetted and golden St. Edmund's Pippin, the aniseed flavoured Ellison's Orange, the savoury, juicy James Grieve and the Egremont Russet, the russet of the high street which has a curious, addictive flavour that Morton Shand described as 'a slight suggestion of the scent of crushed fern' ...
Joan Morgan, in *Orchards*[3]

... and so the list goes on, through the autumn, winter and into spring, through the counties and regions of the land, through a wide range of subtle flavours.

Although the apple takes pride of place for the rich diversity and sheer number of its varieties, there are enough varieties of all the commonly grown fruits to make the process of selecting them seem at first like a perplexing maze of choices. The best way to make sense of it is to look at varieties from six points of view:

• locality;
• ease of growing;
• season of ripening;
• pollinators;
• size of tree;
• taste.

It still may not be a simple process. Perish the thought that it should be! The diversity of fruit varieties is a pleasure to be savoured, even luxuriated in. But this scheme can help to guide you through the maze to a selection which will work in your garden.

The first step is to send off for a number of nursery catalogues, the more the better up to a point. Nurseries tend to specialise, one in top fruit, another in soft fruit, another in nuts. A nursery with the widest selection of, say, apples may only offer a handful of blackcurrant varieties, and these not necessarily the best ones. Even an apple specialist will not offer every lesser-known apple variety; each of the major specialists will offer something that no-one else does.

Some catalogues are a mine of information about varieties. Occasionally they disagree with each other, which is another good reason for getting a number of different ones. Books on fruit growing also give useful information on varieties, though it is often restricted to the more popular ones due to lack of space.

It is certainly worthwhile buying fruit trees and shrubs from specialist mail order nurseries rather than a garden centre. They offer a much wider range, and

the quality of the plants should be of a high standard – something which cannot be said about every garden centre. Also they are usually happy to advise you on your selection over the phone. It is in their interests to see that you get plants that fit your requirements perfectly.

Locality

Until recent times you could tell which county you were in by the shape of the farm waggons, by the breed of sheep in the fields, or by the varieties of fruit growing in the orchards. Today all the farm machinery is mass produced in centralised factories, and if there are any orchards left they will contain a few market-leading varieties which are as mass-produced and as centralised as the tractors.

These orchards are dependent on the chemical industry to keep them going just as much as the tractors depend on oil. The old local varieties were adapted to local conditions of climate, soil and so on, and were much better able to look after themselves. Choosing local

---

CATALOGUE CHECK LIST

The ideal catalogue would give you the following information about each variety on offer:

• season of ripening;
• use and qualities of the fruit, i.e. flavour, cooking qualities etc.;
• appearance of the fruit;
• pollination group, or other pollination information as appropriate (*see pages 81-82*);
• whether tip-bearing – for apples and pears;
• relative size of tree;
• rootstocks on which it is available;
• growth habit – e.g. upright, spreading – if different from the norm;
• whether heavy or light cropper;
• disease susceptibility or resistance – if different from the norm;
• general ease of growing;
• parts of the country it does well in – for the hardiest and most tender varieties.

No catalogue gives every bit of this information, though some give much more than others. But for apples, pears and plums the *Directories* published by the Agroforestry Research Trust give comprehensive information on every known variety.[3]
See List of Suppliers.

---

3   See Further Reading.

varieties not only helps to preserve and enhance the distinctiveness of local culture, it is also a way of getting trees with the degree of self-reliance that we look for in forest garden plants.

Thousands of old fruit varieties are preserved at the National Fruit Collection at Brogdale in Kent,[4] and a number of suppliers still stock the old varieties alongside the newer more popular ones. Thornhayes Nursery (see List of Suppliers) give the original locality and date of introduction of all the hundred plus varieties of apples in their catalogue. Common Ground, in their delightful little book *Orchards, a Guide to Local Conservation*, give a list of apple, plum and cherry varieties which are associated with particular counties, but the most comprehensive information on the origin of apple varieties is to be found in Joan Morgan and Alison Richards' *Book of Apples*.[5] If you have an unidentified tree and would like to know whether it is an old local variety, the Royal Horticultural Society[6] provide a fruit identification service.

Locally adapted varieties are not always old ones. New ones have been bred for specific regions. They will more likely be bred for a specific feature which is prevalent over a large area rather than evolved to suit the all-round characteristics of a small locality. An example is the apple Sunset, which is similar to Cox's Orange Pippin but will succeed in wetter western areas where Cox would succumb to disease. Another is Winston, a Cox substitute for areas where late frosts may be a problem.

An old variety which comes from a different area with similar conditions may also be a good bet. For example the old Cornish Aromatic, which is said to be particularly tolerant of high rainfall, may well be successful all up the west coast.

The microclimate of the garden can be as important as the general climate, extending or restricting the possible choices quite as much as locality. There may also be differences in microclimate within the garden itself, so it may be possible to grow tender varieties, but only a few of them.

Soil type is another local factor which can change completely over short distances, even from one end of a garden to the other. And as a general rule, the less suitable the soil the more robust the variety, as well as the rootstock, must be.

Ease of Growing

To a great extent this point is covered by the previous one. A variety bred for local conditions will certainly be easier to grow than one chosen at random. Nevertheless there are some varieties which are generally easier to grow than others, and this is usually a matter of their resistance to disease. Disease resistance is a double blessing. It saves work and worry, and also means that we can grow fruit successfully with a minimum use of poisons.

Scab is the main disease which resistance is commonly bred for in apples and pears. This disease is doubly important since around half of all canker infections enter via scab wounds. Varieties which are resistant or immune are noted in good nursery catalogues. Other varieties show a general resistance to disease, and these are probably the ones to go for, as long as they have the other qualities you are looking for as well.

Virus diseases can seriously affect soft fruit. There is a government certification scheme for virus-free planting material which covers all the most popular varieties of soft fruits. This includes many varieties of blackcurrants, raspberries and strawberries, but only a few of red currants, gooseberries and hybrid berries. It is certainly worth buying certified stock if the varieties you want are available in it, or even choosing a variety partly because it is included in the scheme. The plants are not immune, but are guaranteed free of virus diseases when you buy them. Since these diseases are slow to infect established plants, certified stock will stay virus-free for virtually all its productive life.

Gooseberries can get mildew, especially in the sheltered conditions of a forest garden, and there are resistant varieties to this.

On the whole, cooking varieties are easier to grow than eaters. The main distinction between the two is how sharp they taste, and there are some borderline varieties, like the redoubtable Newton Wonder apple, which are dual purpose. But this is very much a matter of personal taste, and many, perhaps most people find them too sharp to eat raw. These dual purpose apples tend to become more acceptable as eaters towards the end of their storage period. Damsons are hardier than normal domestic plums, and on the whole much easier to grow.

DISEASE RESISTANT FRUITS AND NUTS

Crab apple	Hazels	Worcesterberry
Mulberry	Black walnut	Blueberries
Elders	Chestnut	Guelder rose
Fig	Rowan	Beach plum
Kiwis	Hawthorns	Wild strawberry
Medlar	*Elaeagnus*	Juneberries
Quince	Ramanas rose	Oregon grape

---

4   See List of Suppliers.
5   See Further Reading.
6   RHS Gardens, Wisley, Surrey GU23 6QB. (01483) 224234.

An alternative to choosing disease-resistant varieties is to choose kinds of fruit and nuts which are not much troubled by disease at all. Of course this restricts what you can get out of the garden, but is an option to consider if low maintenance is a priority.

Pruning
Ease of pruning is another point to be considered. For example, varieties of top fruit which are particularly prone to biennialism are going to need more careful pruning, whereas tip-bearers can get by with little or none. A good catalogue will note which varieties have these characteristics.

Season of Ripening

Different varieties ripen at different times, and some varieties ripen over a longer period than others. The picking season for most fruits can be lengthened both by planting a succession of varieties, and by choosing varieties with a long picking season.

Apples have the longest eating season of any temperate fruit, followed by pears. The others all have a much shorter season, which can only be extended by bottling, making jam or some other kind of preserving.

Apples

The earliest dessert apple varieties are ready to pick in August and the first part of September. Perhaps the earliest of all is George Cave, which is sometimes ripe before the end of July. None of these varieties keep for more than a week or ten days. The early autumn dessert apples, which ripen through September, only keep for a little longer, around two or three weeks.

Because these early apples do not keep there is no point in growing too many of them in a home garden. A row of cordons is a good way of growing a succession of early ripening apples, as these are the most compact trees with the smallest yield per tree. Unfortunately tip bearing varieties cannot be successfully grown as cordons, and this excludes one of the best tasting of the early autumn varieties, Worcester Pearmain. A family tree is another possibility for varieties which are wanted in small quantities.

The rest of the apple crop is picked in October, and different varieties keep for different lengths of time. The late autumn varieties are ripe when picked, or shortly after, and may keep till November or December. The later varieties are unripe when picked and ripen in succession in store. Some will be ready in November, others will keep till March, or even later if storage conditions are ideal.

All these varieties have a much longer season than the early ones. If you only have space for a small number of trees, three, or even two, well-chosen varieties could be enough to keep you in apples from picking time till spring. If there is only room for a single fruit tree in the garden, and you do not fancy a family tree, a keeping dessert apple is the obvious choice – as long as there is an apple in the neighbourhood to pollinate it (*see page 81*). It will keep you in fresh fruit for longer than any other kind of tree, and at a time when apples are more expensive in the shops.

The keepers are obviously the apples which are worth growing in greater quantities, and if any large apple trees are planned for the forest garden they should be keeping varieties.

Cooking apples also come in both early and late varieties, though this is not so critical as it is with eaters because they can be bottled for storage with no loss of quality.

Others

The season for desert pears runs from late July through to January. Unlike dessert apples, they are also suitable for cooking. The only pear varieties which are single-purpose cookers are very late varieties which keep into the spring, longer than any dessert variety will keep. This means that any surplus eating pears can be bottled, so it is not so critical to avoid over-production of them as it is with early apples. The later varieties keep for longer than the earlier, though the difference in keeping time between early and late ones is less than it is for apples.

Plums do not keep, so a succession of three or four varieties would be needed to supply eating plums over the whole season, from July to October. But there may not be space for this in many gardens, even if small trees are grown. As they are tip-bearing they cannot be grown as cordons. Most plums are dual purpose to some extent, though some are more recommended for cooking and others more for eating, so any temporary glut can be bottled. Many varieties can be dried.

The sweet cherry season is between mid to late June and early August, with most varieties ripening in late July. If you have room for more than one you can plant for a succession, but as there is no really dwarfing rootstock for cherries this may not be possible.

Of course the opposite is true of soft fruit. As they are such small plants it is easy to plant a succession of varieties, even in a small garden. The only danger of going for too many different varieties is that you may not have enough fruit ripe at one time to make a meal for the whole family.

On the whole there are fewer varieties of the less commonly grown fruits, and there is less scope for extending the picking season by choice of varieties.

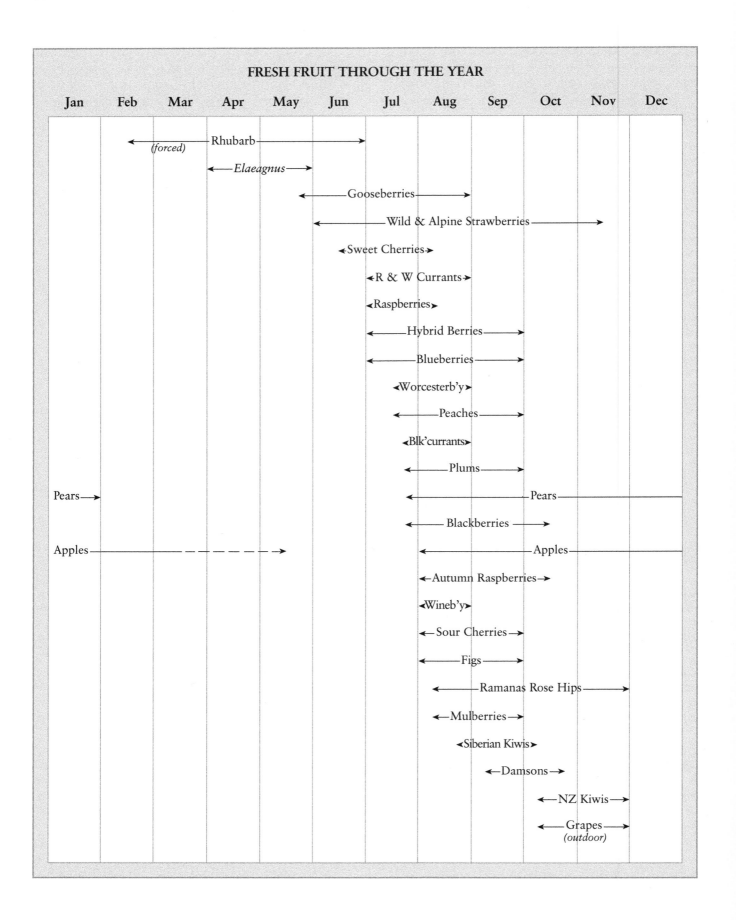

FRESH FRUIT THROUGH THE YEAR

| Jan | Feb | Mar | Apr | May | Jun | Jul | Aug | Sep | Oct | Nov | Dec |

Pollinators

Most commonly grown fruits need pollen from a tree of another variety to pollinate them. It is not possible to grow a single variety of these fruits on its own.

Every individual fruit or nut starts out as a flower. More strictly speaking, it starts out as the female parts of the flower. This develops into a fruit only when it is fertilised by pollen from the male part of a flower of the same species.

Some plant species have separate male and female flowers on different individual plants, for example most varieties of kiwi fruits. These will only produce fruit if both male and female plants are grown together. All the other plants which concern us here have both sexes on the same plant, whether in separate male and female flowers or in hermaphrodite flowers.

Some plants are wind-pollinated, for example hazels, which have separate male and female flowers. The male flowers are the catkins, and the female flowers are tiny little red tufts which you may not have noticed unless you knew they were there. Pollen is blown from the male flowers to the female ones, which then start to develop into clusters of nuts.

Most fruits are insect-pollinated, and these usually have hermaphrodite flowers with petals. The insects are attracted by the sight and smell of the flower and rewarded with food in the form of nectar and pollen. In their passage from flower to flower they transfer some of the pollen from the male parts of one flower to the female parts of another. But having both sexes on the same plant does not necessarily mean that a plant can pollinate itself. Some can, but others can only be fertilised by pollen from another plant of the same species but a different variety.

Those which can fertilise themselves are called self-fertile or self-compatible and those which cannot are called self-infertile or self-incompatible. Self-fertility varies from variety to variety, but some fruits are predominantly self-fertile while others are self-infertile (*see box on the right*).

In fact it is not quite as cut and dried as the lists would suggest. Many self-infertile plants will produce a small crop with their own pollen, but usually not enough to make the plant worth growing. Most self-fertile plants will produce a good crop on their own, but an even better one if they have a pollinator nearby.

Since the pollen to fertilise a self-infertile plant must come not just from another plant but from one of another variety, at least two varieties must be planted together. Different varieties flower at different times, so varieties must be chosen which flower at the same time.

This is more crucial where only two or three trees

SELF-FERTILE FRUITS

Plums	*many varieties*
Damsons	*most*
Cherry plums	
Sweet cherries	*few*
Sour cherries	*most*
Peaches	
Mulberries	
Quinces	
Medlars	
Grapes	
All soft fruit	*except blueberries*
Native elder	

SELF-INFERTILE FRUITS

Apples	*almost all varieties*
Pears	*almost all*[†]
Plums	*many*
Sweet cherries	*most*
Hazel	*in effect*
Blueberries	*partially*
American elder	
Chestnuts	
Walnuts	

[†] A notable exception is the popular variety Conference, which is self-fertile.

of the same kind are to be planted than where a large number of trees of different varieties are grown together. It is also less crucial where there are other trees in the neighbourhood which can act as pollinators – though you can never be sure your neighbours will not decide to grub out their fruit trees at some point in the future.

The further away the pollinators are the less effective they will be, though it is hard to be precise about distance. Something like 100m is probably a good rule of thumb with apples. But pears and plums flower earlier, and they should really be as close as possible to their pollinators as there are fewer insects on the wing earlier in the year.

Pollination Groups

To make the process of selecting pollinators easy, varieties are divided into pollination groups. Apples are normally divided into seven groups, Pollination Group 1 being the earliest flowering, and 7 the latest. Two varieties in the same group will pollinate each other, and they will also pollinate members of adjacent groups, so a variety in Group 3 will pollinate varieties in Groups 2, 3 and 4.

Some catalogues ignore this system and use one of their own, based on a smaller number of groups, often three. This is probably accurate enough to get an adequate crop in most years.

Since pears blossom over a shorter period there are only four pollination groups for them. There are five for sweet cherries, and five for the plum family – plums gages and damsons, which are all one species and hence pollinate each other.

Self-fertile varieties will act as pollinators to other varieties in the same pollination group. Crab apples are particularly useful, as they are self-fertile and some varieties have such a long flowering season that they can pollinate most domestic apple varieties.

The time of flowering is not strongly correlated with the time of ripening. Thus an apple in Pollination Group 1 is not necessarily an earlier fruiting apple than one in Group 6. So it is possible to select a number of trees which will give a succession of fruit throughout the season, but all flower at the same time.

Incompatibility Groups

Some varieties will not pollinate each other even though they flower at the same time. They are called cross-incompatible, and are divided into incompatibility groups. They can only be pollinated by a variety which is *not* in the same incompatibility group, but which *is* in the same or an adjacent pollination group.

- There are no incompatibility groups of apples (though the ever-popular Cox is cross-incompatible with two varieties, Kidd's Orange Red and Holstein).

- There are two incompatibility groups of pears and three of the plum family.

- There is so much cross-incompatibility among sweet cherries that it is easier to list the varieties that do go together rather than the ones that do not, and this is what it usually done in catalogues. Fortunately there are self-fertile cherries, such as the popular variety, Stella.

Some varieties of apples and pears need two pollinators. These are the triploids, which have one and a half times the normal number of chromosomes. They are often very vigorous varieties, Bramley being an example. If one of these varieties is grown, two others in the same pollination group must be grown along with it to pollinate the triploid and each other.

Some varieties of pears are generally unreliable pollinators, and should be treated as triploids. The same goes for varieties of any fruit which are particularly prone to biennialism, as they cannot be relied on to pollinate every year.

Many cross-incompatible, triploid and other awkward varieties are well worth growing for their other qualities. It can be worth taking the trouble to find them pollinators, as long as the pollinators are also varieties which are worth growing for their own sake.

Nuts

The hazel family, cobs and filberts, are strictly speaking self-fertile, as a tree can pollinate its female flowers with its own pollen. But male and female flowers are not always active at the same time, so pollination can be poor in some years. Pollination can be improved by shaking the branches at flowering time, in February, and this can be done at no extra effort by choosing this time for pruning. Nevertheless planting of two or more varieties is recommended.

As there are so few varieties available there are no pollination groups for the hazels, but some varieties are particularly compatible with certain others.[7] If space is limited it is possible to grow a family hazel in order to get more than one variety for pollination. Although they are two different species, cobs and filberts can fertilise each other. Some commercial growers simply rely on the wild hazels in the hedgerows to make up for incomplete self-pollination.

Much the same is true of walnuts. They are self-fertile, each tree bearing both male and female flowers. But in most varieties the male and female flowers mature at different times, in some varieties the male flowers first, in others the female. There are some varieties which can pollinate themselves, but even these do better with a companion.

Young walnut trees tend to produce only female flowers for the first few years, so planting near an existing older tree can help to ensure earlier fruiting. As they are wind pollinated, the young trees should be downwind of the old, and preferably within 80m, though a more distant tree will have some effect.

Size

Although the rootstock is the biggest influence on the size of the tree, the variety has some effect too. Different varieties grown on the same stock will grow to different sizes, and a good nursery catalogue will give an indication of the relative size of different varieties. If there is a variety which suits you in every respect except its size you can choose to grow it on a different rootstock, but there are some varieties which are so vigorous that they cannot be really dwarfed,

---

7   See *The Fruit Garden Displayed*, in Further Reading.

for example Bramleys, and others so weak of growth that they never make more than a small tree.

Some varieties have a distinctive shape, or growth habit, and a good catalogue will give indications of this with remarks like 'upright' or 'spreading'.

Taste

All the above considerations need to be balanced with those of taste. There is no point in creating an eco-logically harmonious and productive forest garden if the children then turn round and say "Eurr! That's horrible. We want our Golden Delicious." If one aim of growing a forest garden is to interest the next gener-ation in more Earth-friendly ways of producing food, it may be best to play safe on taste.

Most fruit tastes pretty good anyway, but some of the older varieties of apples have a taste or texture which is quite unlike that of the half-dozen mass-produced varieties available in the shops. It can be great fun to extend the boundaries of our taste, but it is better to do so by choice than to accidentally buy a tree with fruit which we only get to like after years of religiously munching through tree-loads of it because we hate to throw it away.

Actually finding out what different varieties of fruit taste like can be difficult. Nurseries do their best to describe what each one is like, but flavour is not something which is easily put into words. Even tasting the fruit cannot be relied upon, because so much depends on whether it was picked at the right time and how well it has been handled and stored. The taste of fruit you buy in the shops is often nothing like the true potential of the variety. Shops are also unlikely to offer more than a very small number of the varieties we might like to choose from. But a few shops are beginning to specialise in the niche market of old fashioned varieties. Often these are farm shops attached to orchards where the old trees are growing, so a good deal of travelling may be involved. Perhaps a few visits to Brogdale or some other fruit collection during the picking season is the answer, but several visits would be needed to catch all the fruits and varieties.

Aesthetic appeal is also a matter of taste, and may influence your choice if the ornamental aspect of the garden is important to you. Varieties vary in their blossom colour and scent, and apples in particular have a wide range of fruit colours, from greens through rus-sets to striking reds and stripey ones. Some varieties of pears are noted for the autumn colours of their leaves, while some hazels have specially beautiful catkins. There is a purple-leaved filbert which has red catkins – though it is not a good yielder – and also a couple of varieties of purple-leaved cherry plums.

Chapter 7

THE TREES

THE OBVIOUS ONES

These are the fruit trees most often grown in this country, often referred to as top fruit. They are the ones to consider first for a tree layer of reliable, tasty and easily grown fruits. A wide range of varieties is available for most of them, and information on how to grow them is widely and easily available.

Apples (*Malus domestica*)
The apple is our national fruit. It has been around for so long that we tend to think of it as a native, but its ancestors are probably various species of *Malus* from the mountains of central Asia, though there may be a dash of the native crab apple in some strains. There is hardly a spot on this island where the climate is too tough for at least some varieties of apples to thrive, and in good fruit areas they are one of the easiest fruits to grow.

At the same time they are a gourmet fruit. Victorian aristocrats and *bon viveurs* would wax as lyrical about the subtleties of different apple varieties and years as they would about wine. The apple store was often as prestigious a part of a great country house as the wine cellar. The apple's decorative qualities were appreciated too. They were often planted with an eye to the effect of their blossom, sometimes interplanted with pears for contrast, or roses to give a longer season of colour. A few fruit were sometimes left on the tree for their decorative effect, and those which were brought into the house were valued as much for their visual beauty as for their subtle and rich flavours.

Apples also keep for much longer than any other temperate fruit. Before the days of chemically-controlled storage and imports from all over the world, they were the one fruit which could be eaten fresh for nine or even ten months of the year. Other fruits tend to be a juicy treat for a few weeks and a bottled preserve or jam for the rest of the year.

The huge number of apple varieties which used to exist up and down the country is witness to the success of this one fruit in fulfilling a wide range of human needs in a wide range of environments. Some 2,000 varieties are preserved at Brogdale, and there may be yet more which survive in other collections or unrecorded

HOME-PRESSED APPLE JUICE

Fruit for juicing does not need to be in quite such good condition as desert fruit, especially desert fruit which is to be stored, so juicing can be a good way of using up the imperfect apples at harvest time. It is a good stand-by for a garden where low maintenance is a priority, or for years when for some reason it is not possible to pick the crop at the ideal time.

Bramleys are one of the hardiest and best juicing varieties, but the flavour is better if one or two other varieties are added to the mix.

In addition, there are many old apple trees which survive in ones or twos in back gardens in both town and country. Nine times out of ten this fruit is regarded as nothing but a nuisance by the owners. I'm sure many of them would be only too pleased to have someone in to clear it away and make good use of it. Hopefully this will help more people see the value of the old fruit trees in their gardens, and start using them themselves. In the meantime it could make a nice little seasonal earner for an enterprising individual, or a charitable group looking to raise some funds.

Juicing machines are available from home-made wine-making suppliers, and you can hire them by the day or by the week. The juice must be preserved by freezing or pasturising or it will quickly ferment and become cider.

Rootstock	Habit	Size* *in metres*	First Fruit†	Main Uses	Notes
MM111 M2 M25	Vigorous	6-8	7-8 years (standard 8-10)	Standard, half standard, espalier	Large on good soil, medium on poor
MM106	Semi-dwarfing	4-6	3-4	Bush, cordon, espalier, fan	Bush needs staking for first 4-5 years
M26	Dwarfing	2.5-4	3-4	Bush, cordon	Bush needs staking for first 4-5 years. Good on average soil
M9	Very dwarfing	2-3	2-3	Dwarf bush, dwarf pyramid, cordon	Needs good soil, and staking throughout its life
M27	Extremely dwarfing	1.2-1.8	2-3	For very vigorous varieties, or very small gardens	Needs good soil, and staking throughout its life.

Table 7.1 Rootstocks for Apples

* Height and spread when grown as bush tree. Will be modified by soil and fruiting variety.
† Years from planting when grown as bush.

in old orchards and back gardens. The number of apple varieties available to the home gardener from nurseries is nothing like this, but they outnumber all other available fruit varieties put together.

Forest gardeners who want a reliable, trouble-free supply of fresh fruit over the longest possible time will probably choose apples as the mainstay of their tree layer.

Desert apples, cooking apples and cider are the three traditional uses of apples, with the damaged ones going for chicken or pig food. Another use which the forest gardener might like to consider is making apple juice. Most of us drink a fair amount of fruit juice, and why shouldn't we make use of our native fruit before going to the shops to buy imported citrus?

Apples blossom during the first half of May, when there is still some chance of frost. But most other fruits flower earlier, and it is not normally worthwhile to plant apples in the most favoured microclimates unless none of the more tender fruits are being grown. In a garden which is prone to late frosts the best defence is late-flowering or frost-tolerant varieties.

Shelter is needed, especially at blossom time, as apples are self-infertile and the pollinating insects do not like strong winds. On an exposed site a windbreak is necessary. Apples will tolerate some shade, but need to be in full Sun for at least half the day. Sunshine gives apples their full flavour and colour, so it is more important for desert varieties than cookers.

Figure 7.1

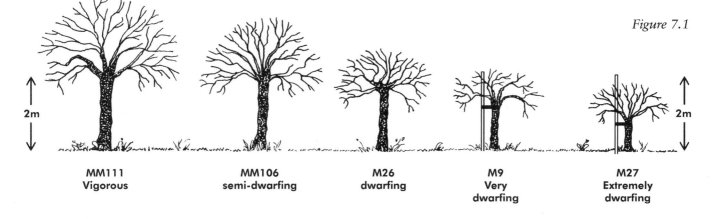

| MM111
Vigorous | MM106
semi-dwarfing | M26
dwarfing | M9
Very
dwarfing | M27
Extremely
dwarfing |

The ideal soil is the same for most kinds of tree fruit: at least 60cm depth of well-drained, fertile, friable loam. But apples are not as fussy as most other fruit, and a more vigorous rootstock can be chosen if conditions are less than ideal. Poor drainage can be a major problem, leading to general unthriftiness and an increased incidence of canker disease. Cookers are more tolerant of poor drainage than dessert varieties. The rootstock M25 does better than others on a damp soil.

There are more different rootstocks for apples than for any other top fruit, but only a few are in common use (*see Table 7.1 and Figure 7.1*). M26 is a popular medium-vigour stock for garden trees, and may be the most suitable for the tree layer in medium sized forest gardens.

Cordons should be spaced 75cm apart on good soil and 90cm on poor. If there is more than one row of cordons they should be 1.8m apart.

The sort of yield to be expected from an apple tree depends on a combination of factors: rootstock, variety, pruning form, soil, situation and the amount of care and attention it receives. The following figures give some idea of what to expect per year from a mature tree of various forms. Note that the smaller forms will reach their maximum yield much sooner than the larger ones:

Tree	kg	lb
Standard	45-180	100-400
Bush on M2	90	200
Bush on M26	27-55	60-120
Dwarf bush on M9	18-27	40-60
Dwarf bush on M27	4-7	10-15
Dwarf pyramid	4-7	10-15
Cordon	1-4	3-8
	depending on rootstock.	
Espalier, 2 tiers	half the yield of a bush on the same rootstock.	

Pears (*Pyrus communis*)

Cultivated pears come from the Mediterranean, though the wild form does exist as an extremely rare native in Britain. They are more delicate than apples, so their geographical range is more restricted, and where both are grown together the pears should be given the more favourable sites in the garden.

They flower about a fortnight earlier than apples, starting in late April, and there are no late flowering varieties. This means they cannot be grown where late frosts are common, and if one part of the garden is less prone to frost than another pears should have it in preference to apples. They also need more warmth and sunshine than apples, and shelter is even more important, partly to make things as easy as possible for the limited number of pollinating insects which are active earlier in the spring, and also because the young leaves and soft-skinned fruit are susceptible to wind damage. The microclimate offered by a south-facing wall often fulfils these conditions, so pears are sometimes grown as cordons or espaliers up the south side of a building.

In a wet climate they are more prone to scab, which is the disease most likely to trouble them.

However, there is a considerable range of pear varieties, some hardier than others. If you live in the north or west or have a sunless garden it is not so much a matter of not being able to grow pears as being restricted to the most hardy varieties.

They favour a slightly heavier range of soils than apples: they are more tolerant of clay or imperfect drainage, but less able to cope with sandy, drought-prone, shallow or limey soils. If pears are grown against a wall special care must be taken to see the soil does

Table 7.2 Rootstocks for Pears

* Height and spread of bush tree. This is very variable, as some pear varieties have a vigorous upright habit of growth, while others are weak and spreading.

Rootstock	Habit	Size* *in metres*	First Fruit	Forms	Notes
Pear	Very vigorous	20	10-20 years	Standard (other forms on poor soil)	The only one for poor soils
Quince A	Medium vigour	3-7	4-8 years from planting	Bush, cordon, dwarf pyramid, espalier	If in doubt, use it. Needs good soil
Quince C	Moderately vigorous	2.5-6	Slightly earlier	Bush, cordon, dwarf pyramid, espalier	Only on the best soil

not dry out. Generous mulching is called for, and possibly watering, especially in the tree's early years.

Bullfinches can be a major pest, eating the fruit buds off pear trees – and to a lesser extent plums – in the winter. Ash keys are their favourite winter food, but ash trees fruit biennially. In years when few ashes are fruiting bullfinches can completely strip the fruit buds of pear trees, causing a total crop loss in that year. Bullfinches do not like to venture far from cover, so pears are only vulnerable if they are right beside a woodland, or in a suburban area with dense tree cover. In these situations it may be wise to consider leaving pears out of the planting plan.

Uses of pears are very similar to those of apples, but they don't keep as long.

Pear rootstocks are all vigorous, and produce magnificent trees. Shaped like a hand pointing to the sky, they can grow taller than a house. In the spring, when they are covered in shining white blossom, they are one of the most remarkable and beautiful features of the traditional landscape. (*see Figure 7.2*) These trees are far too big for most gardens, and take a decade or two before coming into fruit. Hence the old saying that you plant pears for your grandchildren.

Pear rootstocks are used for trees in orchards on poor soil, or to give full sized trees for ornamental purposes. But pears can be grafted onto quince rootstocks, and these are used for garden trees.

Figure 7.2

Yields of pears are slightly lower than those of apples, and rather more variable from season to season. Where a well grown bush apple on a less vigorous rootstock may be expected to yield 25-55kg of fruit a year, a pear of similar size and state of health would be more likely to yield in the range of 15-45kg.

Plums (*Prunus domestica*)

Gages are included with plums, because they are the same species. They are particularly sweet and delicious plums, with a green or yellow coloured.

The plum probably originated as a hybrid between the blackthorn or sloe (*Prunus spinosa*) which is native to Britain, and either the cherry plum (*P. cerasifera*) or its close relation *P. divaricata*, both of which come from the Caucasus. Their ideal climate is one of cold winters and hot, dry summers, so they do better in eastern areas of Britain. But there are many varieties which thrive in the west. All plums blossom early, so they should not be planted where there is a chance of late frosts.

Gages are among the least hardy of plums. They are especially sensitive to rain when ripening, as it can cause the fruit to split and rot. They are most successful in the southern half of Britain, unless a specially favourable microclimate can be found or created. As they tend to be small trees they are particularly suited to wall growing. They breed fairly true from seed and can crop better on their own roots than when grafted.

Wall-grown plums are grown as a fan, never as an espalier. Since plums are tip-bearers, when grown in unrestricted forms they need very little pruning once a good strong shape has been established. This is usually done by about the third year after planting. But the branches may need supporting as the weight of fruit is borne ever further from the trunk as the tree grows.

The preferred soil is a fairly heavy clay loam, as they do not like to dry out at the roots, especially the gages. Lighter soils need plenty of organic matter added to improve moisture retention. A slightly more acid soil is acceptable to plums than to most other top fruit, with a pH of 6.0 to 6.5 being ideal.

Plums do not keep, though they are excellent for bottling and jam. It is also possible to dry, or half-dry them. This increases their sweetness and flavour, and they will

Table 7.3 Rootstocks for Plums

† The rootstock Mussel is sometimes used by nurseries, but should be avoided because it suckers freely.

* Height and spread of bush tree.

Rootstock†	Habit	Size* in metres	First Fruit	Forms	Notes
Brompton, Myrobalan B	Vigorous	5.5-6.5		Standard, half standard	Too big for most gardens
St. Julien A	Semi-vigorous	3.5-4.5	3-6 years	Half standard, bush, fan	The usual choice for gardens
Pixy	Dwarfing	2.5-3	3-6 years	Bush, dwarf pyramid	Needs good soil and heavy feeding

keep till Christmas. The earliest varieties start ripening in July and the latest may still have fruit in October. Fortunately there are many self-fertile varieties, so it is possible to grow a single tree if that is all there is room for.

Yields are variable – they vary from year to year because of frost damage, and between varieties – so any figures given can only be a rough guide.

Tree	kg	lb
Bush on St. Julien A:		
first 10 yrs of fruiting	15-25	40-50
full bearing	40-50	100-120
Fan on St. Julien A	7-14	15-30

Two-thirds of these yields can be expected from trees on Pixy, and from less prolific varieties, including most gages, on St. Julien A.

Damsons (*Prunus domestica* sub-species *insitita*)

The damson is a somewhat wilder version of the plum, less intensively bred. The trees are smaller, tougher and more able to look after themselves. They also lack some of the advantages of more highly domesticated strains, having smaller fruit, which is less sweet, and they lack early varieties to extend the picking season.

The bullace is an even wilder version of the same sub-species, tougher, with smaller, less edible fruit. It is only a step away from the blackthorn.

Damsons certainly have their uses. They produce good yields of fruit for cooking and preserving, which is edible raw if you are not fussy, and they are one fruit tree which also doubles up as a windbreak tree. They give effective shelter in both summer and winter, as the growth of twigs is dense enough to slow down the wind when the leaves are off the trees, and can still yield reasonably well themselves in an exposed position. The Farleigh damson is a variety particularly recommended for windbreaks. Damsons should be mixed with other trees and shrubs in a windbreak, as a monoculture is asking for trouble from pests and disease, even with a tough plant like this.

Apart from use in windbreaks, they are the plums for the wetter and cooler areas of the country, though well worth growing in any area. They are definitely a first choice for a forest garden where low maintenance is a priority. But, like all plums, they flower early and can be caught by a late frost.

On their own roots they make a tree of 3-6 metres height and spread, and are inclined to sucker. Trees bought from nurseries are usually on one of the normal plum rootstocks. They make smaller trees than a domestic plum on the equivalent stock.

Most varieties of damson are self-fertile, and come fairly true when grown from seed. Yields vary greatly from year to year, mainly in response to the weather at blossom time. Harvest is in September or October.

Cherry Plums or myrobalans (*Prunus cerasifera*)

A mature cherry plum makes a magnificent spreading tree. They are sometimes found as hedgerow trees, especially in Somerset, where they make a distinctive and beautiful contribution to the landscape.

The blossom comes out as early as March, and has a degree of frost tolerance. They are more often grown as ornamental or hedging plants than for their fruit. There are red-leaved varieties which are particularly decorative, and cherry plums have occasionally been planted as a street tree. In a good year they produce a heavy yield of fruit which is small, good for cooking, and quite pleasant to eat raw, though not quite as tasty as a domestic plum.

The varieties of cherry plum sold for fruit production are self-fertile, and breed true from seed. Cuttings also take well. They make a tree some 6 metres high and wide. The fruit is ripe in late July or August, and yields are very variable, often tending to be biennial. Separate ornamental and hedging varieties are available, but these also produce edible fruit.

Since it needs very little attention, and is not a reliable cropper, perhaps the best place for the cherry plum is in the hedgerows rather than an intensive forest garden.

Sweet Cherries (*Prunus avium*)

The sweet cherry is a direct descendant of the wild cherry, which is native to much of Europe and West Asia. This includes all of Britain, though wild cherries become rarer the further north you go. It is not common anywhere, and tends to pick out the best soils and microclimates. The beauty of the wild trees, with masses of snowy blossom in spring, exquisite leaves in autumn and beautiful bark in winter, has not been bred out of the cultivated varieties. They are worth planting in a forest garden for their beauty alone.

They are not always small trees in the wild. They can grow as tall as oaks and ashes and take their place with them in the high woodland canopy. Although the cultivated forms are much smaller than this, their large size can be a problem. There is not as yet a really dwarfing rootstock generally available for cherries, so sweet cherries are often too big for a garden.[1] Growing them against a wall is one way of restricting their vigour enough to fit them in, and you need a fairly

---

[1]   Two dwarfing stocks from Belgium, Damil and Inmil (or GM9), are currently under trial in Britain. Most reputable nurseries will not stock them till trials are completed.

Rootstock	Habit	Forms	Spread *in metres*	Height* *in metres*	Notes
Malling F12/1	Vigorous	Standard, half standard	10-12		For specimen trees or commercial orchards
		Bush	8-11		
		Fan	5.5-8	3	
Colt	Semi-vigorous	Standard, half standard, bush	6-8		The stock for gardens
		Pyramid	4-5		
		Fan	4.5-5.5	2.5	

Table 7.4 Rootstocks for Sweet Cherries

* Minimum height of wall needed.

tall wall even then. The fan form is always used rather than the espalier or cordon.

Some sweet cherry varieties are self-fertile, which is fortunate as only large gardens really have space for more than one tree. On the other hand, two different varieties will extend the picking season if they are well chosen.

Although a bunch of juicy, fragrant cherries straight from the tree is a rare treat, too many sweet cherries coming ripe at one time is not a good idea, because they must be eaten fresh. They do keep for a short while, but they soon lose their quality. Even a fairly small tree may produce more than many families can get through in a couple of weeks. They freeze well, but are not suitable for bottling.

Birds are particularly partial to cherries. Netting is fairly straightforward with wall-trained trees, but difficult with free-standing ones as they are so big. Growing unnetted cherries is probably not worthwhile. In most areas the birds get 90% of them in a good year and all of them in a bad one.

Sweet cherries do best in a climate with warm, dry summers, which is why Kent is the home of most commercial cherry orchards. They blossom early, and so are vulnerable to frost. Wall-trained trees can be protected from frost with netting or hessian just as they can be from birds.

Size, birds and frost are three good reasons for growing a fan-trained tree rather than a free-standing one.

A well drained soil is essential. By preference it should be slightly more alkaline than for most other fruit trees, ideally between pH6.7 and 7.5, and somewhat deeper, with at least 75 cm of fertile, friable loam. But cherries are fairly tolerant and will do well on a variety of soils, as long as they are well drained. They root very close to the surface and have been known to break up paths and patios.

Yields can vary enormously according to the size, age and form of the tree and the climate:

Tree	kg	lb
Standard or bush	15-55	30-100
Fan	5-15	12-30

Duke cherries are intermediate between sweet and acid cherries, and probably originated as a cross between the two.

Sour Cherries (*Prunus cerasus*)
One great advantage of sour cherries over sweet cherries is that they are smaller trees, and so fit better into a garden. They are primarily cooking fruit and make good jam, though people with a strong palate may like to eat them straight off the tree. By far the commonest type is the morello, with fruit such a dark red that it is almost black. The amarelle, or Kentish red, has red fruits.

Another advantage is that they are tolerant of shade. Growing a morello cherry up a north-facing wall has almost become a cliché of permaculture design. But clichés only become clichés because they are true, and this really is one kind of tree that can fruit quite happily without any direct sunlight. They do of course need some light, so when grown on a north wall they must not be crowded out by other plants or structures that will rob them of indirect light.

They have the same vulnerability to late frosts and birds as sweet cherries do, but being smaller they are easier to protect. Birds are more of a problem when the fruit is truly ripe, and there are usually a few days between the time they ripen and the time the birds start taking them. If you are quick on the ball you can get away without netting, especially if you want them for bottling or preserving because then they can be picked slightly unripe.

They prefer the same kind of soil as sweet cherries, and the same rootstocks are used. On Colt, bush trees and fans have a spread of 3.5-4.5m; a fan needs a wall at least 2m high, and a bush may grow to 3.5m tall. Fans on F 12/1 spread to 4.5-5.5m and need a slightly higher wall. Half-standards and pyramids are also sometimes grown.

Yields can be heavy for the size of the tree compared to sweet cherries, 5-10kg (12-20lb) from a fan, and 13-18kg (30-40lb) from a bush. They start yielding well in the fourth year after planting, and crop regularly as long as they are not caught by a late frost.

THE LESS OBVIOUS ONES

These are trees which are either less suitable for forest gardening than the commoner top fruits, or simply less well known. None of them is regularly grown in commercial orchards in Britain, but they are all worth at least a second look.

Peaches and figs are really out of their climatic range here, but can yield delicious fruit given a favourable microclimate and some extra care. Other trees in this section are natives, which offer the opposite deal: they are very easy to grow, but the fruit is not as appetising as cultivated kinds. Others, such as mulberries, quinces and medlars, are occasionally grown in gardens, but more often for their decorative or curiosity value than for their fruit.

Asian Pears or Nashi (*Pyrus serotina*)
These trees make it into the 'less obvious' list because they are a recent introduction into this country, and there is still a great deal to learn about how to grow them here. They come from Japan.

According to Chris Bowers & Sons, one of the nurseries which sell Asian pears:

The varieties we offer are hardy, despite flowering early, and grow on average to about 13 feet [4m] with long, arching sometimes pendulous growth. The white, frost resistant flowers are very orna-mental. Golden fruits are ready for picking in late September, and will store until the New Year if required. They have the shape of an apple, the flesh of a pear, but taste like neither; crisp and juicy, with an excellent sweet flavour. . . Any two varieties will ensure good pollination. It is known that the pear variety Williams will also pollinate all [the varieties offered]. Other varieties of pear will probably pollinate, but as yet have not been trialled... Asian pears are an ornamental delight.

The fact that the flowers are frost resistant should make them particularly attractive to growers in areas which get late frosts.

Peaches (*Prunus persica*)
Despite the Latin name, which suggests an origin in Persia, peaches come from China. The climate of their homeland gives a clue to the kind of climate they need to fruit successfully: a warm, sunny spring to ensure safe pollination of their early blossom; a hot summer to ripen the fruit; a dry autumn; a short, cold winter; and just enough rain but no more. It doesn't sound much like Britain! Nevertheless, peaches can be grown as free-standing trees in East Anglia and the south-east of England, and in favoured microclimates further north and west. Elsewhere they can be grown against south- or west-facing walls

The nectarine is a mutation, or sport, of the peach. Its fruit is smaller, with a smooth skin and a more delicate taste. It needs even warmer conditions and has a lower yield, but is otherwise similar to other peaches.

Peaches flower very early in the spring, when hardly any insects are on the wing, and to be sure of getting a crop every year you need to pollinate them by hand. This means transferring pollen from one flower to another with a tuft of cotton wool, and it should be done daily over the whole flowering period. Frost is also likely at this time of the year, and they need to be covered up on any night when it is likely. If they are not sprayed, open-grown trees will almost inevitably get peach leaf curl, and will produce very little. Wall-grown trees can be protected from the disease with a polythene cover from December till late May. As the fruit develops it is usually hand-thinned on two separate occasions in order to get good-sized fruits.

It is possible to grow peaches in this country without all this care and attention, but then you cannot expect to get a harvest every year. Just how often you can depends on your local climate and microclimate and on the run of the seasons. New varieties are constantly being bred, and no doubt later-flowering and generally hardier ones will appear in due course. For the time being, if you want a reliable crop without a lot of work,

Rootstock	Habit	Forms	Spread *in metres*	Height* *in metres*
Brompton	Vigorous	Standard, bush	5.5-7.5	
		Fan	4.5-6	2
St. Julien A	Semi-vigorous	Bush	4.5-5.5	
		Fan	3.5-4.5	2

Table 7.5 Rootstocks for Peaches

* Minimum height of wall, though they can be trained lower with much tying down and pruning.

it is better to grow another kind of tree.

Peaches are self-fertile, so a single tree can be grown.

The soil should be deep and well drained, preferably a medium to heavy loam. Light soils need to have plenty of organic matter added, as well as mulching, to improve moisture retention. A pH of 6.5 to 7 is preferred, but peaches are particularly sensitive to lime, so shallow soils over chalk are not suitable.

Peaches and nectarines start to bear fruit two years after planting and should be into full production by year five or six. Yields are enormously variable, depending on environment, care and size of tree. A rough guide is:

Tree form	kg	lb
Fan	9-15	20-30
Bush	15-27	30-60
Standard	15-55	30-120

Nectarines yield from half to two thirds of this.

Successful peach trees can be grown from stones, though they will not be identical to the parent. A stone from an early-ripening variety will have most chance of success. The tree will not come into fruit till something like the fourth or seventh year after planting, and the size is likely to be similar to grafted trees on Brompton stock. It can be great fun if you enjoy experimenting with plants.

Figs (*Ficus carica*)

Figs are natives of the Middle East. With careful siting and some protection from winter cold they can produce fruit in southern Britain. You may feel the extra effort is worthwhile for the luxury of tasting their delicious, sweet fruit straight from the tree rather than dried and imported from the south.

They are extremely vulnerable to winter cold, because the fruits are initiated in the autumn and grow to maturity in their second year. This means there are tender little fruits on the tree through winter and any cold weather can completely destroy the crop. (They do also produce fruits which are initiated and ripen in the same year, but in our climate these never get enough time to mature.)

In most areas they really need to be grown in a greenhouse, but they can fruit successfully outside in areas which have mild winters. This means the south and west of the country, especially in gardens which are close to the sea. It helps if a fig is fan-trained against a wall, and some crop regularly in this situation with no further protection. To make 100% sure of a crop the whole plant can be covered with an insulating layer of straw or hessian through the winter.

If the temperature problem can be overcome figs are easy to grow, needing little attention in other respects.

They are very tolerant of poor soil, as long as it is well drained. Indeed, in all but the poorest soils their roots must be restricted, or they will put on masses of vegetative growth and very little fruit. This can be done by growing the tree in a large pot – which also means the tree can be taken indoors for the winter. But more often it is done by digging a hole where the fig is to be grown, filling the bottom with rubble, walling the sides with concrete slabs and refilling with soil. They are tolerant of a high pH, and can be grown on a thin soil over chalk.

Figs can grow to quite a large size, but if necessary they can be kept small by pruning. A wall space of 2m high by 3m long is suitable.

Crab Apples (*Malus sylvestris*)

The crab is native to Britain, widespread as a wild tree south of the river Forth, and occasionally found further north. In gardens crabs are most often grown as ornamentals, but they also have more practical uses in a forest garden.

Firstly, they can be edible. The most edible variety, John Downie, can be eaten raw straight off the tree. It has pretty, red-striped fruit the size of a plum and the shape of a pear. Many a dessert apple has a sharper taste. But most crabs are much too bitter to eat raw.

Figure 7.3 John Downie crab apple

Their main food use is in making jam. They are unusually high in pectin, which is one of the substances needed to make jam or jelly set. Fruits vary greatly in the amount of pectin they contain, so a few crab apples are often added to jams made from low-pectin fruits, such as strawberries or blackberries. If you intend making much in the way of preserves from the produce of your woodland garden, a crab tree is a good asset.

Secondly, some varieties of crab can be used as a universal pollinator for apples (*see page 81-82*). The best known of the universal pollinators is Golden Hornet. It is named after the masses of little yellow fruits which it bears in autumn. These stay on the tree well into winter, and the variety is often grown as an ornamental for the sake of them.

Thirdly crabs can be used as a hedging plant. They can make a useful contribution to an edible hedge or windbreak for a forest garden.

Most varieties grow 3-4 metres tall, and have a bushy habit of growth. But some, including the two mentioned here, have a slender, upright habit and can be fitted into a forest garden without taking up much space. Trees bought from nurseries are usually grafted onto one of the usual apple rootstocks. Soil, climate and microclimate requirements are similar to those for cooking apples, as are cultivation techniques.

When selecting a crab variety for a forest garden it is better to look in a list prepared for fruit growers rather than one prepared for ornamental gardeners.[2]

Mulberries (*Morus* spp.)

The black mulberry (*M. nigra*) is the species commonly grown for fruit. It comes from western Asia, and is grown all over Europe. The white mulberry (*M. alba*) comes from China, and though the fruit is edible its main claim to fame is as the food plant of the silkworm, which eats the leaves. The North American red mulberry (*M. rubra*) does not crop well in Britain, but hybrids of the red and white species have been imported into Britain and are said to be doing well:

Several years ago we imported the original plants of these mulberries from America and have been delighted by their performance over here. They are fast growing and come into bearing at a very early age, producing excellent quality, usually seedless, fruit.
Clive Simms[3]

These hybrids are similar in most respects to the black mulberry, and what follows can be taken to apply to both black and hybrid kinds.

The fruits are rather like raspberries or loganberries, sharp-tasting at first, but sweet when fully ripe. They ripen over a relatively long period in August and September, and are best eaten fresh, but can be picked slightly unripe for cooking. They can also be dried and ground into a sweet-tasting flour. This flour is a minor staple food in some Asian countries, such as Afghanistan. They are also suitable for free range pig and poultry fodder, because they fall off the tree once they are fully ripe, which avoids the need for any human handling of the crop.

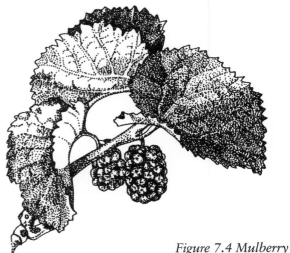

Figure 7.4 Mulberry

One disadvantage of mulberries as fruit trees is the small size of the fruits, which means more time spent picking than is the case with large fruits like apples. Picking soft fruit at ground level is one thing, but when working from a ladder it is nicer to be able to fill your basket relatively quickly.

Mulberries are a low-maintenance crop, as they have no disease problems, and no pests other than birds which take the ripening fruit. Netting is possible with wall-grown trees, but once the tree is yielding well there

---

2   Chris Bowers & Sons have a good list of crabs for fruit growers in their catalogue.
3   See List of Suppliers.

will hopefully be enough for both humans and birds. They also need no pruning once the shape of the tree is established.

Two characteristics make them particularly useful for multi-layer growing: they are tolerant of competition from other plants in their root space, and are late to come into leaf – though they do cast a moderately dense shade once in leaf.

They are attractive trees, with large, heart-shaped leaves and a bark which becomes gnarled with age. They have often been planted as ornamentals. Since the flowers are wind-pollinated, they do not need shelter at flowering time to provide a microclimate for insects. This means they can also be used as a windbreak tree, but some reduction in yield must be expected in this situation.

The flowers are frost hardy, so this is one tree that can take the odd late frost without losing a year's production. They need full Sun for good fruiting. In England and Wales they fruit well as free-standing trees, but in Scotland they really need the micro-climate of a south- or west-facing wall. As a wall-trained tree they are normally espalier trained. Occasionally the ripening fruit may be caught by a very early frost. This makes the fruit unfit for human consumption, but they can still be eaten by pigs and poultry.

A mulberry can cause inconvenience by dropping its dark, staining fruits on washing-lines, patios and garden seats. For these situations there is a white variety which does not stain. This is not *Morus alba*, but a white-fruited variety of *M. nigra*, known confusingly as 'Alba'.

Mulberries are tolerant of a wide range of soils with a wide range of pH, but ideally they like plenty of water to the roots and good drainage.

They are slow-growing, long-lived trees, eventually reaching a height and spread of 6-9m, though smaller in the north, with an irregular shape, tending to be upright in habit rather than spreading. They are not trees for small gardens. They are always grown on their own roots rather than grafted, and it is comparatively easy to grow a new tree from a cutting.

A single tree can be grown, as all mulberries are self-fertile. The black mulberry is slow to come into fruit, taking as much as eight to ten years. It may be erratic during the next decade, producing mostly male flowers in some years and mostly female in others. But we hear the new hybrids avoid these problems.

Quinces (*Cydonia oblonga*)

The true quince is not to be confused with the oriental quinces (*Chaenomeles* spp.), also known as Japonicas. These are normally grown as ornamental shrubs, but do have edible fruit which can be made into jelly. They can be grown in light shade, free-standing or against a wall or fence, including a north-facing one. They reach a height of around 1.8m.

The true quince comes from central and south-west Asia. It is at the northern end of its fruiting range here, and the fruit does not ripen fully. It can be used for making preserves and adding flavour to dishes like apple pie and stewed rabbit. They are probably not worth growing purely for their fruit in a small or medium sized garden, where the space could be taken by something which produces a more popular and versatile fruit.

They do have curiosity value, though, and are quite decorative. They make small, spreading, crooked-shaped trees, with large flowers rather like a dog rose which open in May, large grey/green leaves, and fruits shaped like an apple or pear according to variety, which ripen to an attractive yellow colour in November. As they are self-fertile a single tree can be grown.

Quinces are not fussy as to soil, but do like to have plenty of water at the roots. In fact they are unique among temperate climate fruits in actually preferring a poorly drained soil. They do well beside a pond or stream, where they can make an attractive part of the waterside scene. In southern areas they can be grown in the open. Further north they prefer to be fan-trained up a sunny wall. But this favoured microclimate could be put to a more productive use.

They need little pruning, and though they are susceptible to many of the same pests as apples and pears, on the whole they do not need a lot of attention. Flowering in May, they are not often troubled by late frosts.

They eventually grow to about 4m height and spread when unpruned, though they can be half as big again on a favourable soil. They come into fruit in the third or fourth year, and can live for a hundred years.

Medlars (*Mespilus germanica*)

Like quinces, medlars are curious, somewhat decorative trees. They come from south east Europe and Turkey and are grown all over Europe. In southern England they have naturalised, and can occasionally be found growing in hedgerows. They are related to the quince and the hawthorn, and are usually grafted onto a stock of either species.

They have a crooked, rather picturesque form of growth, sometimes weeping, and the bare branches in winter can be quite ornamental. They bear flowers similar to the quince in May or June, pleasant autumn leaves, and the most curious-shaped fruit of any edible tree. They occasionally flower a second time, in August or September. Though the wild trees are thorny, the cultivated varieties are usually thornless, or nearly so.

Medlars are self-fertile, so a single tree may be grown. They are slow-growing, and may grow to 3.5

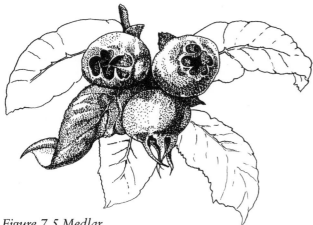

Figure 7.5 Medlar

or 6m according to soil, situation and variety. They are not fussy about soil, and need little pruning. They do reasonably well in most parts of Britain, and with their late flowering time they are most unlikely to be caught by frost. The first fruit can be expected from two to five years after planting, according to the size of the young tree when planted out.

As they can stand some shade they could be used as an understorey beneath really tall standards, but they would eventually grow too tall for the shrub layer of a normal forest garden unless they were pruned to a low shape. This would be a shame, as their value is perhaps greater as a decorative plant than as a food producer.

The fruit ripens on the tree in warmer climates, and it can do so here in a very warm summer such as we might expect once in ten years. But usually we need to let them 'blet'. Bletting is a softening process, almost like a partial rotting. The end product has a sweet flavour remarkably like baked apples and custard. They should be picked in late October or early November, while still hard, and stored for the two or three weeks it takes them to blet. They are ready to eat when the flesh softens and turns brown. If allowed to blet on the tree, they will usually fall off or be eaten by birds.

They can be eaten raw, with a little sugar and cream, baked whole like apples, or made into jelly.

Hawthorns (*Crataegus* spp.)

The common native hawthorn (*C. monogyna*) is in fact edible: the young leaves can be eaten raw, and the haws can be made into a jelly. But the leaves are so tiny it takes an age to pick a mouthful, and most forest gardens produce more than enough fruit for making preserves. It is best used as a hedgerow plant.

The azerole (*C. azarolus*) is a hawthorn from the Mediterranean which has been grown as a food plant. The haws are much plumper, like a tiny red apple, and can be eaten straight off the tree, though they are rather dry.

Much more worthwhile as a food plant, although it is normally grown as an ornamental, is *C. arnoldiana* from north-eastern North America. It is a small tree, eventually growing to 6 or 7m tall, with perhaps half that spread, and a good length of clean stem before the first branch. The fruit is like a large cherry, 2cm in diameter, and has been described as having 'a delicious flavour, sweet with a soft juicy flesh'. It can be eaten raw or cooked. It is ripe in August and yields abundantly, though no figures are available.

Although it can stand a little shade, it fruits best in full Sun. It tolerates exposure, pollution and a wide range of soils, from thin chalky to imperfectly drained. Altogether it sounds a very promising plant for forest gardening.

C. schraderana is similar, with silvery foliage.[4]

Siberian Pea Tree (*Caragana arborescens*)

This is a small tree, often known as the Siberian pea shrub. It is a member of the legume family, and as well as fixing nitrogen it has a place as a food producer and windbreak tree.

The trees are usually grown here as ornamentals, on account of their graceful foliage and clusters of bright yellow flowers, but in Siberia they are used to produce poultry feed. The little pea-like seeds are edible for humans too. The young pods can be cooked like greens, and the dried seeds, which contain 36% protein, can be used like lentils. There is no reason why they should not become an important source of food.

They can grow to a height of 6m and a spread of 4m, but are usually smaller. Dwarf varieties are available, including one called Nana. No pruning is necessary.

They are among the toughest of all plants, and can be used as a hedge or windbreak in very exposed positions, including on coasts, or even grown in a frost pocket. What they do not like is a mild, wet winter, so they are much more likely to succeed in the eastern parts of Britain than in the west. They are not shade tolerant, but only cast a light shade themselves, so they are suitable for the canopy layer of a forest garden.

They prefer a dry, alkaline soil and can tolerate both drought and shallow soils over chalk. They are a good choice for poor, marginal soils, but should do well in any soil suitable for fruit trees.

Other Trees

If the purpose of your forest garden is as much to attract wildlife and please the eye as to produce food, there is no reason why every tree should have an edible product. There are a number of attractive native trees which can be included. Ideally they should be small trees,

---

4   Both are available from Thornhayes Nursery. See List of Suppliers.

ones which cast a light shade and are not too competitive.

The two native birches fulfil these requirements. Usually a small to medium tree of slender habit, they cast a light shade and can be beneficial to neighbouring plants because they improve the soil with their leaf-fall. They will grow in almost any soil or climate, with the single exception of salty winds. They are beautiful at all times of the year, especially the semi-weeping silver birch. In winter both kinds give life to an otherwise grey-brown landscape with their beautiful bark. Birch is also one of the best trees for wildlife, and supports many kinds of fungi. It also has an edible, or rather drinkable, product – birch sap wine.

MAKING BIRCH SAP WINE

For just three to four weeks each and every year in March or April the sap rises up the trunks of the trees. Precisely when this happens is clearly temperature dependent. A warm winter will bring forward the flow. Frost will cut it dead. It starts as suddenly as it stops and the tree gives no warning. So it is that the Moniack Castle folk, on whose livelihood it all depends, make sure they have set up their taps in the surrounding birchwoods during mid-February. To miss the flow would mean to miss a year's production...

The taps are hand drilled just into the area under the bark about an inch in depth and about the same width. Tubes in a cork plug the hole and down flows the sap into a five gallon drum. When full, it is carted back to the castle, simple as that. Occasionally a tree will produce 5 gallons in 24 hours. A more average figure is 2 gallons for the whole flow of one tree. The hole is carefully plugged after use and painted with 'Arborex'. No ill effects have ever been observed from the operation but no single tree is tapped in consecutive years.

The precious liquid is fermented in drums at 72 degrees Fahrenheit for four to five weeks without the addition of any water. Just yeast and sugar and birch sap. The bottled wine is dry and slightly woody and most importantly (for some of us) is said to cure baldness.

Bernard Planterose, from 'Fruits of the Highland Forest' in *Reforesting Scotland*, No. 9, Autumn 1993.

Making birch sap wine sounds like fun. But it is probably not worth including a birch just for the sake of producing the wine – your forest gardener is not exactly short of material for making home-made wine! Although small when compared to oaks and ashes, a mature birch would take up a large proportion of the space available in most gardens. But it can be coppiced when it starts to get too big, and if you choose you can single the regrowth to one stem after a couple of years.

Bird cherry is another hardy native, considerably smaller than the birches. It is found in the wild mainly in Scotland, Wales and the north of England. The fruit is not edible to humans, though birds like it, but they are very attractive trees and cast only a light shade. They produce suckers, but as with all suckering trees, a real mass of suckers is only likely when apical dominance is interfered with by the tree being cut down, pruned at the apex or damaged, or by root damage, which can be caused by too many feet.

The native maple, or field maple, is another small tree and it has the advantage to the landscaper of growing fast to begin with and then slowing down. They can be very beautiful in the autumn, their lemon yellow or gold leaves providing contrast with the vivid reds of cherry leaves. In Britain they only grow wild in the lowland areas of England and Wales, and prefer neutral to alkaline soils. They cast a moderate shade. Although it is possible to make maple syrup from the sap, it is so dilute that the amount of energy needed to drive off the water to concentrate the syrup is too great to make this worthwhile.

A tree which has an edible fruit, but which is probably not worth growing as a serious food plant, is the wild service or chequer (*Sorbus torminalis*), which is native to England and Wales, though rare outside south-east England. They are beautiful trees, with white blossom in late May and June, and unusually-shaped palmate leaves (*see Figure 7.6 right*) which may turn deep red in the autumn. They can reach a height of 15m when mature, but are often smaller, and they are slow growing.

Figure 7.6

They tolerate shade, but flower and fruit best in a relatively light position. In the wild they favour clay soils, but will grow well on most kinds, and they are tolerant of coastal conditions.

The fruits are round or oval, about the size of small cherries, and appear in September. Like medlars, they need to be bletted. Richard Mabey[5] says they then become very sweet. "The taste is unlike anything else which grows wild in this country, with hints

5   *Food for Free*, see Further Reading.

of damson, prune, apricot, sultana and tamarind." He gives a recipe from a Kentish pub which used to serve 'chequerberry beer':

> *Pick off in bunches in October. Hang on a string like onions (look like a swarm of bees). Hang till ripe. Cut off close to berries. Put them in stone or glass jars. Put sugar on – 1lb to 5lb of berries. Shake up well. Keep airtight until juice comes to the top. The longer kept the better. Can add brandy. Drink. Then eat berries!*

Personally I cannot see much reason for including trees that are neither edible nor native. By planting edibles and natives we can meet our needs for visual pleasure at the same time as we feed ourselves and the local wildlife. There are many trees of great beauty in these two groups.

Competitive trees to be avoided include poplars, willows and ash. Ash may at first seem compatible with smaller trees because it comes into leaf late and then only casts a light shade, but it has a voracious appetite for nutrients. Like a cuckoo in the nest, it will take the bulk of the plant food intended for the fruit trees and leave them short. Poplars and willows are thirsty, and will out-compete other trees for water, especially in summer when a good supply of moisture to the roots is needed for fruit development. If any of these trees should self-seed into a forest garden it is a good idea to remove them.

NEIGHBOURING TREES

Oak, beech and lime are three trees which are far too big even to consider planting in a forest garden. But if they are growing nearby we can harvest some food from them.

We do not normally think of oak as a food tree, at least not for human food – most people are aware of the ancient practice of feeding pigs on fallen acorns. The main drawback of acorns is their high tannin content, which makes them bitter and probably rather bad for the digestion. But the tannin can easily be leached out by following this simple method:

> Pick the acorns and dry them. De-husk and grind them. (A coffee mill or blender will do.) Put the acorn flour in a bag and pour boiling water over it. Mix the resultant paste half and half with wheat flour, and use the mix instead of pure wheat flour in any recipe for bread. The result is a rich, dark bread with a delicious nutty flavour.

Oaks tend not to produce acorns every year. Some individual trees are more regular producers than others, but a good acorn year only comes once every two to four years, or even less often if there is a succession of poor seasons. The good years are called mast years, mast being a general name for the seed of large trees.

Beech mast years are even less frequent, occurring at intervals of anything from four to fifteen years, though more regularly in the extreme south, the only part of Britain where beech is truly native. The nuts are really too tiny to be worth the labour of shelling. It would take hours of work to get enough to make a worthwhile contribution to a meal. But they can be pressed to yield an edible oil of very high quality:

> *[The mast] should be gathered as early as possible, before the squirrels have taken it, and before it has had a chance to dry out. The three-faced nuts should be cleaned of any remaining husks, dirt or leaves and then ground, shells and all, in a small oil-mill. (For those with patience, a mincing machine or a strong blender should work as well.) The resulting pulp should be put inside a fine muslin bag and then in a press or under a heavy weight to extract the oil... Every pound of nuts yields as much as three fluid ozs (85ml) of oil. The oil itself is rich in fats and proteins, and provided it is stored in well-sealed containers, will keep fresh considerably longer than many other vegetable fats.*
> Richard Mabey, *Food for Free*.[5]

The leaves of beech are also edible when they first come out in spring. They have a soft texture and a mild taste and make a good salad vegetable.

Lime leaves are softer and tastier than beech, and stay edible further into the season. Richard Mabey says they make a good sandwich filling when picked in high summer. The flowers, which are out in June and July, can be dried for lime flower tea. In terms of sheer bulk, the lime is the foremost bee fodder plant that grows in Britain – though a mixture of fodder plants is needed to give bees a continuous supply of food throughout the spring and summer.

THE DOUBTFUL ONES

Chestnuts and walnuts are valuable food-producing trees, but unfortunately they are too big for most gardens – especially chestnuts. Some of the other trees in this section are even more marginal in our climate than figs and peaches, but may be considered in very favourable situations. At the other extreme, rowan and whitebeam should only be considered as fruit trees in places where most other fruits will not grow. But they all have their uses, and all deserve a mention, even if only to note why they are not more widely applicable in forest gardening.

Chestnuts (*Castanea* spp.)

Although the sweet, or Spanish, chestnut (*C. sativa*) grows in the woods of south England and reproduces freely, it is not a native. Its home is on the shores of the Mediterranean, and it was first brought here in Roman times. The Chinese chestnut (*C. mollissima*) is cultivated in North America, though not so far available over here. However a hybrid of the sweet, Chinese and Japanese chestnuts (*C. crenata*), bred in North America, is now available in Britain.

Sweet chestnuts may reach a height and spread of 10m in twenty years, and eventually grow to 20 or 30m. Trees on dwarfing rootstocks may be available in the near future,[6] but even these will presumably be large trees by garden standards. As they are self-infertile more than one tree is needed for pollination, though it is possible to buy trees with a pollinating branch grafted onto a fruiting variety.[6] They also cast a very heavy shade, and so do not lend themselves to multi-layer planting.

They like a light, acid soil, and cannot stand poor drainage. They yield best in south-east England, though not every year, but will bear nuts all over the south and Midlands, and less often further north and west. Severe frosts may damage young trees, but frost at flowering time is not a problem as they flower in July.

Unlike most other nuts, chestnuts are mainly composed of carbohydrate. They typically have a protein content of around 10%, which is similar to that of grains. There is no good reason why they should not one day take the place of much of the grain we presently eat.

Walnuts (*Juglans* spp.)

The walnut we are familiar with here in Britain is the common, Persian or English walnut (*J. regia*). It is native to China, the Himalayas, Iran and south-east Europe,

and has long been grown all over Europe for its nuts. The black walnut (*J. nigra*) is a North American tree, which is hardier, faster growing and bigger, but its nuts are not so well flavoured. It is rarely grown in Britain. Some confusion can arise when reading American books, as in America 'walnut' can mean *J. nigra*, while In Britain it invariably means *J. regia*, as it does in this book.

Common walnuts can reach 10m height and spread at 20 years, and 20-30m height by 12-18m spread eventually. The recommended spacing in orchards is 10m x10m, and at least two trees are recommended for good pollination.

They are also allelopathic, the black walnut extremely so and the common only mildly. Apples are particularly badly affected, pears and plums hardly at all. But apples coexist quite happily with common walnuts in traditional English orchards. Since the common walnut is the best one to grow for nut production, allelopathy should not be too much of a problem. Though whether one would want to introduce a large allelopath like this, however mild, into a diverse polyculture like a forest garden is doubtful.

Ideally they like the same soil as apples, but are not fussy as long as it is well drained, and they can do well in a shallow soil over chalk. Frost is the great enemy. Young trees can be killed by it, as can the flowers, which come out in April and May. Full Sun and a warm, sheltered microclimate are essential. Given that, common walnuts can produce nuts as far north as South Yorkshire, the black walnut probably further north.

Never buy a tree described simply as 'common walnut' or '*Juglans regia*' it will be one of the old English trees, which take a decade or more to come into bearing and then yield very little. The standard modern varieties are Buccaneer, Broadview and Franquette. They can bear as early as two years after planting, if pollen is available from an older tree nearby, and typical yields are as follows:

Age of Tree	kg	lb
3-5 years	5	10
10-15	50	110
20, full production	75	165

Nutwood Nurseries are now offering a range of varieties and seedlings from North America and eastern Europe which have been selected for cooler climates. These may well be worth trying.

The flavour of home grown fresh or air-dried nuts is far superior to imported kiln dried ones. The common walnut has a protein content of around 18%, and the black walnut around 30%.

---

6   From Nutwood Nurseries. See List of Suppliers.

Other Nuts

Three other members of the walnut family are available in Britain They are: the heartnut (*J. ailantifolia cordiformis*) from Japan, the butternut or white walnut (*J. cinerea*) from North America, and the buartnut, a hybrid of these two.

These trees are similar in size to the true walnuts, and said to be hardier than the common walnut, with better flavoured nuts. Presumably they have a degree of allelopathy.

Almonds are closely related to peaches, and their requirements and growth are more or less the same. The two species grown for nuts are the sweet almond (*Prunus dulcis*) and the bitter almond (*P. amygdalus amara*). There are some almond species grown purely for their ornamental value, and many of these have edible nuts. In fact the sweet and bitter almonds themselves are more often grown for their blossom than for their nuts in this country. They blossom in March or even February, and though they seem to have some ability to avoid flowering during frosty spells, cropping on unprotected trees is inevitably erratic.

Some people suggest that it may be a good idea to plant a few almonds and other heat-loving trees in anticipation of global warming caused by the greenhouse effect. This is not a safe bet. Climate change due to the greenhouse effect is unlikely to be anything as simple as a general rise in temperatures over the whole planet. It will certainly destabilise many of the systems which we are used to, and the effects of this are impossible to predict with any certainty. One possibility is that the Gulf Stream (or rather its offshoot, the North Atlantic Drift) could change course. This ocean current is what keeps our climate so mild for its latitude. If it no longer washed our shores our climate could become more like that of Norway. Not very good for an almond!

Apricots (*Prunus armeniaca*)

Apricots, like peaches, come originally from China, despite the Latin name suggesting Armenia, and their climate requirements are similar to those of peaches. But they flower even earlier – usually in March or April, and occasionally in February. They will grow in south-east England, but certainly need covering at night during the flowering season. They also like a limey soil, with a pH between 6.5 and 8, so they can be grown on the shallow chalky soils found in parts of south England.

A fan trained tree on St Julien A may reach a height of 2.5m and a spread of 4.5m. A bush – which may be feasible in very warm areas – has a spread of 4.5 to 6m.

Rowan (*Sorbus aucuparia*)

The rowan is the hardiest of all our native trees. In Scotland they grow on mountainsides at over 1,000m, which is higher than any other native tree. In south-east Britain they are rare as natives, but often planted as ornamentals.

A sharp-tasting jelly can be made from the fruits of wild rowans. But the sub-species *S. aucuparia edulis*, the sweet rowan, is more edible. It makes a sweeter preserve, but is still too sharp to be eaten raw.

Rowans tolerate all kinds of soil and climatic conditions, but do not tolerate shade. They may be worth growing for their fruit in a forest garden in an extremely cold site where little else will do well, but in most areas they are more use as a windbreak tree, for their ornamental value, or possibly as a decoy to draw thrushes away from other fruits.

Whitebeam (*Sorbus aria*)

Whitebeams are large shrubs or small trees. They are rare natives over most of Britain, found most frequently on limestone or chalk in southern England. They will grow on less alkaline soils and in more northerly locations if planted there. They are light-demanding and cast a fairly heavy shade, so they are not really suitable for either the shrub layer or the tree layer of a forest garden, but they are one of the fruits which can be grown on a shallow soil over chalk.

The fruit varies from tree to tree. I have eaten quite pleasant ones straight off the tree in July, although received wisdom is that they need to be bletted. They are often planted as ornamentals. The undersides of the leaves are covered in white hairs, and when the wind blows the flashing alternation of green above and white below makes the foliage dance.

Chapter 8

THE SHRUBS

THE OBVIOUS ONES

These are the hazels and all the commonly grown soft fruit, including bush and cane fruits.

The temperate world has a great range of shrub species with edible fruits, many of which may be just as useful to us as the few kinds that we commonly grow now. But the very fact that these plants are commonly grown gives them some advantages:

- a great deal of knowledge about how to grow them has been accumulated over the years, and is readily available;

- there is a greater choice of varieties, both to fit individual situations and to give a succession of fruit through the picking season;

- well-grown planting material is readily available, whereas some less common kinds are only available as seed or as expensive specimen plants;

- also, they are generally smaller than the lesser known kinds and so are easier to fit into a small forest garden under moderately dwarf trees.

Hazels and soft fruit are both much less sensitive to cold than the great majority of top fruits. Witness the fact that they can be found growing wild all over Britain, and the centre of commercial cane fruit growing is in central Scotland.

A disadvantage of soft fruit is that they are all to varying degrees popular with birds. When soft fruit is grown on a field scale this is not too serious, because the local bird population cannot make much of a dent in such a big concentration of berries. But a small number of bushes in a garden is another matter. If they are not netted there are always heavy losses to birds. What to do about it in a forest garden is discussed below under Red and White Currants.

Hazels (*Corylus* spp.)
The native hazel, *C. avellana*, is found almost everywhere in Britain, as well as throughout Europe, west Asia and parts of north Africa. Its cultivated forms are known as cob nuts. The filbert, *C. maxima*, is not native this far north, but grows here under cultivation as successfully as the cob. All information given here applies equally to both kinds.

The thing that distinguishes the two hazels from each other is the husk, which in the cob covers part of the nut and in the filbert covers all of it. The name filbert probably derives from 'full beard', after its long husk. Rather confusingly, one of the most commonly grown varieties, the Kentish Cob, is in fact a filbert. Equally confusing, in North America cobs are known as filberts and filberts as giant filberts.

Cobs and filberts used to be grown on a fairly large scale in Kent, often interplanted with vegetable crops. But the 3,000ha recorded in 1913 have now dwindled to some 150ha, though the area is steadily increasing once more. The decline has been due to competition from imports, which can be sold at half the price of home-grown nuts. Much of the imports come from Turkey, and it may be the lower cost of labour for pruning and picking as much as the difference in climate which gives the imports their competitive edge.

Hazels do well in all parts of Britain, though they do need a certain amount of shelter in order to yield well. Flowering time for the cultivated varieties is usually in late January and February. Although the wind-pollinated flowers are fairly hardy, they are sensitive to very wet and windy weather and to severe frosts. But any site which is good enough for top fruit will be more than good enough for hazels.

Hazels can tolerate partial shade. My own observations of wild hazels growing in woods suggest that if they get no significant light from the side they need to be exposed to at least half the day's direct sunlight in order to yield a moderate crop. If they get good indirect light from one side they can give the same yield on a couple of hours' direct sunlight. This is suggested by hazels in hedgerows and on woodland edges, which can yield quite well despite being entirely under the canopy of a vigorous oak. The nuts do all tend to be on the lightward side of the bush, but no doubt the shade side could be induced to contribute by judicious pruning of both tree and shrub.

The hazels are not fussy about soil, as long as it is well drained. In fact they do not yield their best on very rich soils, because too much fertility encourages vegetative growth rather than nuts. The ideal is a light sandy loam of moderate fertility with a pH between 6.7 and 7.5. Liming is beneficial on soils more acid than this, and they do particularly well on chalk and limestone soils.

Cobs and filberts are always grown on their own roots. In fact it is quite easy to propagate them, either by taking a sucker from an existing tree in autumn or by layering in spring. Layering is pegging a young branch down into the ground, where it takes root. Once established it is cut away from the parent to make a new plant.

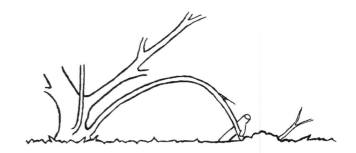

Figure 8.1 Layering

They are traditionally pruned to a shape like a wide, shallow bowl, not unlike the bush form of fruit trees but wider in relation to its height, typically 4.5m wide by 1.5m high, but sometimes as much as 6m x 2m. 4.5m is the normal spacing in nut orchards, or plats as they are known. This shape is quite unlike the natural shape of a woodland hazel, which is much more upright, and it takes a good deal of pruning to form it and maintain it. But it has two great advantages:

GREY SQUIRRELS AND HAZELS

The only serious pests of hazels in this country are grey squirrels. They impose more of a limit on where hazels can be grown than any other factor, such as climate or soil.

Since squirrels only live where there are plenty of large trees, the amount of squirrel damage is closely related to the local vegetation. Where a garden adjoins mature woodland with a high population of squirrels every nut will be stripped from every bush in August, long before they are ripe. In many urban and suburban areas dating from the last century there are now almost as many mature trees as there are in a woodland, and at least as many squirrels. If you regularly see squirrels in your garden you can expect them to take all of any hazelnuts which might be grown there.

Squirrels like to travel around by jumping from tree to tree, and are reluctant to cross open ground. So if your hazel bushes are separated from big trees by a stretch of treeless ground the damage is less intensive. In some years the squirrels may strip them, but more often they will take a proportion of the nuts as they ripen through September and October, and in some years they will leave them alone.

How often they cause serious damage depends on a combination of two factors: how much other food is available that year, and the distance of open ground. My own experience suggest that hazels around 50m from woodland may be stripped in some years and untouched in others, whereas hazels 200m from woodland or other mature trees are safe in any year.

These observations must be taken as indications only. Things like this vary widely from place to place, and there is no substitute for local knowledge and experience. Other factors, like the presence of cats and dogs, can affect the distance of open ground that squirrels feel safe about crossing.

There is very little that can be done about squirrels. It may be possible to fan train hazels against a wall and securely net them with galvanised wire, but I do not know of anyone doing this successfully. You can pick the nuts when they are immature, in early August, and pickle them, but this is a meagre and unappetising harvest. It would not be worth planting bushes for it, though it is a way of getting some yield from existing ones. Where grey squirrels are abundant there is really no alternative but to give hazels a miss.

All this only applies to grey squirrels. If you are fortunate enough to live in one of the remaining areas where the native red squirrels survive then you can certainly grow hazels. Grey squirrels are an introduced species, from North America, and a good example of the havoc which can be wrought by the careless introduction of exotic plants and animals.

it makes the whole bush easy to get at, and it allows hazels to be fitted under standard trees.

It makes a wide plant, though, and if two or three varieties are grown, as recommended for good pollination, they will need a big garden to fit into and the trees above them will need to be full standards. There is one compact variety available, Pearson's Prolific, or the Nottingham Cob. This has a spread of around 3m and could probably be grown under half standards. It is a popular variety, and a good pollinator. Two other varieties, the White Filbert and Ennis are variously described as 'dwarf' and 'vigorous', which sounds contradictory and does not inspire confidence in their compactness. Where there is only room for one hazel, a family tree is possible.

In small gardens hazels could be grown in the canopy layer, pruned into a more upright shape. But they do cast a rather heavy shade, and although this can be lessened by pruning, it would be hard to grow a shrub layer beneath them. They can be left unpruned, but the yield will be lower and they will form a dense bushy mass, filling all three layers and casting a heavy shade. Fan trained hazels are possible, but this is not commonly done.

Hazels come into leaf later than most shrubs; the leaves are not fully expanded till some time in late April or early May. So although they cast a fairly heavy shade once they are leafed, winter-growing greens such as ramsons and winter purslane can be grown beneath them.

The first nuts can be expected in the second year after planting, but full yield may not be reached for ten or even fifteen years. Yields are very erratic from year to year, averaging about 5kg (10lb) per full sized bush with 10kg (25lb) in a good year.

This may seem like a rather low yield for such a big plant. In fact, on a per hectare basis it compares well with the dry weight of other high protein crops, such as beans. If this level of yield can be achieved where there is also a yield of tree fruit above and vegetables below, it comes up to the high levels we expect to get from an intensive garden. When comparing the yield of nuts with that of fruit it must be remembered that most of the weight of fruit is water. As a rule of thumb, a pound of unshelled nuts has at least three times the dry weight of food as a pound of fresh fruit. It is rich food, too, high in oils and protein.

Whatever the quantity of food, the taste of fresh-cracked home-grown nuts is so much better than the dry, woody imported ones that you would hardly think you were eating the same thing. It is worth growing your own hazels simply to discover what a nut really tastes like. An added bonus is the leaf litter, which is unusually high in plant nutrients.

Hazels also contribute great beauty to a garden, especially at the time of year when things are at their drabbest. A hazel bush in midwinter, delicate, cup shaped and gracefully hung with yellow catkins, is a sight of exquisite beauty. I have often been stopped in my tracks with wonder when coming upon one unexpectedly in the woods. What better sight could there be from the kitchen window to cheer us up and to remind us that, for one plant at least, spring is already here?

Some old gardens may have an existing wild hazel in them, and this is usually worth keeping if it does not take up too much room. The yield of nuts will be smaller and less regular than from cultivated varieties, and the nuts themselves will be smaller. But it will also act as a pollinator to most cultivated varieties, as long as it is within about 45m of the forest garden. In addition it will throw out the occasional straight sticks, known as Sun shoots, which can be used for bean poles, broom handles and so on.

Bush Fruit (*Ribes* spp.)

Gooseberries (*Ribes uva-crispa*)
Gooseberries are native to many of the cooler parts of Europe. Whether Britain is part of their native range is hard to say, but they are often found growing wild, and are locally common in hedges in some parts of northern England.

Gooseberries are particularly suitable for a forest garden, because they can stand rather more shade than blackcurrants, and are not such favourites with the birds as red and white currants. They need at least some direct Sun each day, or good indirect light for most of the day, and they will ripen earlier and develop better flavoured fruit in a more sunny position. They can be grown on a north facing wall. A particularly shade tolerant variety is Winham's Industry.

They are not fussy about the soil, as long as it is reasonably well drained and not too limey or too acid, a pH of around 6.7 being ideal. They are susceptible to potash deficiency, and if the soil is known to have a low potash level it should be corrected before planting them.

They are prone to mildew, and especially so in the very sheltered conditions of a forest garden. But there are varieties which are resistant to mildew, and these are best for forest gardening unless there are pressing reasons for choosing another. They are more susceptible to mildew if the soil becomes dry, so mulching is especially important for gooseberries.

They blossom early, in late April or early May, but the flowers are somewhat frost resistant. The amount of shelter they get in a forest garden should be enough to protect them from frost without the need for any other protective measures, unless the garden is in a frost pocket. They are a bit more tolerant of wind than other soft fruits, and can even be used as a hedging plant, giving a bit of 'bottom' to a mixed hedge, but they cannot be expected to fruit reliably in an exposed situation. Cold winds at flowering time will mean no crop at all that year, and any fruit from gooseberries in a hedge should be considered a bonus rather than being relied upon.

They are the earliest ripening of all the commonly grown fruits. Towards the end of May the earliest cookers are ready, together with thinnings from the early eating varieties, which can also be used for cooking. If a mixture of varieties is planted the season goes on till August.

They are usually grown as a bush, though cordons, fans and even standards are not unknown. As a bush they can make a plant of 1.5m height and spread when grown in the open, though they are often smaller than this. If grown in a shady position they tend to grow up towards the light, and so adopt a taller, narrower form. Cordons should be spaced 40 cm apart, while a fan may cover a wall space of 2 x 2m. The standard, which has a clean stem of about 1m, (*see Figure 8.2*) may be a good form to grow above a flourishing vegetable layer. But they are more delicate than bushes, and may not be vigorous enough to stand the competition from the vegetables.

A well-grown bush should yield about 4kg (9lb).

Gooseberries are remarkably long lived. They often go on giving good yields for 25 years, and Robert Hart has one which is still fruiting after more than 30 years – which is about the lifetime of an apple on a very dwarfing rootstock.

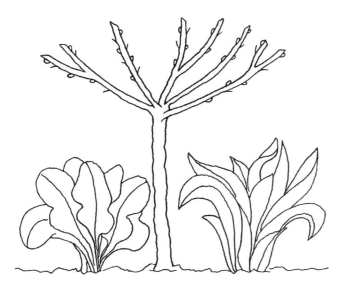

Figure 8.2 Perennial vegetables under standard gooseberry

Worcesterberries (*Ribes divaricatum*)
These used to be thought of as a hybrid between gooseberries and blackcurrants, but are now generally accepted to be a form of the North American species *R. divaricatum*.

They can be seen as a low-input/low-output version of the gooseberry. Hardy, disease-resistant, more vigorous and bigger than gooseberry bushes, they produce lower yields of fruit, and that is only good for cooking and jam. They are an obvious choice where low maintenance is more of a priority than high yield, or for an edible hedge.

Red and White Currants (*Ribes rubrum* and *R. spicatum*)
These are not two separate species, but the white is a sport or mutation of the red. They have been bred from strains of the two closely related *Ribes* species, both of which grow wild in Britain, though there is some debate about whether either is native. In the wild they mainly grow in woods.

Their soil and microclimate requirements are the same as those of gooseberries, except that, like most soft fruit, they are more sensitive to wind, and should not be planted in exposed positions. They have the same shade tolerance.

Unfortunately their fruit is more favoured by birds than any other commonly grown soft fruit. Netting is difficult in a forest garden. Unless the garden resembles pattern A (*see pages 27-28*), the only way to do it would be to net each bush individually. Though this could be done quite effectively to protect the buds in winter and the blossom from frost in spring, it would be difficult in summer when there are vegetables and herbs growing up all around the bushes.

Robert Hart's solution is to allow the nettles to grow up through them. The nettles get to their maximum height when the fruit is ripening and help to conceal it from the birds. Just before picking time the nettles can be cut down with a sickle and added to the compost heap or used for mulch, leaving the fruit exposed to the human eye and hand.

The method is not totally effective, and shading by the nettles can interfere with ripening. But it is a low-input approach, making use of a resource which is growing there of its own accord, with no extra effort needed on the part of the gardener. It is a way of working with nature, seeing nettles as a helping hand rather than as a problem, and not demanding that we harvest every single berry for ourselves.

Red and white currants are normally grown as a bush, but occasionally as cordons or fans to make use of a north-facing wall. This versatility of form is possible because red and white currants, like gooseberries, grow from a single stem, whereas blackcurrants are always

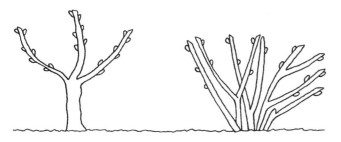

Figure 8.3 Red currant and blackcurrant

grown from a multi-stemmed stool (*see Figure 8.3*). Another advantage of the single-stemmed habit is that it allows for the bush to be grown on a slightly longer 'leg', to leave more room for a vegetable layer underneath.

Size and spacing are similar to gooseberries, that is: bushes to 1.5m high and wide, though often smaller, cordons 40cm apart and fans 2m x 2m. Standards are not grown.

The fruiting season is in July and August. A well-grown bush should yield at least 4kg (9lb) and a cordon 1kg (2.5lb). Plants should go on yielding well for at least ten years. Although they are usually used for pies, preserves, juice or wine, the fruit can be eaten raw, perhaps with a sprinkling of sugar or honey.

Blackcurrants (*Ribes nigrum*)

The native range of blackcurrants stretches from central Europe into Asia, from Scandinavia to the Himalayas. Although they grow wild in Britain, usually in damp woody places, they are probably not native.

Blackcurrants are usually more popular than red or white currants because they are that bit sweeter and so that bit better for eating raw. They also contain the highest levels of vitamin C of any commonly grown fruit, and an added attraction is the fragrance of their leaves – which are also said to be edible. But they are less shade tolerant than the other bush fruits, unable to manage without full Sun for more than half the day, and this makes them slightly less suitable for forest gardening.

Traditional varieties of blackcurrants flower as early as gooseberries but the flowers are not as hardy, so they are particularly vulnerable to spring frosts. They should never be planted where late frosts are common unless you are prepared to cover them during the night at blossom time.

However, a range of new frost-resistant varieties is now available. Some of these flower later, others have greater tolerance of cold. Whether the latter are also more tolerant of shade is not known, but if so

they would be most useful for forest gardening. High yields and many other benefits are also claimed for these new varieties.[1]

One thing blackcurrants do tolerate is a soil which is less than perfectly drained. They prefer a well-drained soil, but they are the obvious first choice for a garden where a soil drainage problem restricts what can be grown. They like a soil which retains moisture well, and light soils need to have organic matter added to improve moisture retention. A pH of around 6.5 is ideal.

Like all soft fruit, they are eaten by birds, but not as much as red and white currants, which are often taken in preference where both are grown together.

They are grown as a multi-stemmed bush, because they fruit best on young wood, and this form encourages new shoots to be produced each year. They are very easy to grow from cuttings, which can be taken in the first summer after planting. So you can save a good deal of money by buying fewer plants than you need and bulking them up yourself. Only certified virus-free stock should be used for cuttings.

The bushes can be as much as 1.5-1.8m in height and spread, but may be much smaller according to variety and situation. They should yield around 4kg (9lb) each. The season is late July and August, and each variety may be ripe over some three weeks. Blackcurrants often go on bearing for a dozen years or more.

Cane Fruit (*Rubus* spp.)

Raspberries (*Rubus idaeus*)

Wild raspberries grow all over Britain, including the Scottish Highlands, often beside running water. The little fruits are quite pleasant to eat raw, unlike the rather sour offerings of wild currants. They are native from Scandinavia to central Asia.

Raspberries are usually grown in a row, supported by wires, making something like a hedge. They will often fit neatly into odd strips of land, such as that left between a path and the garden fence. When several rows are grown together they are normally spaced as much as 1.5m apart to allow space for picking, but a row can fit quite well into a strip of soil 60cm wide beside an existing path. They can grow as tall as 2m, but are often shorter, around 1.5m. They can spread by suckering, and even become quite invasive.

The root system of raspberries is perennial but the canes only live for one or two years. In the summer fruiting raspberries, the canes live for two years, fruiting in their second year and then dying. In the autumn fruiting varieties the canes fruit in their first and only year.

The summer fruiting kind are more reliable in cooler areas, where autumn fruiting ones may not get time to

---

[1]   For an enthusiastic description of these varieties see the catalogue of Chris Bowers & Sons.

ripen fully. But the autumn fruiting kind may do better in dry areas where summer droughts are possible, and they are not usually eaten by birds. They are also easier to prune: you simply cut the lot down when they have finished fruiting, whereas with summer-fruiting raspberries you need to cut out the two-year-old canes and leave the one-year-old ones.

As they flower late in the spring, raspberries avoid problems with frost. But, like almost all soft fruit, they do need protection from wind. They need a minimum of half a day's full Sun, and it is recommended not to plant them directly under trees because they do not like being dripped upon. Autumn fruiting varieties need a sunnier position than summer fruiting, as they are ripening when the sunlight is becoming weaker.

They prefer a slightly acid soil, around pH6.6, and are more prone to chlorosis in very limey soils than any other commonly grown fruit. They need both good drainage and good moisture retention, so organic matter should be dug in before planting, especially on lighter soils. Heavy mulching is also recommended.

Yields are around 2-3kg (4-7lb) per metre of row. Traditional autumn fruiting varieties yield much less, but the popular variety Autumn Bliss yields about the same. With a mixture of varieties it is possible to have fresh raspberries from June till the first frost of autumn. If there is any surplus, it makes good jam, pies and so on. Canes start bearing reasonably well in their second year, and give a full crop in their third. After 12 years yields start to decline due to virus infections. It is always worthwhile to plant virus free stock as raspberries are very susceptible to virus diseases, but it is impossible to prevent the infection slowly coming in as the years go by.

Blackberries or Bramble (*Rubus fruticosus* agg.)
Undoubtedly native, found all over Britain, the rest of Europe and the Mediterranean region, blackberries are surely our most popular wild fruit. They are perhaps the only one whose wild varieties are usually sweeter and tastier than the cultivated ones. They are a very variable plant, and some 2,000 microspecies have been identified worldwide, of which almost 400 grow in Britain.

Wild varieties are not usually recommended for gardens because they are not reliable yielders. But with such wide genetic variation it should be possible to find some wild strains which are more reliable than others. If you know a particularly delicious and productive wild bush it is easy to propagate it in your garden from a stem cutting. But they are big rampant plants and only really suitable for large gardens.

Some of the cultivated varieties are thornless and some are less vigorous, but on the whole their taste is weak and insipid, especially the thornless ones. Even these varieties are fairly rampant, and not suited to small gardens. They are normally grown along a fence, and one plant takes up anything from 3 to 4.5m of fence, according to variety and pruning style. Pruning cannot be neglected, or the blackberry will take over. If more than one row is grown, a spacing of 1.8m between rows is recommended, but if grown against a boundary fence they can be restricted to half that width, depending on variety. The compact varieties may take up something like two thirds as much space.

It might be feasible for blackberries to be grown without support under the trees of a forest garden. But this would only work in a large-scale garden where there is plenty of space. Regular pruning would be essential to prevent them taking over altogether, and they need to be carefully placed so as not to make it hard to get at the trees. No vegetable layer would be possible directly under them. On the whole they are best suited to boundary fences and the like.

Blackberries are only partly deciduous – it varies according to the variety and the severity of the winter. But when they are trained to a fence or wall it is quite possible to grow perennial vegetables around the base of them, especially when they border a path.

They yield quite well in half shade. They are tolerant of a wide range of soils, even slightly impeded drainage, and are particularly useful on dry soils. They are very hardy, and avoid frost by late flowering. If your only possible site for a forest garden is in a frost pocket, then blackberries, together with the hybrid berries, are your best choice among the commonly grown fruits.

A yield of 5-15kg (10-30lb) per plant can be expected, depending on variety and the size of the plant. They can yield heavy crops for 15 to 20 years.

Hybrid Berries (*Rubus* x)
These are similar to blackberries, but more suitable for medium-sized and smaller gardens.

Hybrid is rather a loose term in this context. Most of them are indeed hybrids between different *Rubus* species, usually blackberries and raspberries, but some of the plants listed under hybrid berries in nursery catalogues are species in their own right. Hybrids are often named after the place where they were first bred, or the person responsible. Loganberries have been with us since they were discovered by Judge James H. Logan of California in 1881, and since then a whole array of different crosses have been bred: Veitchberry, Boysenberry, Kings' Acre berry, Tayberry and so on.

Each is slightly different in fruit, growth habit, hardiness, taste, time of ripening and length of fruiting season. But basically they are all closer to the blackberry than to any other fruit. On the whole they are smaller, and less rampant. They are also somewhat less robust, less tolerant of shade and unsuitable soil, and not at all tolerant of poor drainage. But they are nonetheless tough, easily grown plants, and like blackberries they flower late, so they can be grown where late frost may be a problem.

They are a first-class choice for walls, fences and odd strips of land. They are much easier to grow than restricted forms of fruit trees, and come into bearing sooner – which can be an important factor for people who do not expect to live in their present home for many years.

Loganberries are particularly good for medium sized woodland gardens. They are among the most shade-tolerant of soft fruits, doing well on a north wall as long as they get good indirect light. They are also not much taken by birds, always an important point with unnetted soft fruit. Rather smaller plants than blackberries, they need about 2.4m of fence. The fruit is ripe from mid-July, and slightly on the sharp side, though quite acceptable for eating raw, with a distinctive flavour of its own.

Tayberries are a more recently bred equivalent of loganberries, about the same size, a bit less prickly, with sweeter fruit and a longer picking season – early July to mid-August. They are moderately shade-tolerant, but less so than loganberries.

Kings Acre berries are smaller, needing only 1.8m of fence, so they are a good choice for smaller gardens. The fruit ripens a bit earlier than loganberries, and is sweeter and more blackberry-like in flavour.

Yields of hybrid berries vary greatly according to the vigour and size of the different hybrids, but are typically in the range of 3 to 8kg (7-15lb) per bush.

Japanese Wineberries (*Rubus phoenicolasius*)
These delicate-looking plants are probably the prettiest cane fruit you can grow. Instead of thorns, their stems are covered with a fuzz of red hairs, so in winter the whole plant makes a tracery of red against the sombre colours of the quiet season. In summer the green leaves contrast beautifully with the red stems, and the fruit ripens from golden yellow to wine red. Although a species in their own right, they are usually listed among the hybrids in nursery catalogues.

The fruit is very sweet, and delicious eaten raw. Their easy taste and thornless habit make them ideal plants for children to get used to the idea of picking fruit for themselves, and making the direct connection between growing plants and the pleasure of eating. In these days of instant gratification and undemanding, super-sweet flavours not many plants can compete with the sweet-counter. But Japanese wineberries can.

They are moderately vigorous as 'hybrid' berries go.

Each plant needs 2.5m of wall or fence to spread itself along, and produces canes some 2m tall. They prefer a light shade and can fruit well against a north-facing wall. They also do well in colder, upland areas. They are easy to propagate from cuttings. The fruit is ripe in August.

THE LESS OBVIOUS ONES

The plants in this section are either:

* suitable for a limited range of microclimates or soils – such as grapes and blueberries;

* easy to grow but produce fruit which is less popular than common soft fruits – such as elder;

* not well known here in Britain, at least as fruiting plants – such as thimbleberries and *elaeagnus*;

* or rather large for the shrub layer of most forest gardens. In fact most of them are larger than the common soft fruits.

Many of them fall into more than one of these groups. None of them is likely to be the mainstay of the shrub layer in a typical forest garden, but each of them may be useful where circumstances are unusual in one way or another. Some of the larger shrubs could hardly be grown under a tree layer unless very strictly pruned. They may be more suitable for two-layer plantings in places too shady for a full three-layer forest garden.

Elders (*Sambucus* spp.)
A greatly undervalued plant, elder is the easiest fruit to grow and has a wide range of products, though the fruit is not really edible raw.

The common elder (*S. nigra*) is native throughout Britain, except for the highest Scottish mountains. It is a great opportunist, springing up rapidly on bare or disturbed ground, including piles of rubble and even tumbledown walls. The American or sweet elder (*S. canadensis*), from North America, gives a heavier yield of larger fruits, and improved varieties of it are available, though its tendency to sucker is a disadvantage. It is often grown in preference to the native species. The red-berried elder (*S. racemosa*), which is sometimes grown as an ornamental, is not edible.

Elderberry wine and elderflower champagne or cordial are the products of the elder which may first spring to mind. But Richard Mabey[2] reckons there are probably more uses for elderflowers than for any other kind of blossom: made into a cold summer drink, "munched straight off the branch on a hot summer's day [with a] taste as frothy as a glass of ice-cream soda,"

---

2   *Food for Free*, see Further Reading.

as a preserve with gooseberries, made into elderflower fritters, or as an ingredient in skin ointments and eye lotions. My own favourite use for elderflowers is to dry them for tea (*see box below*).

If after all that there are enough flowers left to set any berries, and you don't want to make wine with them, you can add them to jams and pies, or try Richard Mabey's recipe for Pontack Sauce, "a relic from those days when every retired military gentleman carried his patent sauce as an indispensable part of his luggage".[3]

Elders will make small trees, usually to about three metres tall, exceptionally to ten metres. But they will grow well as multi-stemmed bushes too. The bush form is normally used when it is grown for fruit, and this allows elders to be grown under other fruit trees, thus making use of their shade tolerance.

They are amongst the most shade-tolerant of shrubs, and they can produce a worthwhile crop with less sunlight than hazel can. In semi-natural woodland they can flower and fruit below a gap in the canopy which reveals about a quarter of the sky above. In this situation they get sunshine for less than a quarter of a summer day, but it is the brightest, noonday light. The crop here may be something like a third of what it would be if the elder was right out in the open with full Sun all day, and perhaps half what it would be on a woodland edge.

Plate 8.1 Elderberries (Tim Harland)

They are mildly allelopathic, with the effect coming mainly from chemicals released from the leaves as they decompose in the soil. The only plants seriously affected are members of the cabbage family. Other vegetables can be grown beneath elders.

Shelter is not needed. Elders can produce good crops in exposed positions, and can even be used as fruiting windbreak trees in areas of moderate exposure, including coastal sites. They are tolerant of a very wide range of soils, including those two bugbears of most fruit trees and shrubs, chalky soil and poor drainage. They do like plenty of nitrogen, though, and the wild elder tends to seek out high nitrogen soils. But any garden soil is likely to be adequate in nitrogen for elder. There are few pests or diseases to trouble them, and birds do not take elderberries as their first choice.

A mature bush may have a spread of about 3m. It will fit under a standard tree on a rich soil, and a half standard on a poorer soil. If your garden has a rich soil and you are not planning to plant standard trees the best place for elders is probably behind the trees rather than under them, in a north-facing or overshadowed situation. Alternatively they can be grown as standards in the tree layer.

Pruning helps to improve the yield, but is not essential once the bush shape is formed. The common elder is self-fertile, but the American elder is not, so at least two varieties must be grown in order to get a good set of fruit. The common elder is not a reliable pollinator for American elder.

They can also be used to make some productive use of awkward or difficult pieces of land, such as shady

ELDERFLOWER TEA

Pick the flower clusters whole, preferably as soon as the flowers are open. They can be dried anywhere, but ideally not in direct sunlight, laid out singly on newspaper. They are dry enough when the flowers separate from the stalk on being rubbed gently, and resemble a golden powder. They are best stored in brown jars, as all dried plant products keep their vital properties for longer in the dark.

In the middle of winter, take one teaspoon of the magic powder, place it in a teapot and add boiling water. Before your eyes the tiny flowers unfold to their former shape in the hot water, the heady scent of summer fills the room, and you can feel yourself once again under a warm sunny sky, by the elder bushes covered with cascades of frothy white blossom. It is like a spoonful of distilled summer.

Mixed with equal parts of peppermint and yarrow it makes the famous 'flu tea' recommended by many herbalists for minor bugs and maladies. An equal part of coltsfoot can be added if the bug is coldy or chesty.

---

3   *Food for Free*, see Further Reading.

areas under existing large trees. As long as there is a little light coming in, either from above or from the side, they will give some yield. Standard elders fit well under big trees, and do not need pruning at all. Elders can easily be propagated from cuttings, and useful plants may be had free simply by sticking twigs from a local elder bush in the soil. At least half of them should take.

Grapes (*Vitis vinifera* and hybrids)

The origin of the vine lies deep in the history and mythology of the Mediterranean peoples. It is probably a native of Asia Minor, but grows wild all around the Mediterranean. The hybrids are recent crosses with American species of vine. They tend to be more resistant to disease and heavier yielding, though with perhaps lower quality fruit for dessert purposes.

After an absence of many centuries vineyards are now reappearing in Britain, mainly in southern England. In Roman and early Medieval times they were far more common than they are now. The great hiatus in grape growing between then and now has been largely due to climate changes. Before the Norman conquest the average temperature was slightly higher than it is today, but from the late Middle Ages up to the beginning of the last century the so-called Little Ice Age intervened, with colder temperatures than today.

Grape vines are Sun-loving plants, especially here at the northern edge of their range, so they are hardly the ideal plant for the shrub layer of a forest garden. But in many gardens there are sunny situations where they can do well. They are beautiful plants throughout the year, with their graceful tendrils and uniquely shaped leaves, especially those varieties which turn red in autumn. As well as dessert fruit and wine they can provide shade and a gentle, relaxed atmosphere in the garden.

One of the best uses of a vine is as a pergola over a patio which is inclined to get uncomfortably hot in summer. This can easily happen in a very sheltered, south-facing spot, especially in an urban area (*see Figure 8.4*). Of course this kind of super-heated situation is also just what a vine likes for its own growth. They give a dappled shade, letting some sunlight filter gently through, and obligingly drop their leaves to let the full Sun in when the weather turns cooler in autumn.

Wherever they are grown, grapes should be given the sunniest microclimate in the garden, and a very sheltered one. They can stand cold winters, but not late spring frosts or cool summers. In the right microclimate they thrive as far north as central Scotland, though the further north you go the less you can rely on them to fruit well every year. A south or south-west facing wall is ideal, though in the south of England they do well in the open, preferably on a slope of the same aspect. Even in the south it is not recommended to plant them at more than 100m above sea level.

They are tolerant of a wide range of soils as long as the soil is deep, and good drainage is essential. A pH between 6.5 and 7 is ideal, and too much lime will cause chlorosis.

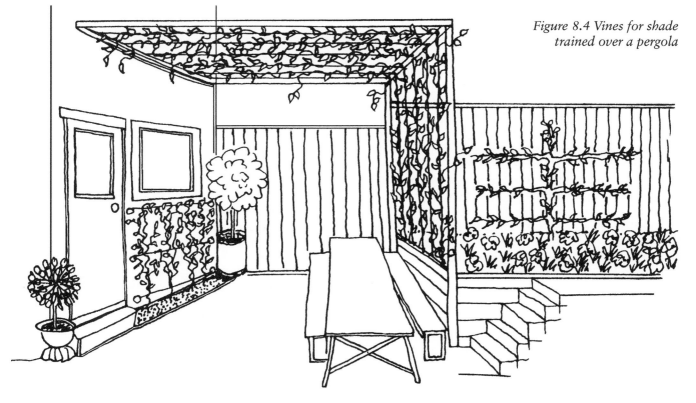

Figure 8.4 Vines for shade trained over a pergola

Along a wall or fence they should be planted 1.2m apart. If more than one row is grown the recommended spacing between rows is 1.5-2m. They cannot be grown without support.

They repay the effort of careful pruning. Yields are very variable, and care should be taken to select a variety suited to the situation and to your needs: some are recommended for walls, others for cooler situations; some are for wine some for dessert fruit, and others are dual purpose.

Kiwis (*Actinidia* spp.)

There are three species of kiwi which can be grown here.

The best known is the one we buy in the shops (*A. chinensis* or *deliciosa*), usually imported from New Zealand. It was given the name kiwi because this was thought to be more marketable than its previous name, Chinese gooseberry, which records its original home. South of a line from the Wash to Shrewsbury it can be grown outside, if it is cared for like a peach, with a cover to keep off spring frosts, hand pollination and so on.

The hardy or Siberian kiwi (*A. arguta*) is native to northern China and Japan as well as parts of Siberia. It is very vigorous, and in the wild it climbs to the tops of the tallest trees. The fruit tastes very similar to that of its more familiar cousin, if anything even sweeter, but it is smaller and has a smooth skin. It is very rich in vitamins and minerals, especially vitamin C.

The third kind is the Manchurian kiwi (*A. kolomikta*), otherwise known as the Kolomikta vine or kishmish, which is also from north-east Asia. This is a smaller plant, and more shade tolerant. The fruit is similar to the Siberian kiwi in taste, appearance and nutritional content. At present it is often grown as an ornamental in this country, but rarely for its fruit.

All kiwis are rampant if left to themselves and they definitely need pruning in a forest garden, where they must coexist with other fruiting plants. They are compulsive climbers, and if no support is provided they will climb up the nearest thing available. In a forest garden this is likely to be one of the fruit trees, which will probably get smothered by its uninvited guest and stop producing any fruit.

They can be espalier trained on fences or walls. The Siberian needs at least 2m height, with as much as 6m between plants. The other two kinds need a little less height and 3-5m between plants. They could all be trained over a pergola, and the smaller two perhaps over an arch.

Most varieties of all three species bear male and female flowers on different plants, so male plants must be grown for pollination. One male will pollinate about seven females within a range of about 15m. It is also possible to graft a male branch onto a female plant. But self-fertile varieties of New Zealand and Siberian kiwis have been bred, and at least one of each is available in this country.[4] This means a single plant can be grown on its own.

All three kinds can stand hard winters, but to varying degrees they are susceptible to spring frosts. The flowers do not bloom till July, but the young shoots which bear the flowers come out in spring, and if they are frosted then the plant is severely set back and will not fruit that year. The New Zealand kiwi is the most vulnerable; the Siberian starts growing a little later in spring, usually in early May, and so has a better chance of avoiding frosts, while the Manchurian is the most frost tolerant and escapes frosting most years. The Siberian kiwi should have no trouble ripening its fruit in our summers, though it cannot tolerate much shade. The Manchurian is more shade tolerant. All three kinds need shelter, but especially the New Zealand kiwi.

Soil conditions are not critical, and the ideal soil is the same as for apples and other fruit.

Because they are cross-pollinated, kiwi plants grown from seed are extremely variable (though presumably this does not apply to self-fertile plants grown well away from any other kiwi). Plants of named variety and known qualities should always be bought if at all possible. Unfortunately the Manchurian kiwi is, at the time of writing, only available as seed,[5] except for the purely ornamental varieties which are usually only sold as male plants. But this is certainly the best one for a forest garden in our climate, as it is more tolerant of both shade and spring frosts than either of the others, and less rampant than the Siberian.

Plants with desirable qualities can be reproduced vegetatively by taking cuttings in late summer or by layering in spring.

Pest and disease problems are rare with kiwis, except that they are extremely vulnerable to slugs when young. Another problem is cats. Apparently kiwis contain a substance which cats find irresistible, and they can rub, chew and claw a young plant to death if they are not kept off. A sleeve of wire netting around the plant should do the job.

The first fruit is borne two to four years after planting. A Siberian vine can produce up to 50kg (110lb) of fruit when mature. It ripens over a long period between late August and early October, so the fresh fruit does not all come in a rush, which is good for the home gardener. Any surplus can be made into jam, jelly or even wine.

The New Zealand kiwi has a more moderate yield, and ripens over a shorter period. The fruit must be stored for 4-6 weeks before eating to get the full flavour.

---

[4]   From Buckingham Nurseries, see List of Suppliers.

[5]   From Future Foods and the Agroforestry Research Trust, see List of Suppliers.

They are decorative plants, and until recently the New Zealand kiwi was grown more for its appearance than for fruit in this country. It has big, heart-shaped leaves and creamy flowers. The Manchurian kiwi often has leaves with pink, white and green variegation, especially the male plants. But these varieties are probably less productive.

Roses (*Rosa* spp.)

The dog rose (*R. canina*) is common throughout Britain as far north as Shetland, and is a true climber, while the more shrubby field rose (*R. arvensis*) is found mainly south of the Tees. The sweet briar or eglantine (*R. eglanteria*) is similar to the dog rose, but exudes a delightful scent from its leaves, especially when they are gently rubbed between finger and thumb. It is naturalised in Britain.

The ramanas rose is these days more often referred to by its Latin name, *Rosa rugosa*, which seems a shame when the common name has such a romantic, far-away ring to it. It is a short, shrubby rose, with many fine thorns. It originates in north-east Asia, and is much used in this country by landscape architects as a tough, low-maintenance, yet attractive hedging and border plant.

In the Second World War, when supplies of imported fruit were interrupted, British people went out into the countryside to scour the waysides and hedgerows for wild rose hips to make rose hip syrup as an emergency source of vitamin C. In fact rose hips contain some 20 times the amount of vitamin C as oranges, weight for weight. They were commonly used in pies and puddings in the ages before intensive fruit production made larger and less fiddly fruit more widely available.

Rose hips are fiddly to use because the pith around the seeds contains sharp hairs, which can cause intense irritation to the digestive system. They have even been extracted from the fruit for use as itching powder! They must be removed before the fruit can be used for food or drink, either by individually opening the tiny fruit and removing the pith, or by reducing the fruit to a liquid and then straining.

Enter the ramanas rose. This species has such large hips, often a good 3cm across, that it is relatively easy to scoop out the pith. It is even possible to eat them straight off the bush if you are careful not to bite into the pith (*see Figure 8.5*). It also has a far higher yield of hips than any other rose, so it is more worth growing as a source of stored vitamin C.

No-one who grows a forest garden is likely to be deficient in this vitamin, but it can also be used in very high doses as a tonic to the immune system, a useful adjunct to the healing of almost any ill. A few

Figure 8.5 Dog rose (left) and ramanas rose (right)

bottles of rose hip syrup on the pantry shelf are a good stand-by.

As well as the hips, the petals of both wild and ramanas roses can be eaten. They can be added to salads, or made into a variety of concoctions, from rose-petal wine and jelly to Turkish delight. The petals of ramanas roses are taken in China as a medicine to soothe the liver, and its young shoots and leaves are said to be edible when cooked.

Ramanas roses can tolerate almost any weather, including cold winters, strong winds, coastal conditions, and air pollution. As regards soil they can thrive on anything from lime-rich clays to the poorest sandy and stony coastal soils. They can tolerate a little shade, but production of hips is soon affected as shade increases. They are certainly more suited to a hedge or even a windbreak round a forest garden than to the shady parts under the trees.

They can grow to 2m, but normally stay at around 1m, especially if they are getting plenty of light. They have large, pinky flowers in summer, and the big orange-coloured hips make a long-lasting display in autumn – though you may prefer to pick them before too long to ensure you get them in good condition. There are double-flowered varieties, but these have smaller hips, so they should be avoided if fruit production is a priority. The variety Scabrosa is said to be large in all its parts, including the hips.

With ramanas roses as a powerhouse of vitamin C production, there is surely still room in many a forest garden for one or two dog roses, or even an eglantine to fill the summer months with its delicate scent. Nothing brightens up the brown twigs of winter more than the little scarlet hips of the dog rose, dotted around like tiny Chinese lanterns until eventually a hungry thrush comes and takes them. If they are pruned occasionally they can live in the boughs of a fruit tree without seriously affecting its yield.

Elaeagnus species

There are many species and hybrids of *Elaeagnus* which can be grown successfully in this country. Like the legumes, they have a symbiotic relationship with nitrogen-fixing bacteria (*see page 46*). Most are very tough plants, and can stand any extremes of climate and soil likely to be found in Britain except waterlogging. They are all tolerant of wind, and are excellent windbreak plants, including in coastal situations. The bulb fields on the Isles of Scilly are protected by tall hedges, often of *Elaeagnus*. Many of them bear edible fruits, but they are normally grown as ornamentals.

E. angustifolia, the oleaster or Russian olive is a deciduous shrub or tree, growing to 20m tall. Its fruit is edible and can be pressed to yield an edible oil. It is not tolerant of shade. *E. commutata*, the silverberry, is also deciduous and produces edible, if mealy, fruits. It is much smaller, growing to 2-3m, more tolerant of shade and very decorative, with silver foliage and fruits in addition to the fragrant, silver-yellow flowers which it bears in May.

The one most suitable for forest gardening is probably *Elaeagnus x ebbingei*, an ornamental hybrid with no common English name. Although it is evergreen, which means that no vegetable layer can be grown beneath it, it is extremely tolerant of shade and can do well beneath trees. It may be suited to a part of the garden where the trees cast too much shade to allow both a shrub and a vegetable layer to thrive. It grows to a height and spread of about 5m, but can be kept as small as 1.5m high and 1m wide by pruning. It is said to be a good companion plant in orchards, increasing yields of fruit trees by 10%, presumably due to nitrogen fixation.

One of the great merits of this plant is that its fruit is ripe in April and May, when there is very little other fruit about. As it has not been bred specifically for fruiting, the fruit is variable in size, yield and taste, but it usually has a rich flavour when fully ripe. It is said to produce a fair crop in most years when grown in Britain. The variety Limelight is one which crops particularly well, even on small bushes.

Like all *Elaeagnus* it prefers a well-drained soil of only moderate fertility, and can succeed in very dry and poor soils. It can survive very low temperatures, and thrives at least as far north as Glasgow, but may become deciduous in cold winters. Sometimes a whole branch can die back for no apparent reason. If this occurs the branch should be removed.

Since this is a hybrid it will not breed true from seed, but it can be propagated from cuttings. Half-ripe and mature cuttings, taken in summer and autumn respectively, can both be successful, as can layering.[6]

Blueberries (*Vaccinium* spp.)

These are the fruit to grow in soils which are too acid for anything else.

The bilberry or blaeberry (*V. myrtillus*) is a common native throughout the moorland and mountain parts of Britain, and right across the north of Europe and Asia. They grow both in the open and in light woodland. The fruits are tiny and it takes ages to pick enough to make a mouthful, let alone a meal. The species normally cultivated in gardens are the high bush blueberries (*V. corymbosum* and *V. australe*), from North America. These give a higher yield of larger sized fruit. The fruit is rather bland when eaten raw, but good when cooked or bottled. They are also attractive plants, especially in autumn, when the leaves turn to a medley of reds and golds.

They cannot stand a pH above 5.5. In a garden with a more alkaline soil they can only be grown by strenuous efforts to turn the soil into what it is not. This is done by removing the soil, either from the planting holes or over the whole blueberry patch, and replacing it in with a mixture of acid peat and the original soil. Chemicals may also be used to reduce the pH, and peat must be added regularly over the years.

This kind of gardening is a good example of working against nature. It requires a great deal of work both to set up and to maintain, and using peat contributes to the destruction of peat bogs, ecosystems of great diversity which are being rapidly destroyed. On the other hand, where the soil is naturally acid, blueberries are one of the few fruits that can be grown *without* making great changes to the soil.

They need a high level of organic matter, as they depend on a symbiotic fungus which needs plenty of organic matter to feed on. They also need a moist but well-drained soil. Growing them in raised beds is often enough to improve the drainage. They will stand slight shade, and should be sheltered from strong winds. They are hardy in all parts of the British Isles, but they do need at least five months without frost. Ideally they like a warm summer with plenty of rain. They are only partially self-fertile, and set a poor crop if only one variety is grown. Pruning is not really necessary. There are no disease or pest problems other than birds, which take the fruit, and rabbits, which are particularly fond of blueberry bark.

When mature the bushes reach a size of 1.5-2m, and they should be planted this distance apart. They are slow to come into full bearing, giving about 2.5kg (5lb) in the fifth year after planting and some 5kg (11lb) when mature, but they can go on bearing for up to 50 years.

---

6   For more information on *Elaeagnus*, especially *ebbingei*, see *Permaculture Magazine*, No 9.

Two other blueberries which may be of use in acid soils are: the thin leaved blueberry (*V. membranaceum*), which is particularly drought-resistant, growing to about 2m tall; and the box blueberry (*V. ovatum*), a spreading evergreen shrub, also to 2m, which can be used to make a hedge.[7]

Thimbleberries and Salmonberries (*Rubus* spp.)
The northwest of North America, from Oregon to British Columbia, is very similar in climate to the north-west of Europe, and its natural vegetation is woodland. It is also the world's great storehouse of berry-bearing woodland shrub species.

Two which are currently available over here[8] are the thimbleberry (*R. parviflorus*) and the salmonberry (*R. spectabilis*). Both are tolerant of part shade, but the full flavour of the fruit is not always developed in the cool summers of Britain. So perhaps these plants are most suited to the sunnier parts of the garden, or the south-eastern part of the country, if they are wanted for eating raw. The young shoots are also edible, peeled and eaten raw or cooked, and the flowers can be added to salads.

Thimbleberry bushes bear large white, fragrant flowers in June, followed by red berries, and maple-shaped leaves which turn yellow in autumn. The fruit is variously described as 'luscious', 'insipid' and 'of good flavour although sometimes a bit seedy'. They are vigorous shrubs, growing to a height of 2.5m and a spread of 2m. They have a suckering habit of growth and can form dense thickets. With their late flowering date they may be of most use in gardens subject to late frosts.

Salmonberries are a bit taller, up to 3m, and flower in the early spring. But they make a beautiful display when in bloom, and bear fruit rather like raspberries.

Juneberries (*Amelanchier* spp.)
These are also woodland shrubs from North America, but their home is further inland, so they are used to a more continental climate than ours. Two of the species most commonly available in Britain[9] are *A. canadensis*, the true juneberry, and *A. alnifolia*, the saskatoon. But naming is very confused. In America they are often collectively known as chequerberries, and in Britain, where they are often grown as ornamentals, as snowy mespilus or shadbush.

The saskatoon is the kind most often grown for its fruit. Several fruiting cultivars are available in America, where it is cultivated in orchards. The juneberry is more often grown as an ornamental, but is similar in most respects, and the two can be considered together.

They are slow-growing, multi-stemmed shrubs, growing to a height of about 5m and a spread of 3m, though some varieties are smaller. Prince William is a good fruiting variety of juneberry which is 3m tall and 2m wide. They can spread by suckering and form thickets. The flowers come out in April or May, saskatoons slightly later than juneberries, and they have some degree of frost tolerance. The fruit is ripe, as the name suggests, in June. It is blue-purple in colour, sweet, tasty and rich in vitamin C. It can be eaten fresh, cooked, preserved or dried like raisins. It tends to ripen all at once.

Cultivated varieties of saskatoon come into fruiting within three to four years, and reach full production after 8 years. Full production can be around 4kg (10lb) per plant in an orchard, where they are planted in rows 4m apart with 1m between plants. In less formal plantings a spacing of 3m each way is recommended. At least two plants should be planted for good pollination – not necessarily two varieties, though this may be a wise insurance. They can be propagated both by seed and by suckers.

As they stand light shade they deserve consideration for the shrub layer of a forest garden. But they are potentially very big plants, and will need hard pruning even to fit under standards. They are very hardy and not troubled by disease. Although they prefer a moist, fertile soil they can tolerate both poor soils and heavy clays. They are also relatively tolerant of both wind and drought. The fruit is taken by birds.

Chinese Dogwood (*Cornus kousa chinensis*)
This shrub comes from China and Japan, and is related to our native dogwood (which does not bear edible fruit). It is very ornamental, with showy flower clusters in summer, and red strawberry-like fruits which ripen in September. They are juicy, and often have a good flavour, suitable for eating raw or cooked. If left unpruned the shrub grows to 3m or more, and it likes an acid, moisture-retaining soil.

It is probably a more useful plant than the rather better known cornelian cherry (*Cornus mas*). This is a very big shrub, growing to 8m. It flowers early in spring, which makes it susceptible to frost, and bears a fruit which is usually only good enough for preserves.

Salt Bush (*Atriplex halimus*)
Otherwise known as shrubby orache or tree purslane, this shrub is in fact a relative of the native vegetable, common orache. It comes from southern Europe and is hardy in the milder parts of Britain. It is particularly useful in gardens near the sea.

It is evergreen, growing to 1-1.5m, and is very resistant to salty winds. But it must have a sunny position and a well-drained soil. It can be used as the shrubby element

7   Seed available from Future Foods, see List of Suppliers.
8   As seed, from Future Foods and Chiltern Seeds, see List of Suppliers.
9   From Future Foods, see List of Suppliers.

in a windbreak, and can be trimmed to form a hedge. The leaves are edible cooked or raw. They have a pleasant, slightly salty taste, and are a welcome addition to winter salads.

Beach Plum (*Prunus maritima*)

This shrub grows on the sand dunes of the east coast of the USA, so it is a good plant for a forest garden very near the coast, where many fruiting plants find the salt-laden winds intolerable. In fact it cannot be recommended for inland areas as the fruit seldom ripens away from the coast in Britain.

It is a thorny bush, with a height and spread of about 2m, bearing masses of white flowers in April or May, followed by small juicy fruits in late summer which can be eaten raw or made into preserves and pies. It is a useful component of an edible windbreak or hedge. It is a disease resistant, low-maintenance plant, late-flowering and tolerant of both cold and poor sandy soils.

Guelder Rose (*Viburnum opulus*)

Not a rose despite its name, this is a thornless shrub, native throughout Britain, though less frequent in Scotland. It prefers moist, alkaline soils and thrives in situations too wet for other shrubs, though it tolerates a wide range of soils. It can survive quite well in deep shade, but flowers and fruits best on an edge.

The white flowers come out in June or July, and are bunched together in a compact inflorescence that gives the shrub its alternative name of snowball bush.[10] The bright red berries are ripe in September and October, and the maple-like leaves often turn beautiful shades of red before they fall later in the autumn. The berries are not edible raw, but make a jelly or pie filling with a distinctive woodsy taste. The flavour improves after the berries have been frosted, but if you want to get them before the birds do you can pick them before the first frost and put them in a freezer overnight.

This is the plant for soils which are too poorly drained for other fruits. It is typically 2m high and 1.5m across. It does not need pruning, but can be pruned to control its size without much loss of yield, because the berries are borne on new twigs as well as last year's. It can start bearing within one or two years of planting, and heavily within five to seven years. A typical bush yields enough berries to make 10 or 12 jars of jelly. It is self-fertile. (See colour illustrations.)

Oregon Grape (*Mahonia aquifolium* or *repens*)

Another shrub from the west of North America, mahonias are often grown in Britain as ornamentals, and have naturalised in a few places. They are evergreen, with holly-like leaves, and bear beautifully-scented yellow flowers from the New Year till April and May,

followed by blue-black berries from July to September. The flowers are edible, and can be made into a sweet drink. The fruit is rather too tart to be eaten raw unless it is very ripe, but it makes good jam and jelly.

They are small shrubs, about 1.5m high by 1m wide, tolerant of shade and dry soils, and generally tough and maintenance-free. They produce suckers, and could become invasive if left entirely to their own devices, but there is a non-suckering variety called Apollo. They are probably most worth growing where drought-tolerance or low maintenance are high priorities.

Edible Honeysuckle (*Lonicera caerulea edulis*)

When people hear about this plant they often think "Aha. An edible climber.", but in fact it does not climb. It is a different species to the native honeysuckle, and makes a compact bush of 1-1.5m height and spread. It is often grown as an ornamental, for its yellowish-white flowers in spring and conspicuous dark blue berries. These are similar to blueberries, and best used in pies or crumbles.

GROWING A NATIVE SHRUBBERY

Producing food is not everyone's main priority in growing a forest garden. Beauty, wildlife, a play area for children, and the interest of having a living ecosystem in the back garden were all mentioned as possible reasons for forest gardening in Chapter 1. Some of these things go better together than others – an intensive play area, for example, is not likely to be a great haven for wildlife – but all of them can be had from a shrubbery composed of native plants just as well as from a full-blown forest garden.

On the whole native plants support many more kinds of insects and other invertebrates than exotics, and thus more of the birds and other predators that live on them. Natives are usually easier to grow, as they have evolved to suit local conditions. Many of them are as beautiful as any exotics, and some have edible or otherwise useful parts. They are also worth growing for their own sake: there is something dignified and harmonious about growing the plants which have co-evolved with this land. There is a way in which they are 'right' which can be felt and intuited more easily than it can be explained in words.

A shrubbery composed entirely of natives will not yield as much food as a forest garden composed of plants which have been bred over generations for human food. But it is not necessary to be purist about it, and a combination of natives and serious food producers can be chosen to suit the needs of the individual family.

---

10   Not to be confused with snowberry, *Symphoricarpus racemosus*, which bears white berries in the autumn and is not edible.

The design may fall anywhere along a continuum from pure forest garden to pure native shrubbery.

Alternatively, where there is enough space a food oriented forest garden can be grown in one part of the garden and a native shrubbery in another part, perhaps further from the house. Or the one could merge into the other.

A native shrubbery can be very flexible in its purpose. We may plant the shrubs with the intention of picking the nuts and berries, making preserves and wine, and weaving baskets. But some years we may not have the time, or be away from home at the crucial time of year. All is not lost, though. The nuts and berries will be eaten by birds and small mammals, and the willow will flower in the spring to make an early meal of nectar and pollen for butterflies and bees. Nothing is wasted, all is gained.

The layout of a shrubbery can be very similar to that of a forest garden proper. The best overall shape will depend on the main purpose. For children, a dense planting with plenty of deep places to hide and make dens may be best, while a shallow crescent or horseshoe with plenty of edge could be best where enjoying the beauty of the shrubs is a high priority.

The ground layer can be planted with native edibles, such as ramsons and wild sorrel, or with woodland wildflowers. It is also good to have at least one tree. Apart from the visual effect that the vertical dimension gives, some birds prefer to forage up in trees rather than down in the shrubs, and others will only nest where the male has a high perch to sing from.

On the whole native trees and shrubs are larger than the more usual forest garden plants. Native trees are not grown on dwarfing rootstocks, and most native shrubs are much bigger than currants and gooseberries, in fact many reach a similar size to a dwarf apple tree. But there are a number of small trees, and most of the shrubs can stand hard cutting. A native shrubbery can be fitted in to all but the smallest gardens.

Occasional maintenance is necessary in large gardens as well as small. If the whole shrubbery is left untouched for many years, not only will it grow very tall, but eventually the more vigorous shrubs will suppress the less vigorous, and diversity will be reduced. Also, no light will get to the ground, and the herb layer will suffer. Selective coppicing is probably a better way to cut things back than pruning. It is easier, and it creates a diverse structure which is good for woodland flowers and wildlife. The fastest-growing shrubs, such as willows, may start to crowd out their neighbours only three or four years after planting, and they will need regular coppicing from this time. Very slow growing ones, like holly, may not need touching for a lifetime.

[11] See Further Reading.

Plate 8.2 A native hawthorn in full bloom. Is any exotic ornamental more beautiful than this? (PW)

Plants

If the shrubbery is to be native in a real sense the plants should be native to the locality, not just to Britain as a whole. They should also be ones which would naturally occur in the soil and microclimate found in the garden. This kind of shrubbery will be something like a natural community which might have occupied that site – something close to the natural grain of the land. The book *Planting Native Trees and Shrubs*[11] gives comprehensive information on which species occur together naturally, as well as maps showing the natural distribution of each one in Britain and Ireland.

It is also worthwhile to plant local varieties if at all possible. A hawthorn which is native to East Anglia, for example, will have evolved in a very different ecosystem, and be genetically distinct from one which comes from North Wales. A few nurseries are beginning to specify the origin of their native trees and shrubs, but most do not. Indeed many 'native' shrubs are in fact imported from Germany or Poland.

The surest way to get really local plants is to collect your own seeds or cuttings and grow them on. This is not only a very satisfying thing to do, but gives you a couple of years to contemplate your design, and probably change it for the better.

Whatever plants you do buy should come from native plant specialists rather than suppliers of ornamentals. Many native trees and shrubs have been bred as ornamentals, and these are very far removed from the original wild stock.

Trees

Crab apple, rowan, birch, field maple, bird cherry, wild service and whitebeam are all described elsewhere in this book (*see Plant Index*).

Shrubs

Bilberry, broom, gorse, blackberry, wild roses, hawthorn, guelder rose, hazel and elder are all described elsewhere. These include all the native shrubs with significant edible fruit.

Hazel can be grown as a coppice plant in large gardens, giving bean poles and pea sticks on a seven year rotation. They should be spaced 2m apart, and surrounded by other shrubs or trees to encourage them to grow upwards and produce good straight sticks.

Willows are excellent wildlife plants, second only to oaks in the number of insect species they support. The spring-flowering or pussy willows are shrubs or small trees, and their beautiful catkins not only brighten up the early spring with their display, but provide the most abundant source of food for bees and other insects at that time of year.

The osier (*Salix viminalis*) is the traditional basket willow, growing tall and thin when coppiced regularly, almost more like a large reed than a shrub. It can reach over 2m tall and is usually grown in rows 60cm apart with 30cm spacing within the rows. Other spring willows, of which there are several species, are more shrubby and not really suitable for basketry. They need a spacing of 2-3m each way. All willows can be easily propagated from cuttings. As they are sensitive to weed competition in their first year, a good way to establish them is by sticking cuttings straight through a sheet of black plastic mulch.

All willows are competitive and only suitable for larger gardens. The large tree willows, including crack (*S. fragilis*) and white (*S. alba*) willows should be avoided altogether.

Native dogwood is a medium-sized suckering shrub, which can form a dense thicket. A common wild variety has purple-red stems These can be used in basketry to add another colour to the buffs and browns of willow, and they give some colour to the garden in winter. The white flowers are out in June and July.

The native honeysuckle is a joy to have in the garden. It is very pretty, and you can pick a flower, bite off the bottom of the trumpet and suck out a little drink of honey-flavoured nectar. It should never be planted near young trees or shrubs as it will seriously constrict their growth and even kill them. But it can climb up a mature fruit tree without harm, or cover a wire fence or trellis.

Ivy is a much maligned climber. It often does well on trees which are already sick or dying, and people think that it is causing the trouble. But it can only do any harm to trees when they are very young, and it is not in any way parasitic. It will grow in places which are too dark for anything else, and has great value for wildlife: it flowers in November, and is the most abundant source of food for flower-feeding insects at that time of year; its berries are available in early spring, when there is little for berry-eating birds to eat; and it makes a good dense nesting and roosting site for small birds.

Spindle is the most exquisitely beautiful of native shrubs. It is a slender plant, usually growing to about 3m tall by 1.5m wide, with a pleasantly textured bark, green twigs and elegant pointed leaves. The white flowers are small and inconspicuous, but as autumn draws on the pink fruits form, then split open to reveal the orange seed inside. The two colours complement each other perfectly. The leaves sometimes stay green till falling, but usually turn to a range of reds, oranges, pinks and purples that defy description. No part of the plant is edible or particularly useful in any other way: It is worth growing purely for its beauty.

Chapter 9

THE VEGETABLES

There are over 1,000 herbaceous plants which grow wild in Britain, but less than 100 trees and shrubs. In a semi-natural woodland there is usually a much greater diversity of plants in the herb layer than in the tree and shrub layers, and the same is true of a forest garden, at least potentially. There are many, many plants which could be included in this chapter. To include them all would require a book of its own.

Even the number which have been included may seem excessive if you are looking for somewhere to start. They are all useful plants, though many of them fill specialist niches and will not find a home in every garden. For a good basic selection I recommend those in the box below. They are my personal favourites, listed in the order in which they appear in the text, not in order of preference.

---

15 FAVOURITE VEGETABLES

Greens	Salads	
Good King Henry	Chickweed	Dandelion
Fat hen	Lamb's lettuce	Nasturtium
Sea beet	Salad burnet	Lemon balm
Nine Star broccoli	Land cress	Ramsons
Perennial kale	Hairy bittercress	Welsh onion

Classification
The vegetables are divided up into Greens, Salads and Others for convenience, but the distinction is not absolute. Most of the greens can be eaten raw, many of the salad plants can be cooked, and many of the plants listed under Others can be added to salads in one form or another. Those included under Herbs are mainly plants which are used in smaller quantities, but some of them can be used in salads in the same proportions as the salad vegetables.

GREENS

Spinaches

Strictly speaking spinach is a single species, *Spinacea oleracea*, but there are many other plants which can be grown and eaten in the same way. Most of them are members of the goosefoot or beet family (*Chenopodiaceae*). Some are self-seeders, and two, Good King Henry and sea beet, are perennials.

If more than one member of this family are allowed to self-seed in the same garden, there is a distinct possibility of cross-pollination. This means that the new generation of plants will not necessarily be like their parents. This could be fun, or it could mean you end up with a whole lot of plants which are not nearly as productive as the ones you started with. If you want to keep them the same you need to choose which species and variety you want to grow and stick to it. Even then there is a possibility of pollination from wild plants or neighbours' gardens, as pollination can take place at a distance of 150-300m.

Most spinaches, including common-or-garden spinach, contain a high level of oxalic acid, which is harmful if eaten in excess because it interferes with the uptake of iron and calcium. Plants with high levels of it should not really be eaten more than two or three times a week. Chard (*Beta vulgaris*) has much lower levels than other spinaches, so can be eaten more frequently. Presumably the same goes for sea beet, which is the same species as chard, but this has not been confirmed.

All spinaches are tolerant of some degree of shade. They also like to have a constantly moist soil; if it dries out too much they tend to go to seed. On both these counts they are suited to the kind of microclimates they may find in a forest garden.

Good King Henry (*Chenopodium bonus-henricus*)
Good King Henry was cultivated all over Europe in medieval times and earlier, and has naturalised in many

places, including Britain. Just where it was originally native is obscure. It is now enjoying a modest revival as a garden vegetable, and seed is available from various suppliers.

The fact that it is perennial gives it that early start in the spring before the trees and shrubs come into leaf. The tiny new leaves, like a bunch of miniature pixie hats, can emerge as early as the end of February. So Henry can probably do better in shadier parts of the garden than the annual spinaches. Don't be put off by the instruction you may see on the seed packet – depending on where you buy them – saying 'full Sun'. Like most plants it will probably yield better with more light, but it is actually one of the most shade-tolerant of vegetables.

The mature leaves have the characteristic leaf shape of the goosefoot tribe, like a webbed foot. They are the same size or slightly smaller than the familiar annual spinach. They taste very good, but have a slightly bitter overtone if cooked alone. When added to stews, stir-fries and other mixed dishes the sharpness is lost, and they add a rich, savoury flavour to the food.

It is said that the young stems can be cooked like asparagus if picked in the spring when not more than 20cm high – an alternative name for the plant is Lincolnshire asparagus. The unopened flower heads can be eaten boiled or steamed, and both they and the leaves can also be added to salads if picked young.

There is a possibility of harvesting the ripe seeds as a grain crop, though it would need to be grown in a sunny position to ensure ripening. Henry's relatives, fat hen and quinoa (pronounced keenwa), have both been used for grain. In fact quinoa, which comes from South America, has recently been introduced into this country as a garden grain crop and is giving reasonable yields.

Mark Burton of Manchester has tried Henry as a grain crop. He reports that "Unselected plants gave me a yield of six ounces per square yard from one picking of seed (this extrapolates to 1,815 pounds per acre, although grown broadscale there would be greater losses from birds etc.). More could be collected by picking two or three times... We would not be able to make bread from it, but it is alright, if a little hard, in stews, pilaffs and the like. Fat hen flour has been used for cakes and porridge."[1]

As a leaf crop it keeps going for seven or eight months of the year. In winter it dies down, and if you cover it with some mulch this will encourage it to sprout earlier the next spring. Mark Burton finds that less than two square metres of Henry is enough for his family of four.

The plants should be 30cm apart each way. In the first year the leaves should be picked lightly if at all, but flower heads should be removed as they form.

The plants will last for about five years before they need replacing, which they are quite capable of doing themselves by self-seeding. Alternatively, you can detach a piece of lower stem with roots attached and plant it, or divide the plants in spring.

It is not fussy about the soil. Once established the plants need very little attention. They can grow to a maximum height of about 1m, but are usually kept shorter by picking.

Fat Hen (*Chenopodium album*)
A close relative of Good King Henry, but annual, fat hen has if anything a longer pedigree as a food plant. Remains of it have been found in settlements of the New Stone Age all over Europe. It was important in the Middle Ages but its popularity declined after the introduction of common spinach.

The reason for its decline is probably the rather smaller size of its leaves. It can't be the taste, which is somewhat superior to that of common spinach. They have a savoury, slightly salty taste, which is partially lost when they are cooked, so the younger leaves are better put into a salad than into the cooking pot. The young flowering shoots can be cooked along with the leaves. The grain can be harvested and used in a similar way to that of Good King Henry. The picking season, for leaves, is from the end of May till the beginning of autumn. It can be harvested young as a cut-and-come-again crop, or progressively thinned to leave a few large plants at 30cm spacings or thereabouts.

Although not a woodland plant, fat hen can stand some shade. It's main preference as to soil is for a high level of nitrogen. In fact it is often found on old compost and manure heaps, and when found growing in open ground is taken to be an indicator of a soil with a high nitrogen content.

Orach or Orache (*Atriplex* spp.)
In the USA orach is called fat hen and fat hen is called lamb's quarters. The confusion is understandable, because they are very similar plants, and both occur in a variety of forms. To a great extent the wild orach can be regarded as interchangeable with fat hen, but there are also cultivated varieties of orach.

The cultivated oraches are sometimes referred to as mountain spinach, and are varieties of the species *A. hortensis*. There are both green and red forms, and they are valued as ornamentals as well as food plants. They can be used as spinach or in salads. The taste is very mild and a touch sweet, so they are often mixed with stronger tasting leaves, such as sorrel.

Like all spinaches orach tends to run to seed in

---

[1]   From an article 'Good King Henry' in *Permaculture Magazine*, No. 2.

hot dry weather, though rather less readily than the common spinach. The process can be delayed by picking the flower heads as soon as they form. One or two plants should be allowed to flower and self-seed. The cultivated forms can grow up to as much as 2m, but only need to be spaced some 20cm apart.

Chard (*Beta vulgaris* ssp. *cicla*)

Otherwise known as leaf beet, sea kale and a number of other names, this widely-cultivated spinach has several advantages. Firstly, it has lower levels of oxalic acid than other spinaches, so it may be eaten more often. Secondly, it yields very well given good conditions. Thirdly, it has great big leaves, with thick fleshy midribs, which makes picking easy and quick. Fourthly, it is biennial, so it will not normally go to seed in its first year of growth.

In fact if the winters are not too cold chard can provide green leaves to pick for much of the year. The main crop is in the plant's first summer, and it will provide some pickings on into the autumn, even after the first frosts. It will survive most winters, and start producing leaves fairly early in the spring. The leaves decrease in size as its second summer comes on, a sign that the plant is approaching flowering. When this happens the flowering shoots can be picked too and added to the pot, leaving a couple of plants to self-seed. Just as the supply of leaves begin to run out, the next generation, the progeny of last year's self-seeding, is well into leaf.

This cycle can be broken by an exceptionally hard frost, which will kill the overwintering plants. Then there will be no early bite of chard the coming spring, though the following generation will already be seeded. The microclimate of a forest garden will help a little, but beware of covering chard with mulch in the winter to protect it from frost. If the weather turns unexpectedly mild the mulch will encourage slugs, which will finish it off as surely as the frost would have done.

It is a vigorous, if not a prolific, self-seeder. It does not cover the ground with a carpet of little seedlings as some self-seeders do, but the plants which do establish are well capable of looking after themselves.

The plants should be about 30cm apart. Vigorous specimens can sometimes grow as tall as 2m when in flower, but the rest of the time they are only as tall as their biggest leaf, usually about 30-40cm. They should be picked hard, because the more you pick them the more they produce. Like all spinaches, they like plenty of nutrients, especially nitrogen, and plenty of water. If you are short of manure, mulch material or water, chard should get a high priority on what you have. It will repay you well.

Sea Beet (*Beta vulgaris* ssp. *maritima*)

This plant is a native. It is the same species as beetroot and chard, but a different subspecies, and is probably the plant from which they were originally bred. Sea beet is normally a perennial, though there are annual and biennial forms as well. It is an extremely coastal species, not usually found more than a few metres from the high tide mark. It grows all round the coasts of England and Wales, though not in Scotland.

Figure 9.1 Sea beet in early May (PW)

The leaves are large towards the beginning of the season, becoming smaller as time goes by, and very thick. This means it is relatively quick and easy to pick enough to make a meal. The flavour is good, similar to cultivated spinaches. The season is long. On mild western coasts there is not a month in the year when you cannot pick a meal's-worth of sea beet. In the colder east the season runs from April to October. Peak production is in mid-May. The taste is delicious, very much like chard, and presumably the level of oxalic acid is low.

No doubt the moderating effect of the sea on winter temperatures helps to keep it green through the winter. This may be a limitation on taking this plant into cultivation in inland areas which get severe winter frosts, as it is too slow-growing to be worth cultivating as an annual. But no doubt more winter-hardy varieties could be bred if this should prove necessary.

It is shade-tolerant. In the wild it grows in a wide range of situations, from exposed cliff tops to sheltered and shady creek-sides. The plants tend to be much bigger in the more sheltered situations. It can grow well under trees and shrubs. In areas where the winters are mild enough for it to stay green all year round, it can do very well with deciduous overhead cover and side light from the north only. In colder areas, where it can make less use of winter sunshine, it needs a proportionately more open situation.

Seed gathered from the wild is often reluctant to germinate, but there is no problem with seed from a wild flower seed supplier. It will also grow from offsets. Growth is slow in the first year compared with chard. Plants grown from seed should not be picked in the first year, and in the second care should be taken not to overpick. They can eventually reach a size of 1m tall by 60cm across, but a spacing of 30cm apart is probably best for plants which are picked regularly.

Other Spinaches

Perpetual spinach sounds like a perennial, but is in fact a biennial form of *Beta vulgaris*, the species which includes chard and sea beet. It is called perpetual to distinguish it from true spinach, which has a shorter season. Its alternative name is spinach beet. It is probably the most resilient self-seeder among the cultivated spinaches: it is often the only cultivated plant to survive a year or two after a vegetable garden has been abandoned. Chard which is left to self-seed often reverts to a form very much like perpetual spinach.

New Zealand spinach (*Tetragonia expansa*) is not a member of the goosefoot family but it still contains oxalic acid. Its advantage is that it can stand dry conditions and poor soil better than the other spinaches. On the other hand it is not tolerant of shade nor frost hardy. It often self-seeds.

The Cabbage Family (*Cruciferae*)

Cabbage, cauliflower, broccoli, Brussels sprouts, kale and kohl rabi are all varieties of the same species, *Brassica oleracea*. The ancestor of them all is still occasionally found growing wild beside the coast. It is usually perennial and occasionally biennial, but virtually all of the thousands of cultivated varieties are sold as annuals or biennials. Two perennial varieties which do exist are Nine Star broccoli, and perennial kale. Sea kale is not a brassica but a closely related perennial which has been taken into cultivation in much the same form as it grows in the wild.

Self-seeding of brassicas is not a realistic proposition. They are avid cross-pollinators, so you can never be sure what the progeny will be like. Young brassicas are also very vulnerable plants, which need the protection we give them in a nursery bed, and they are not likely to succeed in the shady, competitive conditions of a forest garden.

However, some hardy brassicas can be grown as perennials in shady conditions. Spring cabbage is the most suitable kind, but it can be done with kale, purple sprouting broccoli and savoys, and probably various other brassicas too. All you do is harvest the edible parts and allow the plants to regrow from the stem. If they flower the flowers should be removed before they open, and can be eaten as broccoli. Spring cabbage can eventually grow into a huge green spider with a little cabbage at the end of each 'leg'. The plants can be very productive, and the green leaves sit there throughout the year, fresh whenever you want to eat them.

Although the plants tend to grow towards the light, a certain amount of shade seems to be necessary to get them to go perennial. It should not be assumed that the process will be successful in every garden, but it is surely worth a try.[2]

A possible problem with perennial brassicas of any kind is the soil-borne disease, clubroot. If brassicas do poorly, have discoloured leaves and wilt easily in hot weather clubroot should be suspected. It can be confirmed by pulling up the plant and looking at the root, which is swollen in infected plants – hence the name. If it is present no members of the cabbage family can be grown in that soil for at least seven years – some say twenty.

The main means of control in annual brassicas is strict crop rotation, with no members of the cabbage family grown on the same ground for two years running. But obviously this is not possible with perennials. Liming the soil to a pH of about 7 also helps to control the disease, together with maintaining good drainage and a high level of organic matter.

It is not necessary to take special precautions against clubroot in a garden where the infection does not exist. But if you are moving into a new garden it is impossible to know whether clubroot is present. If no brassicas have been grown there for around seven years clubroot is unlikely to be there, though it can survive on wild or ornamental members of the same family. If you have grown brassicas for a number of years without seeing clubroot you can be fairly sure it is not there.

The best way to keep the garden free of the disease is never to buy in brassica seedlings or accept them as gifts from neighbours, but always raise your own from seed. If you are not sure that your garden is free of it the best precaution is to lime all perennial brassicas regularly. When they need renewing they should not be replanted in the same place. Perennial kale does not

---

2   I am indebted to Phil Corbett of Nottingham for this information on perennialising brassicas.

need replacing as it can maintain itself indefinitely. If it becomes infected you can take stem cuttings and plant them in another part of the garden, being careful not to transfer any root or soil with the cuttings. The old plants should be burnt.

'Nine Star' Broccoli (*Brassica oleracea*)

You can buy Nine Star seed in many garden shops. It is the only variety of perennial brassica available commercially, though there is no technical reason why more should not be bred.[3]

In its first year it is rather like a cauliflower, producing a big white curd in the middle, surrounded by a number of little ones (perhaps they are the nine stars?). In subsequent years the distinction between the one big head and the little ones becomes less and the plant becomes much more like a sprouting broccoli. If it is well cared for it can go on producing useful crops for some five years, though they get lighter as the years go by.

Like all brassicas, it needs a fertile, moist but well-drained soil. It much prefers a sunny site, on the edge of the forest garden rather than within it.

Cultivation is the same as for any broccoli, sown in a seedbed in April and planted out when the plants are big enough, usually in June. The curds are ready to pick over a relatively short time in spring, typically four to six weeks in April and May, so there is no point in growing many plants. It is capable of growing to a height and spread of 1m if well husbanded on a good fertile soil, and a single plant may be enough for a small family with plenty of other vegetables in the garden. But it is often smaller, and quite healthy plants may be half this size.

In order to keep it going from year to year it is essential not to let it flower. All the curds must be picked, even if you have a glut of vegetables at that time and don't need to eat them. Otherwise they will develop into flowers and from them into seed, whereupon the plant will think it has accomplished its life's task and gracefully die. The leaves should not be picked at all, so as to give the plant the maximum chance to build up reserves for next year.

It can also be killed off by very cold winters, and can build up pest and disease problems over the years. Some growers say they can never get it to last more than three years, and in any case it must be raised again from bought-in seed when a new generation is needed. It is not a really low-maintenance plant, but certainly a rewarding and delicious one to grow.

---

3   There are, however, commercial and political reasons why it is difficult for a new variety to come on the market – or for an old one to stay there – unless the seed can be sold in very high volumes, i.e. to commercial growers. This would be unlikely in the case of a perennial vegetable. See *Saving the Seed*, Renée Velvé, Earthscan, 1992, for a clear account of the present situation with regard to plant varieties in Europe.

Perennial Kale (*Brassica oleracea*)

This is a real low-maintenance perennial vegetable, tough, productive and good to eat. It is a multi-stemmed plant, with stems that tend to grow horizontally for a while then curve upwards. Any part of a stem which touches the ground can put out new roots. The variety most often found is Dorbenton's, which grows to a height of 60-75cm. It hardly ever flowers. Some plants never do, others may do so once in ten years. They do not die after flowering.

Plate 9.2 Dorbenton's perennial kale. (PW)

It is green all through the year, and starts growth early in the spring. The leaves are rather small, about the size of well-grown common spinach, and have a nutty taste which is much better than the annual varieties of kale.

It is very easy to grow. Stem cuttings will take any time from spring to autumn, and should be planted at around 60cm apart. In a few years they will have grown to form a thick clump, and though it will spread it is not invasive. It is susceptible to attack from the common pests of brassicas, including whitefly and cabbage white butterflies. Though these can reduce the yield they do not normally affect the general health of the plants. If no pest control is carried out the plants will simply shrug off the pests and carry on growing as before.

It will tolerate a wide range of soils and climates, and a light seasonal shade, but not heavy shade. No doubt a well-established clump will cope with gradually increasing shade better than young plants will cope with being planted out under existing trees or shrubs. So if it is established at the same time as the upper layers, it may do better than if it is added when the trees and shrubs are mature.

Sea Kale (*Crambe maritima*)

Not to be confused with chard, which is sometimes known by this name, sea kale is a very hardy native perennial. In the wild it grows in sand and shingle beaches, sometimes forcing its way up through as much as a metre depth of pebbles. The grey-green wavy-edged leaves and clusters of white flowers make it attractive, and it is sometimes grown as an ornamental.

The main edible part is not the leaves but the stems. These are blanched (i.e. deprived of light) as they grow in springtime, and are eaten raw. The blanching can be done by covering them with a traditional rhubarb forcing pot or a length of pipe with some covering at the top, or by simply heaping soil or mulch up around the stalks. The very young leaves and shoots can be eaten raw, and the leaf midribs can be cooked.

It prefers full Sun, but can grow adequately in partial shade. The soil should be deep, sandy, well drained, fertile and around pH7. It is a good plant for an excessively dry soil.

It can be raised either from seed or from root cuttings, known as thongs. Raising from seed is difficult. It should be sown 2.5cm deep in spring. Germination is erratic, and can take as long as three years. Plants raised from seed are very variable, and only the strongest-looking plants should be selected for planting out. They should not be blanched and picked till they are in their third year of growth, but in the long run seed-grown plants are the more vigorous.

Thongs are planted 2.5cm below the soil surface in March. They can be blanched and picked the following year, but it is better to wait till their second year of growth.

Mature plants can be a metre wide and 60 cm high in summer. They die back in winter, and blanching, or forcing as it is also called, can be started at any time once this has happened.

Umbellifers (*Umbelliferae*)

This family includes many root vegetables, such as carrots and parsnips, and many culinary herbs, such as angelica and sweet cicely. It also includes many wild plants, of which cow parsley is the best known. Some of the wild plants are poisonous, especially the ones that grow in or near water, but identification of the common edible ones is not difficult.

Apart from their value as food, all this family have the added benefit of attracting pest predators into the garden. They are also dynamic accumulators, and with their deep taproots they are good soil conditioners.

Many are monocarpic perennials, plants which, like annuals and biennials, flower and seed once in their lives and then die. They may live for anything from two to five years, depending on environmental conditions.

Most complete their life cycles quicker in conditions of good light and soil fertility. Some true perennials may become monocarpic in certain conditions, like wild angelica, which becomes monocarpic in shady conditions.

Alexanders (*Smyrnium olustratum*)

This is a Mediterranean plant, reputedly introduced by the Romans. It has naturalised itself, mainly in coastal areas, as far north as central Scotland. After centuries of neglect it is now being revived as a pot herb, and seed can be bought from a number of suppliers.

The main edible parts are the leaf stalks, especially the thickest ones at the base of the plant, and these can be blanched by heaping up mulch material around them. The pinkish part should be taken, not the green part, and lightly boiled then served with butter. The main stems can also be used, but they need to have the fibrous bits peeled off the outside. Like many umbellifers, it has a slight anise taste, and the texture is delicate. All parts of the plant can be used in salads, including the young flower buds, but sparingly because the taste is strong. It can also be grown as a cut-and-come-again crop. The dried seeds are said to be a pepper substitute.

It is monocarpic, and as it successfully maintains itself in the crowded vegetation of hedgebanks it should have no trouble doing the same in a forest garden. It does all its growing between early autumn and about May, when it either flowers and dies or retreats underground – an ideal annual cycle for a forest garden plant, growing beneath deciduous trees.

Although mainly a hedgerow plant, it can occasionally be found in woods beside the sea, even under a closed canopy. The mature plant grows to about 1m in the open and up to 2m in the shade.

Hogweed (*Heracleum sphondylium*)

Although usually a grassland plant, hogweed will stand light shade, and like most natives it is very easy to grow. It is monocarpic, and will hold its own in vigorous perennial vegetation. The edible parts are the bases of the young shoots, which can be boiled, but it is essential to get them while they are still young.

Lovage (*Levisticum officinale*)

This is best known as a cultivated herb, but there is a naturalised form (*L. scoticum*) which grows on rocky sea cliffs in parts of Scotland. Lovage dies down in winter but is one of the first garden plants up in the spring, and grows to as much as 2.5m. So it does well in shady places, but not directly under trees and shrubs. The plants should be spaced about 60cm apart. It does best in a rich, moist soil. It will self-seed, but young plants are vulnerable to slugs.

It can be regarded as a perennial celery and used in the same way. The leaf stalks can be blanched by mulching up (the forest garden equivalent of earthing up) and boiled as a straight vegetable. It can also be used in soups, stews and casseroles and the leaves can be added to salads. The flavour is similar to celery, but with a hint of yeast. The seeds can also be eaten, and an oil can be extracted from the roots.

Ground Elder (*Aegopodium podagraria*)

On the face of it ground elder sounds like an ideal plant for a forest garden: it produces edible leafy greens, is perennial, thrives in shade and is low enough to grow under a shrub layer. But who in their right mind would introduce such an invasive plant into their garden? Gardeners who have it have to expend constant energy keeping it within bounds. It is tempting, but the temptation is probably best resisted.

Rock Samphire (*Crithmum maritimum*)

Not to be confused with marsh samphire (a completely different plant which grows on salt flats and is also edible), rock samphire is a perennial plant native to sea cliffs in south and west Britain. It deserves mention as an edible plant which can grow in walls and other rocky places. If your garden has a wall with enough crevices in it to allow plants to grow, this is an edible one you could try there.

It is best eaten boiled or steamed. The flesh of the leaves and stems can then be sucked away from their fibrous centres.

Other Greens

Stinging Nettles (*Urtica dioica*)

Whether you like it or not, nettles will probably make an attempt to colonise your forest garden. They do well in soils with high levels of nutrients, which is something every garden soil has relative to the world at large, and as a perennial they will appreciate the conditions in a garden devoted to perennials. They are also very tolerant of shade.

Although they will outcompete most other vegetables in the garden, and therefore give you some weeding work, nettles do not have to be seen as a problem. If their many and various uses are appreciated they can be one of the most useful plants in the garden. They can help to hide ripe fruit from hungry birds (*see page 102*); they are an excellent source of mulch or compost material; they provide alternative food sources and overwinter shelter for pest predators; they are an important wildlife plant, with more than 40 species of insects, including caterpillars of several butterflies, either partially or totally dependent on them for food

and shelter; they also yield a green dye, and fibres as fine as silk, which can be spun and woven into cloth.

As a food plant, they come into their own in the spring. Indeed, in a mild year they can start growing in winter, and be up to harvestable quantities by February. By the beginning of June they are past their best, becoming coarse in texture, bitter tasting and somewhat laxative. But if they are cut down early in the year the regrowth can be picked for eating.

They can be eaten as a straight green vegetable, boiled lightly in no more water than sticks to them after washing, and mashed to a purée with a little seasoning. They are inclined to be somewhat bland, though, so they are better used as an addition to other dishes. When the first leaves emerge from the ground in spring they do not sting, and can be eaten as a salad vegetable.

Comfrey (*Symphytum uplandicum*)

There are several different species of comfrey. Common comfrey (*S. officinale*) is a native perennial plant of streamsides and other wet places which has long been used as a medicinal plant. It can be mildly invasive.

Russian comfrey (*S. uplandicum*) is a hybrid, made famous by the Henry Doubleday Research Association as a dynamic accumulator. It is also perennial, but does not spread, either by root or by seed. It contains higher levels of potassium and other plant nutrients than common comfrey, starts growing earlier in the year, yields more heavily and stands cutting better. It is the best kind of comfrey for the garden.

Comfrey is the dynamic accumulator *par excellence* (*see pages 48-49*), and can be planted round the edge of the garden to keep out perennial weeds (*see page 54*). These are its main uses in a forest garden, but it can also be eaten.

Plate 9.3 Comfrey in April, showing the remarkable amount of growth this plant can make in the spring. (PW)

It begins to show above the ground in March, or February in very mild areas, and the little leaf spears can be sliced raw and added to salads. Through the spring, summer and early autumn the leaves can be lightly boiled as greens. But the taste is not that special and the texture is slightly furry, so they are better when made into fritters, dipped in batter and deep fried. Comfrey is probably not worth growing purely as a food plant, but if you are growing it for other purposes you can eat it if you are short of other vegetables.

It is also useful as a first aid plant for cuts and bruises. To help heal a small cut, cover it with a small piece of comfrey leaf, furry side down, held in place with a sticking plaster. Healing is then very quick, but be sure the cut is clean because any infection will be sealed in. For bruises and strains, use a comfrey poultice or a dressing containing comfrey oil.

It will do quite well in shade, though the yield of leaves may be greater when it is grown in a sunny position. But the limiting factor to its growth is more likely to be the supply of nitrogen than the degree of sunlight. Comfrey has an almost unlimited appetite for nitrogen, to complement the other minerals it is so good at extracting from the soil, and thus fuel the enormous growth which it is capable of. It can handle nitrogen in a much more raw state than most other plants can – even unrotted chicken manure is grist to its mill.

It can grow to a height and spread of 1m, but if it is constantly cut for use as manure it will not reach this size, and a spacing of 60cm is about right. It can be established from root cuttings, bought at considerable expense from seed suppliers, or from offsets, obtained from friends and neighbours who already grow comfrey. This can be done at any time of the year except December and January, but spring or autumn planting will give the best results.

Before you plant comfrey be quite sure you have it where you want it and will continue to want it for some time to come, because once established it is a very difficult plant to eradicate. On very light soils it can be possible to dig the whole plant up, even after a few years' growth; but on most soils there will always be at least a little bit of root left behind, and a whole new plant can easily grow from that little bit. The only way to ensure complete eradication is by using a poison.

Goosegrass or Cleavers (*Galium aparine*)

This is better known as a children's toy rather than a food plant. It will stick to any clothing, and there can hardly be one of us who didn't throw it and have it thrown at us when we were little.

It is another of those greens you wouldn't put top of your list for taste, but it is almost impervious to cold, and the main picking season is through the winter. It is useful to bulk out a pot of mixed greens. It is not worth planting goosegrass, but if it grows along the base of a hedge it is worth leaving some of it there for winter greens rather than tidily weeding it away.

Poultry love it, and it is a good source of calcium for eggshells. Presumably that is how it got its name.

The Plantains (*Plantago* spp.)

These are another useful ingredient of mixed greens, though rather strong to be eaten on their own. Greater or rat's-tail plantain (*P. major*) is a plant of paths and odd corners and thrives on being trampled. Although not a woodland plant, it has broader leaves and thus may be a better bet for shady places than ribwort plantain (*P. lanceolata*) which has narrower leaves and is a common grassland herb. They are also first-aid plants – the crushed leaves give some relief from burns, whether from Sun or fire. Both plants are perennial.

Buck's horn plantain (*P. coronopus*) is a self-seeding biennial which has been cultivated as a salad plant in the past. Joy Larkcom says "The tough but tasty leaves [are] at their best in spring and autumn. Blanch in boiling water for a few seconds to make them more tender."[4] It is not shade tolerant, growing in dry, bare places in the wild, often on sandy soils and usually near the coast.

Golden Saxifrage (*Chrysosplenium oppositifolium*)

This little native plant is comparatively rare in the wild, though in places where it does occur it can carpet the ground. These places are invariably both shady and wet,

---

MIXED GREENS

There is usually something to eat at any time of the year in a forest garden, but it can be a matter of a little bit of this and a little bit of that rather than a whole meal's worth of one kind of vegetable. These can be cooked together to make a dish of mixed greens, just as we put a variety of raw vegetables together to make a salad.

In fact there are some kinds of greens which are better as an ingredient of mixed greens than on their own. These include strong-tasting ones like red valerian, or ones with an undistinguished taste like goosegrass. The best flavour, as with a salad of 'herbs', comes from mixing as many different kinds together as are available.

Liquidising them to make a sauce or soup will do even more to even out strong flavours and remove fibrousness.

---

4   *The Salad Garden*, see Further Reading.

so it is an ideal plant for a forest garden on a wet soil. The kind of soil it really thrives on is too wet for the majority of fruit trees and shrubs, but there is no reason why it should not grow well enough in a moderately moist soil.

It is very low-growing, its little leaves making an interlocking mosaic barely more than a centimetre above ground until it flowers, so it can be grown as a ground cover crop beneath taller vegetables. Its yield per square metre is small, but it is an addition to the yield of the plants above it, making use of a niche where very little else will grow. It is perennial and stays green throughout the winter, which presumably explains why it is so successful in shady places. It can even out-compete creeping buttercup in shady conditions, and that is saying something.

It has a rather strong taste at any time of the year, and is best added to a pot of mixed greens. It may be grown as much to protect the soil in winter as for food.

Red Valerian (*Centranthus ruber*)

The name valerian is often associated with sleeping draughts, but it is the white or common valerian (*Valeriana officinalis*) which puts you to sleep, not the red. So you can eat as much red valerian as you like without any danger of nodding off over your plate of greens.

It deserves mention as an edible wall plant. It is not native, but has long been naturalised and grows profusely in walls in south west England, where it makes a vivid display through the summer. It has a slightly bitter taste, with a strong overtone of broad beans. The smallest leaves can be added to salads, to give a sharpness similar to that of chicory, and the larger ones cooked as greens.

SALADS

Many of these plants can also be cooked as greens, but on the whole they are ones which are better eaten raw. All of them have some resistance to slugs, but this is very variable and local, so no guarantees can be given.

Mild Tasting Leaves

Chickweed (*Stellaria media*)

Many wild plants have a rather strong taste, and while they may be welcome additions to a salad, they are not the sort of thing which can substitute for lettuce as the mild-tasting ingredient which is used in bulk. But chickweed is one wild vegetable which can. Before flowering it has a mild, nutty taste, which is if anything better than lettuce. After flowering the taste becomes a little smoky, but it still makes an excellent base for a salad.

It is an annual which self-seeds readily – too readily for gardeners who don't know they can eat it! In fields it is often found where a cow pat has been: the cowpat kills the grass under it, which gives a patch of bare soil for the chickweed to colonise, and it supplies plant nutrients as it decomposes. Another place it is often found is under trees or overgrown hedges in pasture fields, where sheep and cattle seeking shade have bared the ground with their hooves and fertilised it with their dung. It grows well in these shady places as long as there is plenty of light from the side.

In the garden we need to reproduce these conditions for it: bare soil, plenty of nutrients and partial shade or full Sun. Although it can become invasive, it is easy to remove, and makes good compost or mulch material, as long as it is pulled before it sets seed.

It can be picked in every month of the year – you can clear away the snow and find good edible chickweed underneath – though of course it does not do much growing when the weather is cold. In the summertime plants grown in light shade tend to make better eating and stay green longer than those in full Sun. The whole plant can be eaten, stems and all, as it does not become noticeably fibrous. It can be eaten cooked, in which case it should be boiled for less than five minutes.

Lamb's Lettuce or Corn Salad (*Valerianella locusta*)

Lamb's lettuce is another mild-tasting salad plant. It is a low-growing annual, probably native but widely cultivated, which self-seeds as prolifically as almost any food plant.

It is very much a plant of the winter and spring. The seed is reluctant to germinate in warm soil, and most of it waits till autumn. The plants grow slowly, almost regardless of temperature, right through the winter. In late spring they soon go to seed as the temperature warms up, though plants which germinate in early spring can make a worthwhile amount of leaf before they flower. Since they do much of their growing when the leaves are off the trees and shrubs, they can be grown in comparatively shady places. But they are not very shade-tolerant plants, and do not grow in woods in the wild.

It is a small plant, rarely growing above 10cm till it flowers, so it can form an understorey below taller plants, thus making more complete use of the ground and reducing the need for mulch. When it self-seeds profusely, which it often does, it can act as a winter green manure. It is especially suitable because it does not become fibrous, even when it goes to seed, so it decomposes easily when the time comes.

Where it comes up thickly it can be treated as a cut-and-come-again crop, or it can be thinned to about 10-15cm apart and grown on. Larger plants can be picked whole, or they can be cut, leaving behind one growing point which will grow on to form another plant.

It is worth letting lamb's lettuce go to flower for the beauty as much as for the seed which follows. The flowers vary from white to an exquisite pale blue. When contrasted with the bright yellow of land cress in bloom and the lady's smock-like flowers of radishes, the whole effect is as beautiful as any purely ornamental display.

Winter Purslane or Claytonia
(*Claytonia perfoliata / Montia perfoliata*)
Also known as miner's lettuce and spring beauty, this plant is not to be confused with others which share the name purslane. Common or garden purslane (*Portulaca oleracea*) is a half-hardy summer salad plant which, although it sometimes seeds itself, is probably not robust enough for a forest garden. Pink purslane is described below.

If there is a garden plant which self-seeds more prolifically than lamb's lettuce it is winter purslane. It is one of those plants which, as they say, "once you've got it, you've got it for good". It prefers rather acid, sandy soils, but will do well anywhere as long as it does not suffer waterlogging. It does well in light shade.

Although the name suggests it is primarily a winter vegetable, it can be picked all year round, and indeed will be killed by very hard frosts. (The seed in the ground always survives, though.) In milder winters it can do so well that it is possible to get fed up with the sight of the stuff, pleasant though it is to eat. It can be treated as a cut-and-come-again, or thinned to about 12-15cm apart. Even mature plants will resprout from the roots several times. The leaves are an attractive, almost triangular heart shape, and have a fresh, mild flavour with a slightly fleshy texture.

Pink Purslane (*Montia sibirica*)
You would have thought it was a native wildflower, so well has this plant adapted itself to British conditions. In fact it is an introduction from North America. It grows wild in damp, shady places, thriving even under a closed canopy, and forms dense stands in some secondary woods, including ones with poorly drained soils and at high altitudes. It is common in woods on Dartmoor.

It is an annual or short-lived perennial. The leaves have a pleasant mild flavour throughout the year, though they occasionally develop a bit of a tang after flowering. They can be used in salads or cooked. The pink flowers make a bright display in spring and summer.

Salad Burnet (*Sanguisorba minor*)
This is a native perennial salad plant which does well in partial shade and is pickable all year round. It is very tough, and will self-seed readily. In the wild it is most often found on chalky soils, so it has a good degree of drought resistance and a preference for a high pH. But it is not fussy, and will do well on a wide range of soils.

It is a pretty plant, with its double rows of little leaflets topped off with delicate russet flowers, and it is worth growing purely as an ornamental. The taste is mild, with a hint of cucumber. As well as being a tasty and decorative ingredient in a green salad, it makes a good garnish for a potato salad, mixed with an equal part of Welsh onion. The young leaves are best for eating, and the plant is at its best in mid-spring. The older leaves can be eaten if they are dipped in hot water for a few moments, but it is better to discard them, which encourages new young leaves to grow.

Figure 9.1
Salad burnet

The mature plant is about 30cm high and wide, but it does not mind being a bit crowded. Removing the flowers as soon as they form will give a higher yield of leaves, and well-established plants can be rigorously cut back in summer to encourage new, tender growth. The young plants can be picked soon after they appear, and salad burnet can be treated as a self-seeder rather than a perennial.

Strong Tasting Leaves

Chicory (*Cichorium intybus*)
Wild chicory is a native plant of the dandelion family, with a beautiful sky-blue flower. It is a good dynamic accumulator. Organic farmers sometimes include it in seed mixtures for grazing animals because of the minerals it contains, and it can be used in a garden fertility patch.

There is also a wide range of cultivated chicories, bred for a variety of purposes.[5] The wild plant is perennial, as are most of the cultivated varieties, though they are usually treated as annuals. They will self-seed if allowed to, but the resulting plants are very variable, especially if more than one type is grown in the garden. They are tough plants, rarely troubled by pests and diseases. They are resistant to cold, but do not like wet winter weather.

Some chicories are grown for their roots, which may be grated into salads or roasted as a coffee substitute. Others, the Whitloof or Belgian chicories, are grown for 'chicons', those large, pale yellow buds which are grown by forcing the plant in the dark. There are also

---

[5]   For a detailed account of chicories see *The Salad Garden* and *The Vegetable Garden Displayed*.

many chicories which are grown for their leaves, and these are broadly divided into the green-leaved chicories and the red-leaved. Red-leaved chicory, often known as *radicchio*, can provide a year-round supply of attractive, sharp-tasting leaves.

The Grumolo type is particularly suitable for gardening, as it does better than most as a perennial. It is a green-leaved type from the Piedmont region of Italy. It is very resistant to cold, tolerant of poor soils, and well able to hold its own with other perennial vegetation.

During the summer it bears upright leaves, but in autumn and spring it forms a low rosette which persists through winter in mild areas and dies down in colder conditions. The young plants should be thinned to a spacing of 5-7cm. The summer leaves may be cut when they reach a height of 5-7cm.

Like all chicories it has a somewhat bitter taste, which gets stronger with age. This is one reason why chicories are usually cultivated as annuals. Regular selection of young self-seeded plants and removal of older ones may help to keep a younger stock. But chicory is supposed to be strong-tasting. It is a plant to add bite to blander leaves, not something to be eaten in bulk, except by those with a strong palate.

Both red-leaved and Grumolo chicories can tolerate light shade. When they go to seed in their second and subsequent summers, they shoot up to 2m tall, with beautiful sky blue flowers, which are also edible.

Dandelion (*Taraxacum officinale*)

From autumn through to spring dandelions have a mild to pleasantly tangy taste, and can be used liberally in salads. In the summer their taste is too strong for most people. If you like a really sharp taste, you can pop a few summer leaves straight in your salad, but you may prefer to blanch them by putting a plant pot over a dandelion for a few days till the leaves turn pale. The top part of the root can also be used in salads, as can the flowers – a colourful and mild-tasting ingredient in any month of the year.

Sorrel (*Rumex* spp.)

Common sorrel (*R. acetosa*) is a native perennial of the dock family. Sorrels can always be told from docks by the arrowhead shape of their leaves, and the fact that they tend to be smaller. There are various other forms of sorrel, including the broad-leaved French sorrel, and the low-growing buckler-leaved sorrel, which can be used as a ground cover plant. The common and French kinds grow to about 30cm tall, or more if they are allowed to flower, and buckler-leaved to about 20cm.

All kinds have a sharp, acid taste, which adds piquancy to a salad if used in moderation. This taste is caused by a very high oxalic acid content, and for that reason they should not be eaten in any quantity. They can also be cooked in stir-fries, soups or mixed greens. In mild winters they can be picked all year round, and even in cold ones they are among the last plants to die down and the first to reappear.

They can tolerate a considerable degree of shade, especially wild strains of common sorrel, which can be found growing in woods. They are extremely easy to grow, being tolerant of a wide range of soils, though they produce bigger leaves on more fertile soils. Each plant needs about 25cm of space. One plant should be enough for most families if you are using it as a minor ingredient in salads and cooked dishes. If you want to make the occasional sorrel soup you will need perhaps half a dozen.

Figure 9.2 Sorrel

The plants may be hermaphrodite or single sex, but as long as flowers of both sexes are present sorrel will self-seed readily. New plants should be selected to replace old ones every three or four years.

Jack-by-the-Hedge (*Alliaria petiolata*)

Garlic mustard is another name for this plant, and it does indeed have a taste of garlic, especially when the leaves are young and tender in spring. As it matures the garlic taste is somewhat overlain by other strong flavours which are more of an acquired taste. It is at its very best around Easter time. It can be added to salads or used in cooking, either in soups, stews and casseroles, or to flavour an omelette.

It is a native plant, a biennial which germinates in spring with sometimes a second generation in the autumn. In mild areas it is green throughout the year, and in cooler ones it will peep through as early as February. Its natural habitat, as its name would suggest, is hedgerows and woodland edges. But it can also be found well inside secondary woods, and will do equally well in the open.

It is variable in size, but a well-grown plant can be as much as 40cm wide by 1m tall. A plant like this can be very attractive, with a succession of white flowers throughout spring and summer, and its bushy, lime-green leaves. A single plant should be enough for most families. It self-seeds reliably, and can be harvested as a cut-and-come-again plant. Some individuals have creeping roots and become perennial but mobile. It is a member of the cabbage family, so it could possibly harbour or suffer from clubroot.

Turkish Rocket (*Bunias orientalis*)
Although both perennial and large-leaved, Turkish rocket is not particularly tolerant of shade. It is a plant for the sunny edge of the forest garden. It is not a perennial substitute for the common or 'Mediterranean' rocket, as its taste is very different, without the nuttiness of that vegetable. The leaves are hot and fresh when young, but excessively hot and rather unpalatable when they grow big.

Plate 9.4 Turkish rocket in September. Leaves this big are well past their best for eating, but make good mulch. (PW)

So if it grows faster than you can eat it you need to pick and discard the mature leaves to allow younger ones to develop. It is up early in the spring, and it can go on producing into the autumn. It gives heavy yields and withstands both cold and drought very well. Plants need at least 50cm spacing and can grow 90cm tall.

The Cresses

These are all members of the cabbage family (*Cruciferae*). They fall between the mild and strong tasting leaves and all have at least a hint of pepper or mustard flavour to them, which usually becomes stronger as they mature. Many members of this family are to some degree edible, but those listed here are probably the most suitable for a forest garden.[6]

If they are allowed to self-seed on the same piece of ground year after year they can keep a clubroot infection going. But they should not be too much troubled themselves, because they grow quickly and come to maturity before the disease can seriously harm them.

Land Cress (*Barbarea verna / B. praecox*)
Land Cress is very similar to lamb's lettuce in its growing requirements. It crops from autumn to spring, though it does not grow at quite such low temperatures as lamb's lettuce. It is often possible to go on picking it till midsummer, long after the lamb's lettuce is finished. It is reluctant to germinate in warm soil, and soon goes to seed in hot weather. When it is in flower the taste becomes hotter, though still pleasant.

Though mostly biennial, a proportion of plants usually grow on for another year after flowering. It self-seeds readily, though not quite as prolifically as lamb's lettuce. It not only tolerates shade, but actually prefers a light shade to full Sun, especially in summer. It is slightly larger than lamb's lettuce and should be thinned to 15cm apart. On the whole the two plants do well together and complement each other in a salad, as land cress has a sharper flavour, somewhat like watercress.

Watercress
(*Nasturtium officinale / Rorippa nasturtium-aquaticum*)
It is hard to grow watercress away from running water. It does not do at all well in still water, and although it is possible to get it to grow in moist soil it is probably not worth the trouble. It is susceptible to slugs, and if it is not doing very well they can eat it faster than it grows.

If your garden has a spring or brook, watercress will 'grow like a weed'. But in country districts be sure the water has not flowed through an area where sheep graze, because it could be infected with the liver fluke parasite, which affects both sheep and humans. If in doubt always cook it, as 20 minutes at boiling point will kill the liver fluke. Watercress makes good soup, thickened with potato.

It is perennial, and the easiest way to establish it is simply to plant some sprigs of the watercress you buy in a food shop. First check that they have little roots like fine white hairs sprouting from the leaf nodes. If not, suspend them in a jar of water till the roots appear. They should be planted along the edge of the flowing water about 15cm apart. Watercress prefers dappled shade to full Sun.

Hairy Bittercress (*Cardamine hirsuta*)
Despite its name, this little plant is not noticeably hairy and not at all bitter. It is in fact the best tasting of all the cresses, nutty, with just a hint of pepperyness. Its main drawback is that it is very small, a rosette of tiny leaves, usually less than 10cm across. The best way to pick it is to uproot the whole plant and chop off the root and the base of the stems. Even so, it is difficult to get enough to make a bulk contribution to a salad; its contribution is

---

6   See *Food for Free* for some more of the wild ones.

its taste. It is also good as a garnish, or as filling for a cheese and cress sandwich. You can help the plants to grow bigger by thinning them to 10cm or more apart, and by growing them in moist, shady places.

It is an annual and has a great reputation as a garden weed. But the places it really likes to grow are damp woods, wherever there is some bare or lightly-covered soil for it to seed into. It is often found by the sides of paths or streams that go through woods, and in the summer it grows much bigger under a closed canopy than in the open. It does not need shade and wetness in order to grow, but it prefers them. It is green throughout the year, and can be picked in winter in all but the coldest areas.

Despite its great powers of reproduction it is not more competitive than lamb's lettuce, winter purslane, land cress and so on, and is unlikely to take over in a forest garden.

Shepherd's Purse (*Capsella bursa-pastoris*)

This is another native cress that deserves mention. It has a fine, clean taste and can grow to a big size given good soil fertility. It too can be invasive, but should not be any more of a problem in a forest garden than any other prolific self-seeder.

Other Salad Plants

Mitsuba (*Cryptotaenia japonica*)

Otherwise known as honewort or Japanese parsley, this is a perennial woodland plant from the Orient. It is not related to parsley, but its taste has been described as a unique and delicious blend of parsley and celery. The leaves and stalks can be used in salads, stir-fries and soups. The roots are also edible.

It does well in light shade on a moist soil. It grows to about 35cm and can be used as a ground cover. A hardy plant, it stays green all year round, and will self-seed. Plants should be thinned to about 15cm.[7]

Nasturtium (*Tropaeolum majus*)

Nasturtium leaves fall somewhere between the mild-tasting and strong-tasting categories. In fact their rather peppery taste is similar to that of some of the cresses, though the plants are in no way related. The leaves can be used in moderate to large quantities in salads according to taste, the flowers and flower buds make a colourful and tasty addition to a salad, and the seed pods can either be eaten raw or pickled in imitation of capers. All in all it is one of the most versatile and pleasant-tasting of salad vegetables – though it is still best known as an ornamental.

It comes from the warmer climes of South America and cannot stand the slightest frost, so although it is perennial it can only be grown as an annual here. It will self-seed, but not very reliably. It may be worth hand raising a few plants each year and planting them out in the forest garden. It likes a fairly sunny position, but can cope with light shade, especially once it is growing vigorously.

There are a range of varieties. The most vigorous are classed as trailing or climbing, intermediate ones as semi-trailing, and the least vigorous as dwarf. A single plant of a trailing variety can cover as much as 2m square, as long as they get a good start in the spring. As they are frost sensitive they are not among the first plants to get going, but once they do, their exuberant growth can suppress a lot of annual weeds. The semi-trailing varieties only spread to about 40cm and the dwarfs to about 25cm. The trailing or climbing varieties can be grown up a wall or fence.

They are tolerant of poor soil and dry conditions, and generally one of the easiest of plants to grow.

Deadnettles (*Lamium* spp.)

Although they are probably not worth introducing into the garden, these plants are quite likely to appear on their own and should be harvested rather than weeded. They are members of the same family as the mints. Red deadnettle (*L. purpureum*) has a unique aromatic flavour which is rather overpowering if it is eaten on its own, but adds subtlety to a salad. The compact heads of the plant, containing leaves, flowers and stem, can be used whole, sprinkled over the top of the salad. White deadnettle (*L. album*) is much milder-tasting and can be used in larger quantities.

OTHERS

Herbs

The number of useful herbs, including medicinal ones, dye plants and so on, which could be grown in a forest garden is enormous. Those listed here are the ones most likely to be of use to the average forest gardener.

Mints (*Mentha* spp.)

The mints are a group of plants which can easily outgrow their usefulness and become weeds. They spread rapidly by means of runners. They love the shady, moist conditions of a forest garden, and are so vigorous and invasive that a single little plant can soon multiply into a mass of mint far bigger than is needed, and crowd out a lot of other plants in the process. They also have a big appetite for plant nutrients, and can rapidly deplete the soil.

---

[7]   Available from Suffolk Herbs.

The different species of mints vary in their vigour. Applemint is the most invasive, and it should not be planted in a forest garden – unless you either want to eat it by the cart-load or spend your life weeding. Next in vigour are the other ones which grow wild in this country, whether as native plants or garden escapes: garden mint, spearmint, water mint, peppermint and pennyroyal.

The other kinds of mint, such as pineapple, eau-de-Cologne and ginger mints are not much of a problem, but then they are not so useful either. They can be added to salads, contributing a decorative element with their variously coloured leaves, as well as their distinct flavours; they are also used in pot-pourri.

The two mints worth growing in more than very small quantities are probably garden mint and peppermint. Garden mint is the best one for cooking. Peppermint makes a refreshing hot drink which has mild medicinal properties, especially for minor stomach ailments. Both can be added to the salad bowl in liberal quantities.

It is best to plant the more vigorous mints in some shady out-of-the-way corner by themselves than in the forest garden proper. The runners will not cross mown grass or a hard path.

Nor, it seems, will they pass a sage plant. I do not know whether this goes for all species of mint or all kinds of sage, but I have seen the runners of peppermint and pineapple mint stopped in their tracks by a common sage plant in my garden. The foliage of the peppermint would have overwhelmed the sage by now if I did not prune it back fairly regularly, but that is an easy job compared to digging up runners. Perhaps mints could be confined by rings of sage.

They like a soil that is both rich and moist, and should be initially planted at a spacing of 25cm apart in spring or autumn. Small pieces of root are the usual planting material. All mints die down with the onset of winter frosts and sprout again in the spring. But it is not unknown for some plants to survive the winter above ground in a microclimate that is free of hard frosts. A light covering of brushwood or dried herbaceous stems will help to keep them green through winter.

Lemon Balm (*Melissa officinalis*)

Balm is Robert Hart's favourite herb, not just because of its taste but also for its health-giving properties. It is said to be an all-round tonic, especially good for the brain. It can be included in salads and fruit salads, and made into a hot drink. It can be eaten in some quantity without harm. It is also much loved by bees, and will attract them into a garden where it grows.

It is a perennial, related to the mints, and like them it dies down in autumn and is up early in the spring.

In mild areas it can appear as early as the end of January, which is much earlier than any mint. In a sheltered position it can also survive the first light autumn frosts which kill off most mints. It is invasive, but not as invasive as the more vigorous kinds of mint, nor such a heavy feeder. In fact it is a very tolerant plant, doing well in a wide variety of soils, moisture conditions and degrees of shade. Plants should be about 60cm apart and they grow to about the same height.

Other Shade-Bearing Herbs

Most of these plants do better in light shade than in full Sun, especially in summer.

Parsley (*Petroselinum crispum*) is notoriously hard to germinate, and actually seems to do better as a self-seeder than when sown by human hand. But it is biennial and does not always survive the winter, which makes it a rather unreliable self-seeder. Moist conditions are necessary, especially in the plant's early life. The plain, or broad-leaved types are hardier, more vigorous and at least as well-flavoured as the prettier curly types.

Sweet Cicely (*Myrrhis odorata*) is a perennial of the umbellifer family. Its main use is to reduce the acidity of tart fruits, such as rhubarb. A bunch of it included in the cooking pot with the fruit will stop the acid taking the edge off your teeth, without the need to use any sugar. It can also be used in salads, in large or small quantities, and is available early in spring. It has a mild taste with just a hint of anise. The plant is about 60cm high and wide. It likes moist conditions, and will do well beside a stream or pond, but is also drought-tolerant and will stand dry shade.

Angelica (*Angelica archangelica*) is another umbellifer, and another one which is up early in spring. Like sweet cicely it can be used in salads and to neutralise acid fruit, though its more familiar use is in sweet cookery. It is almost as tall as lovage, growing to 2m when mature. It is monocarpic and self-seeds readily, but because it is hard to germinate from seed packets, it is best to establish it from self-sown plants from another garden. It prefers a moist soil.

Chervil (*Antriscus cerefolium*) is a self-seeding annual or biennial umbellifer, used mainly in cooking but also in salads. It has a slight aniseed flavour. It needs moist conditions and plants are some 25cm tall and 10cm across. In mild areas it can remain green over winter.

Its wild relative, cow parsley (*A. sylvestris*), is a perennial alternative. It should be picked as early as possible in the season as it turns bitter later, but the stems can be dried for later use. Although it will stand light shade, a sunny position will give earlier flowering.

Bergamot (*Mondara didyma*) is a perennial of the mint family which makes an excellent hot drink and has some medicinal uses. It is also popular with bees and attractive to look at. It likes a moist, rich soil and is around 60cm high and 45cm across.

Sun-Loving Herbs

What garden could be without borage (*Borago officinalis*)? The cheerful blue-starred flowers spring up here and there all over the garden year after year once you have sown it. Bees love the flowers, and they are edible, adding colour to summer salads. The leaves can also go into salads as long as they are picked young; they get prickly as they get older. Both leaves and flowers can also be used in cool summer drinks. The plants grow to about 60cm tall and should be thinned to 45cm if necessary.

Coltsfoot (*Tussilago farfara*) is one of the most useful medicinal herbs. It is specific for the common cold, and can prevent a cold in the head becoming bronchitis. The flowers emerge from below ground as early as February, like tiny pale dandelions. The leaves appear later, and they can be picked and dried at any time before the frosts of autumn kill them off. But they are best in late spring or early summer, when they still have the potency of youth but are big enough to make picking easy. Whenever a cold threatens they can be used to make a tea, which should be taken with honey three times a day.

Coltsfoot gets its name from the shape of the leaves, like the underside of a horse's foot. It is a native perennial, and although normally a plant of open places, it should be able to cope with some summer shade. It can be invasive.

Figure 9.4 Coltsfoot

Yarrow (*Achillea millefolium*) is a very common grassland plant, present in most lawns. It is a useful plant to have in the garden, being one of the three components of 'flu tea', along with peppermint and elderflower. All above-ground parts of the plant can be dried and used for this. It is rather strong-tasting to put in salads, though quite edible.

Fennel (*Foeniculum vulgare*) is one of the herbs whose leaves can be eaten in large quantities. It is an umbellifer and the anise flavour is quite strong, but overall it has a very fresh taste and blends well with other salad ingredients. The seeds can be collected and dried for a herb 'tea' which is good for minor stomach upsets – a good substitute for peppermint for people taking homoeopathic medicine. It is perennial, dying down in winter, coming up early in spring and reaching a height of up to 1.5m in summer. The plants live longer if the flower heads are removed before they bloom, but it self-seeds readily if they are left. It is slightly allelopathic and other plants growing very nearby may be adversely affected. It is very attractive, and often grown as an ornamental.

The cultivated varieties of marjoram, rosemary, sage, winter savoury, tarragon and thyme come from the Mediterranean or other warmer climes – though the wild forms of most of them can be found in favoured spots in Britain. Although they can survive in light shade they all benefit from full Sun and the stored heat of walls, paving or any other stones. Apart from benefiting their general health, sunshine concentrates the aromatic oils which give them their flavour and medicinal properties. On the whole they prefer light, well-drained soils without too much fertility. Some of them can inhibit the germination of seeds, so they should be kept away from self-seeding areas if possible.

They are all perennials, though marjoram and rosemary are not very hardy and may not survive well in colder areas. On the other hand, these two are more tolerant than the others of partial shade. There is a Russian form of tarragon which is hardier than the French one, and may be more suitable for forest gardening, but it does not taste nearly as good.

Onions

The perennial onions can be divided into those which give a harvest of leaves and those which give a harvest of bulbs or cloves, such as shallots or garlic. The latter group are perennial in as much as the planting material for next year is a bulb or clove from this year's plant, but they are much best grown on rotation with the annuals. Only the leaf onions are really suitable for forest gardening.

One advantage all perennial onions have over annual

ones is that once established they are resistant to slugs – which can mercilessly destroy newly emerged onion seedlings. Growing annual onions from sets does not solve the slug problem, it simply hands it over to the person who grows the sets. Perennial onions are sometimes eaten by slugs, but garlic and garlic chives never.

The perennial onions are an exception to the rule of thumb that larger leaved plants are more shade tolerant than narrow leaved ones. Apart from ramsons, they are narrow leaved and do best in a light shade. In a sunny position they will flower and go to seed, the leaves becoming dry and fibrous and the bulbs woody. In a position which is shaded for much of the day and receives adequate light from the side they will produce succulent green leaves all summer long.

Ramsons (*Allium ursinum*)

Otherwise known as wild garlic, ramsons is one member of the onion family which actually thrives in heavy shade. This is not just because it has a leaf as broad as your tongue, but also because of its annual cycle.

Plate 9.4 Ramsons in the wild creating an extensive ground cover in the shade of beech trees.

A native woodland plant, it sometimes spills out from the woods onto adjacent shady banks but is almost never found right out in the open. It spends winter below ground as a bulb, and the leaves emerge as early as February. By early March there are often some leaves big enough to pick. It usually grows as a pure stand, and in May the brilliant white flowers carpet the woodland floor in a dazzling display. By mid June, when the trees are in full leaf, the plants have died down again and nothing remains above ground.

The leaves are the part usually harvested, as production of cloves is low. If you grow bulb garlic in your garden ramsons can complement it perfectly. It is often ready to pick just as the stored bulb garlic from last year's crop

gets used up, and finishes just when the first green bulbs of this year's crop are ready.

As well as being used in cooking as a direct substitute for bulb garlic, it is excellent in salads, and its mildness allows it to be used in considerable quantities. It can also be used as a garnish, or as a sandwich filling along with things like cottage cheese or peanut butter.

It is obviously a prime candidate for the shadier parts of a forest garden – always remembering that no food plant will grow in total shade – and it does not do well in a completely unshaded situation. It likes a moist soil, preferably with a high lime content, and tolerates very wet conditions.

Plants should be spaced about 15cm apart. It can be invasive, especially in wet, shady conditions where it has the competitive edge over most other herbaceous plants.

Welsh Onions (*Allium fistulosum*)

These do not come from Wales but from Siberia. The Old English word 'welsh' is used here in it's original meaning of 'foreign'. (The 'wal' in walnut has the same derivation and meaning.) They are also known as ciboule. They are a tough, perennial alternative to spring onions, growing in dense clumps up to 50cm tall. They stay green for all or most of the winter, though very severe cold may kill them. The red-bulbed varieties are hardier, nearer to the wild form and tastier than the more common white-bulbed ones.

The plants should be renewed every few years to keep them healthy. They often self-seed, but if they do not a few plants can be detached from the outside of the clump and replanted elsewhere. They should be planted 20cm apart. The leaves regrow vigorously after picking and can be harvested intensively. The bulbs can be picked as well, but they regrow much more slowly, and total production will be more if only leaves are picked. Though their main use is in salads they can be used for cooking if no other onions are available.

Everlasting Onions (*Allium perutile*)

Also known as the ever-ready onion, these are a smaller, somewhat milder version of Welsh onions. They only reproduce vegetatively, so they can be grown in sunnier spots without going to seed. They are also more cold-tolerant and will stay green in areas where Welsh onions may die down over winter.

Tree Onions (*Allium cepa proliferum*)

Sometimes called Egyptian onions, these are rather surreal. They look like – in fact they are – normal bulb onions with a group of little onions growing out of the tip of the stem. They reproduce by bending over till the little bulbs touch ground.

These bulbils as they are called can be harvested,

but yields are low, and peeling such small bulbs is a bit tedious. The plants also produce a single main bulb at ground level, and leaves like Welsh onions. It is probably best to harvest the bulbs and leaves and regard the bulbils as a self-seeding mechanism. If a few plants are left unpicked they will produce bulbils in their first or second year. Tree onions are extremely hardy, and not fussy about soil. They grow to a maximum of 1m, but usually less, and should be spaced 20cm apart.

Chives (*Allium schoenoprasum*)

Chives make a very pretty plant when the purple flowers are in bloom, and can be grown as a decorative edge to a bed. But for fresh leaf production it's best to cut the whole plant to the ground several times through the season, which prevents flowering. Leaving every other plant to flower is a good compromise.

They die down in autumn and are up again in February, though they should not be picked until they have put on a fair bit of growth. They need a rich soil or generous feeding to do really well, and prefer moist conditions. They should be planted about 25cm apart, in either spring or autumn, and will grow 30cm tall if done well.

For maximum vigour they should be lifted after three or four years and bunches of three or four plants detached from the outside of the clump and replanted. A little dry mulch placed over the plants in winter will encourage early spring growth.

Chinese or Garlic Chives (*Allium tuberosum*)

These are similar to chives with a flavour somewhere between garlic and chives. They need a fairly fertile soil. They should be spaced 15-20cm apart. In their first year they should only be picked very sparingly and not allowed to flower. Once established they do not need separating and replanting every few years unless new planting material is required. They die down for a while in winter.

Rocambole (*Allium sativum ophioscorodon*)

This plant is like a cross between garlic, chives and tree onions. It is really a kind of garlic. In autumn and spring it produces fine leaves which can be picked like chives, and in early summer it produces bulbils like tree onions. It's alternative name is serpent garlic, because the flowering stem makes a snake-like coil just below the bulbils.

Plate 9.5 Welsh onion. (PW)

Figure 9.5 Tree onion.

The bulbs can be harvested, though they don't keep as long as other varieties of garlic. In a forest garden it is best used as a winter replacement for chives, as it is green when they have died down. A combination of chives and rocambole can give a year-round supply of tasty fine-leaved onions for adding to salads and many cooked dishes.

Bulbs can be sown in spring, summer or autumn, 1cm deep and 5cm apart. Bulbils can also be used but they are less reliable and give rise to slower-growing plants. Once established it can reproduce by means of its bulbils and may become mildly invasive.

Roots

The scope for roots in a forest garden is limited. This is not just because harvesting them involves digging, but also because there are few root crops which are shade-bearing perennials or self-seeders.

Jerusalem Artichokes (*Helianthus tuberosus*)

This is one plant which is indeed edible, very tolerant of shade, and perennial. Unfortunately the canes grow to a height of 2-3m in summer, so they will not fit under the trees and shrubs of a forest garden. Also, as they are tubers rather than true roots harvesting them involves overall digging of the ground rather than loosening the soil and drawing out a cylindrical root.

The best place for them is either just to the north of the forest garden where the ground is shaded by the trees, or in some place that is shaded by buildings or other tall vegetation. An acquaintance of mine who had an awkward patch in his garden, overshaded by laurel bushes, found that Jerusalem artichokes were the only food plant he could grow there with any success.

In summer when the stems and leaves are fully grown they can make a windbreak for tender plants like tomatoes, as long as they are well grown and only subject to mild winds. Unfortunately this is not much use for a forest garden, where the main need for a windbreak is in spring when the top and soft fruit are in blossom.

Once you have planted them it is very difficult to get rid of them, as even the tiniest tuber left in the soil will sprout and grow, so it pays to be quite sure that you will want them in that position well into the future before planting them. They are also invasive, and it is a good precaution to dig some kind of barrier into the soil around the patch, like a line of slates. A small clump can be grown in a bottomless bucket sunk into the ground.

Tubers sold for eating can be used for planting material. They should be planted 12cm deep and 30cm apart in spring, and the stalks may need earthing up as they grow to make them more wind firm. They are ready in the autumn and winter, and best stored in the ground because they dry out and lose their crispness in the air.

You can decrease the knobbliness of your stock by always returning the roundest one to the ground when harvesting.

They are very tough plants, tolerant of poor soils and needing little in the way of cultivation. It would be nice to think that they could be used as a bulk starch crop, substituting for potatoes. Unfortunately they are too strong tasting to be used as a staple. They are excellent in soups, especially when mixed with other strong tasting vegetables like celeriac or parsnip, or raw, grated into a salad. But you wouldn't want to eat them every day.

American Groundnut (*Apios americana*)

This is a perennial plant that produces tubers which do taste similar to potatoes. It is a low vine, growing to about 1m, and being a legume it can fix nitrogen if the appropriate bacteria are present. As it has not been intensively bred as a food plant it presumably does not yield anything like as much as potatoes.

It is a new plant to this country,[8] and it is not yet clear how well it will do in our climate, and how much shade it can tolerate. But its natural home is moist woods and thickets in Pennsylvania, and one account says it prefers dappled shade to full Sun. It is also said to tolerate acid soils. The tubers are best harvested in the autumn, when the foliage dies down, and they can be taken in the first year, though it takes 2-3 years to accumulate a sizeable crop. They contain 17% protein. The seeds can also be eaten, cooked like peas and beans.

Light-Demanding Roots

Skirret (*Sium sisarum*) is a true perennial root vegetable. It produces a cluster of thin, carrot-like roots in the autumn, one of which can be left in the ground as next year's planting material. Unfortunately it is susceptible to slugs. The foliage dies right down in winter, and if the slugs are really bad in spring they can eat it faster than it can grow. But it should be able to grow away from them in most gardens in most years, and it is less vulnerable to slugs than plants which must be grown from seed each year. The taste is somewhere between carrot and parsnip with a hint of bitterness, and the roots can be eaten cooked or raw.

Dandelion (*Taraxacum officinale*) seeds can actually be bought from seed suppliers. Presumably they are of a strain which is in some way superior or other to the wild plant. But it does seem strange to buy and deliberately cultivate something which is available free for no more trouble than removing it from the ground wherever it chooses to grow – which is more or less everywhere in my garden! Although the roots can be used as a cooked vegetable, they have a very strong sour taste and even a tiny bit can dominate a stew or soup. Their best use is for dandelion 'coffee'.

8   Available from Future Foods and Plants for a Future.

MAKING DANDELION 'COFFEE' [9]

To make dandelion coffee, choose the thickest roots, and put the others in the compost – they're more trouble than they're worth.

Don't bother to wash them; just cut off the leafy tops, and peel the roots thinly with a sharp knife – then give them a rinse.

Cut into chunks about an inch long, and grind in a metal mincer.

Dry roast in a cast iron frying pan on as low a heat as possible, using a heat dispersing mat, if you have one. Roast until the minced root is dark brown, and crumbles between finger and thumb.

Grind in a mortar or surubachi – a Japanese pottery mortar with ridges fashioned into it to make the food grind more easily. They are available from wholefood shops that stock macrobiotic foods.

To make coffee, use a good heaped teaspoon of powder per mug, and bring to the boil. Stand for long enough to let the grounds settle, then drink, adding milk or whatever.

---

[9]   By Cathy Ashley in 'Solutions!', *Permaculture Magazine*, No. 9.

Fruits

Rhubarb (*Rheum* x *cultorum*)

Although it grows well in partial shade, it is doubtful whether rhubarb should be grown directly under fruit trees as it is a very deep-rooted and exhaustive plant and may compete excessively with the trees. It is probably better suited, like Jerusalem artichokes, to a shady spot away from the trees, perhaps to the north of a wall or building. If there is no such spot looking for a shade-tolerant plant to fill it, rhubarb will do just as well in the open.

It is usually established by planting sets, which are had by dividing up an older plant. As rhubarb is prone to virus diseases it is important to get sets from a healthy plant. A two or three year old plant is likely to be healthier than an older one, and if the only plant available is an older one the buds from the outside edges of the rootstock are likely to be the healthiest.

It will thrive on any kind of soil, as long as it is well supplied with nutrients, especially nitrogen, and well drained. 75-90cm is enough space for one plant in a sunny position, but if it is planted in the shade the leaves will expand to cover a wider area than this. The secret of growing good rhubarb is said to be to keep it dry in winter and moist in summer. On heavy soils it is some-times grown on ridges or mounds to help drainage, and in spring a thick mulch of manure will help both to keep it moist and to feed it.

Picking time is from late spring to early summer, but it can be extended back to the end of February by forcing. Forcing is done by placing either a purpose-built clay pot or a length of drain pipe with a lid on it over the plant in winter. This keeps the plant in the dark, which stimulates growth and produces very tender stalks. Later in the year the stalks become more acid, but the season can be extended into the summer by choosing less acid varieties.

Wild Strawberries (*Fragaria vesca*)

The cultivated strawberry is a perennial and can stand a certain amount of shade, but it is a demanding plant, and probably more suited to a conventional vegetable garden than a forest garden.

The fruits of the wild strawberry are tiny by comparison to the cultivated ones, and it takes so long to pick a mouthful that they are fruits to be savoured for their magical taste rather than eaten for serious sustenance. Alpine strawberries are a subspecies of the wild strawberry (*F. vesca alpina*). They have bigger fruit, but it is still small compared to the usual cultivated strawberries.

Both wild and alpine strawberries can tolerate light shade, and both can survive quite happily without much attention. The disadvantage of the alpine kind is that they can get virus diseases – in which case they should be taken up and new plants established in another part of the garden. The alpines also lack runners, which means they cannot colonise new ground vegetatively as other wild strawberries can, though they can spread by seed, and often come up in cracks in masonry and paths.

Both kinds are pretty plants, with bright little flowers in spring and summer, followed by equally bright and cheerful fruit in summer and autumn. Even if the yield of fruit is low, they are a joy to have in the garden.

Rubus tricolor

This is a plant for the very darkest part of the garden. It is said to be able to survive even under the shade of beech trees. In more moderate shade, such as can be found in a forest garden, it can flower and fruit, though not every year. Although the yield may be low and unreliable, it can be regarded as a bonus, something produced in a situation where not much else will grow. It can also be used to cover the ground if not all the area of the forest garden is needed for vegetables. It does well on a variety of soils.

It is a low ground cover plant which does not grow above 30cm in height. The plants should be spaced 1m apart. They can soon cover a wide area and are not suitable for smaller gardens. Even in larger gardens they may need to be cut back regularly.

Mushrooms

Fungi, unlike green plants, do not manufacture their own food, but get their energy by decomposing existing organic matter. This means they do not need sunlight in order to grow, and are thus ideal for the darker parts of a forest garden. They are tasty and nutritious food, mostly higher in protein than vegetables, with especially high levels of vitamin D.

There are an enormous number of edible mushrooms which can be grown in gardens. Full details are to be found in *Mushrooms in the Garden*, by Hellmut Steineck.[10] The following are a few basic kinds which should do well without too much trouble, and are available as spawn in this country.[11]

Wood-Living Mushrooms

These can be grown either on logs or in sawdust. Each kind has a preference for certain kinds of wood, but most will grow on more than one kind. The kind of wood has an influence on the life-cycle of the mushrooms. When they are grown on poplar or birch logs they come into full yield most quickly, but may only last three years. Oak-grown ones last the longest, but there is little yield in the first year. Beech or cherry are intermediate at about five years. Most kinds will not grow on conifers, and sycamore is unsuitable because it is often infected with other kinds of fungi already. Almost any other kind of broad-leaved wood will do.

Freshly-felled wood, or sawdust from freshly-felled wood must be used. It should be cut in winter for inoculating in spring, or in mild areas in autumn for inoculating in winter, ideally from 30 to 60 days after felling. If older wood is used there is more likelihood of other fungi having taken up residence.

Logs 10-25cm thick are ideal, as they have a higher proportion of sapwood to heartwood than thicker logs, and the mushrooms grow best in the sapwood. They can be any convenient length, say around 50cm. Before inoculation the logs should be kept off the ground in a moist, shady place – the interior of a forest garden is ideal. Sawdust can be kept in plastic bags, both before and after inoculation.

30gm of moist spawn is enough to inoculate one log 10cm thick and 50cm long. Five of these should be enough to supply the average family with mushrooms in season. Inoculation should be done with care, following the instructions that come with the spawn. After inoculation the logs do not need to be kept off the ground. They should be kept reasonably moist throughout the life of the fungi, which should be easy in the shadier parts of the garden. In very dry weather they may need watering. The first mushrooms may come in the autumn or spring following inoculation.

Shii-take, or Japanese forest mushrooms (*Lentinus edodes*) are a popular kind of wood-living mushrooms. They are high in protein, and B vitamins, including B12, which is often deficient in vegetarian or vegan diets. They also help to boost the immune system by encouraging the production of interferon. They will grow on many hardwoods, but prefer oak.

The oyster mushrooms (*Pleurotus* spp.) are attractive fungi with a pleasant flavour. The pine oyster mushroom (*P. colombinus*) is particularly useful in areas where logs from broadleaved trees are hard to come by, as it will grow on conifers.

Both shii-take and oyster mushrooms can be dried for out-of-season use. They are tougher than the common mushroom and need fairly intensive cooking to get the best out of them.

Ground-Living Mushrooms

Many of these mushrooms play an important part in reducing leaf litter and herbaceous material down to humus. This is a vital part in the soil fertility cycle, and ground-living fungi are always present in the soil. If some of these are kinds which produce edible mushrooms, so much the better for us. The edible kinds will live on compost heaps and strawy manure heaps, but only once they have cooled down.

Wood blewits (*Lepista nuda*) will grow happily in the mulch of a forest garden. They often appear of their own accord, but if not the mulch can be inoculated with the spawn. The picking season is from September to December. They taste good, but should not be eaten raw, as they can be indigestible.

Shaggy ink caps (*Coprinus comatus*) are less of a woodland species. They are often found on lawns, especially newly made ones, and are sometimes taken as an indicator of disturbed ground. They should be picked as soon as they appear, and cooked immediately, otherwise they can dissolve into a black, inky liquid. Some people discard the stem before cooking, but personally I cannot see why. They are delicious, if rather mild-tasting.

---

[10]   See Further Reading.

[11]   Available from Future Foods. Instructions for growing are included.

Chapter 10

DESIGNING A FOREST GARDEN

The practical process: a step-by-step guide and an actual example

I get a lot of pleasure from designing a garden.
It's more fun than playing chess.
Bill Mollison

A good initial design is more important for a forest garden than it is for many other kinds of garden, because it is composed of perennial plants, some of which will live for a very long time. If, a year after planting, you discover that you've made a major mistake, it is possible to dig the whole lot up and replant it. But most of us haven't got that much energy. We are more likely to find plenty of good reasons to go on for the rest of our lives living with something which does not work as well as it might. In fact a design fault may not show up for several years, by which time the trees will be too big to move anyway.

Designing can be divided up into a number of stages:

*   Collecting information;

*   Recording;

*   Evaluation;

*   Design
        including:
        costing,
        implementation.

COLLECTING INFORMATION

This part of the process is more important than most of us would give credit to. Good initial observation and listening is the foundation of good design. Observing the site through each of the seasons is particularly valuable. Time spent observing can also be used to mull over ideas and search out new information. It is time well spent.

The Land

Things to note about your forest garden site are:

*   its ecological value;

*   its form, i.e. slopes etc.;

*   the local climate;

*   microclimate:
        light and shade,
        wind,
        frost,
        warm walls;

*   water sources;

*   soil;

*   existing vegetation.

Ecological Value

If you feel unable to decide whether there is anything of great ecological value in your garden, the local County or Urban Wildlife Trust will probably be only too pleased to give you free advice.

Landform

This is usually a matter of choosing the steeper slopes, if any, for perennial vegetation, such as a forest garden, to protect them from soil erosion. The landform also affects frost pockets, which are dealt with below.

Climate

The regional climate, as opposed to the microclimate, will mainly affect the choice of plants and varieties.

Microclimate

This affects the choice of plants too, but it also affects the layout of the garden.

Light and shade

It is a complex matter to predict where the shade from buildings and existing trees will fall at different times of the year and different times of day, and the best way to find out is to observe it through the year.

The angle of the Sun is at its highest on the summer solstice, 21 June, lowest on the winter solstice, 21 December and exactly halfway on the spring and autumn equinoxes 21 March and September, when day and night are the same length:

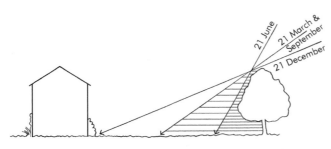

Figure 10.1

The second half of the year is a mirror image of the first half, so if you know where the shade falls at various times during the first six months you can work it out for the second six months. The day which falls, say, 50 days after the summer solstice is just the same length, and experiences just the same angle of Sun, as the day which falls 50 days before it.

Midwinter is not very important, as nothing much is happening in the garden then, but notes of where the shade falls from February to Midsummer, perhaps at monthly or two-monthly intervals, will reveal where the sunny and shady spots are. Since the angle and direction of the Sun change through the day, observations should be made three times a day, mid-morning, noon and mid-afternoon.

The best way to record the observations is to sketch them on a series of maps of the garden. To get an overall idea of the sunniest and shadiest parts of the garden you can make a composite map, with a different kind of cross-hatching for each observation, so that the shadier places get progressively darker as the different layers of hatching build up. Nine layers of shading are about as much as the map will take, so it is best to choose three representative days, perhaps one each in early spring, mid-spring and midsummer.

Wind

It is never safe to assume that the local wind pattern is the same as the national or regional one. The local landform can have a big effect. In a narrow valley or street the wind will almost always blow either up it or down it, regardless of what it may be doing in the sky above.

Frost

To find out whether there are any frost pockets in your garden, and if so where they are, can mean getting up early in the morning a few times when a light frost is forecast.

The places which are frosty first thing are the frost pockets. Those which are still frosty after an hour or two of sunshine may not be. They are the places where frost lingers, because the Sun either reaches them latest or strikes them at a more oblique angle. If the frost was light they may also be in frost pockets, but after an overall frost they are just as likely not. In fact places which thaw slowly after an overall frost can be good spots to plant frost-tender tress, as a slow thaw is less harmful to plant tissues than a rapid one.

Another method is to place frost-tender plants at intervals down the slope, say sprouting potatoes in spring or French beans in pots in autumn. The ones in the frost pocket will die.

A single year's observation may not reveal all, especially if it is a mild year without much in the way of frost. If you want to go ahead with planting you can try to predict where the frost pockets will be from the general principles given in Chapter 3, or rely on memories – your own or other people's. The problem with memories is that we often do not notice things accurately if we are not specifically looking out for them.

Warm walls

Most walls have shade cast on them for at least part of each day, and this must be noted along with which direction they face.

Water

Water Supply

In most gardens the principal source of water for summer watering apart from the mains is the roof of the house and any other buildings. As well as any outdoor taps, the position of the downpipes should be noted, along with potential sites for a water storage tank.

Grey water is the other on-site source of water, and the position and height of outlets should be noted.

Drainage

Patches of poorly drained soil often only reveal themselves after a period of heavy rain. It is sometimes possible to identify potentially wet soil during dry weather by noting which plants choose to grow there of their own accord – in other words the weeds. But this approach must be used with caution. The wetness of the soil is only one of the influences on those plants, and it may not be the dominant one.

In most gardens the main selection pressure on the weeds is their ability to resist the attempts of gardeners to get rid of them. So creeping buttercups may indicate poor drainage, or they may indicate a level of weeding that has put paid to less persistent plants but not to these. The same plants in a pasture field may be a much more reliable indicator of a wet patch, but even here it is wise not to jump to conclusions. Indicator plants are clues to soil conditions, not conclusive proof.

Possible reasons for a wet soil are:

- a leaking water pipe;
- an obstruction in the subsoil such as the floor of a demolished building;
- compaction, which can be relieved by cultivation;
- the soil is a poorly-drained clay which needs land drains under it before you can grow fruit there.

The best way to find out which is responsible is to dig one or more inspection pits.

Soil

It is always worthwhile to get to know your soil well. The better you know the soil the better you can work with it, and if it varies from one part of the garden to another it should be an influence on your planting plan.

The first thing to do is to find out if it is predominantly sand or clay (*see box on this page*).

The second thing to do is to dig a few inspection holes. You should go down at least 45cm, if you can get that far. Look out for signs of chalk, old builders' rubble and compacted soil. If you suspect there may be a drainage problem, look out for orange flecks in the subsoil, which are a sign of bad drainage, or blue clay, which is a sign of worse drainage. If you find either it probably means that you will have to install land drains before you can grow fruit. It is worthwhile getting professional advice.

pH and the plant nutrient status of the soil can be checked with one of the soil test kits available from garden centres. Or you can get it tested professionally for a few pounds by your local branch of ADAS, the government agricultural advisory service, or for a slightly higher fee by Elm Farm Research Centre, the organic research people.[1]

The organic matter level of the soil is reflected in its colour. A dark colour indicates high organic matter, because humus – organic matter which has decayed to a stable state in the soil – is dark brown to black. But beware. Many gardens in both town and country have had coal ash dumped on them over decades or even centuries, and may be dark for that reason. On the other hand gardens like this are usually high in organic matter as well.

---

[1] Elm Farm Research Centre, Hampstead Marshall, Nr. Newbury, Berkshire RG15 0HR. (01488) 658298.

A SIMPLE SOIL TEXTURE TEST

- Take about a teaspoonful of soil in your hand and moisten it gradually while you knead it till it reaches the moisture content at which it holds together most strongly.

- Try to mould it into a ball.

  A sandy soil:
  will not form a ball, or forms one which breaks up very easily; feels predominantly gritty.

  A clay soil:
  forms a strong ball that is hard to deform; has a sticky feel when wet.

  A loamy soil:
  falls between these two extremes; may feel both gritty and sticky when kneaded.

This is a simplified soil texture test. It leaves out the finer distinctions, but it gives you the general picture. It tells you whether to expect excessive drainage or insufficient drainage to be a problem, whether a deficiency of soil nutrients is likely, or if soil compaction may be present.

It is well worth checking that there are no specific soil problems, such as drainage or excess lime. But most soils will grow a reasonable forest garden, and if the garden already grows good crops of vegetables and flowers, that is a good indication that it will be all right.

Existing Plants
These may be important in one of three ways:

- they may be valued garden plants which you want to keep;
- some or all of the garden may have a special weed problem;
- nearby trees, in the garden or over the fence, may influence the garden.

The People

There are two questions to be answered by the members of the household:

- what do you want from the garden? i.e. the outputs;
- what do you want to put into it? i.e. the inputs.

Outputs

It is a good idea to get each member of the family to draw up a list of what they want from the garden, both general and specific, and put some priorities on it.

Quantities are also important for those things which can be quantified. For example, if you want space to sit out in the garden, just how much space do you want? How many people will be sitting there at any one time? You may need less space than you think.

The most quantifiable thing is the output of food. As well as deciding which kinds of food you want to grow in the new garden, it is important to make an estimate of how much of each you are likely to need. You can get some idea of how much by the amount you currently eat. The forest garden may well change the family's eating habits to some extent. But it is important not to overestimate this and end up with a big surplus – unless you have a good idea of how you can make use of it. A family which eats 5lb of fruit a week at present may increase that to 7 or 10lb, but it is unlikely to start eating 20 or 30lb.

Inputs

The design must reflect the amount of maintenance you and your family will realistically want to undertake once the garden is established. There is more about this under Evaluation, below.

RECORDING

Apart from making notes of what you observe and keeping the lists of what the people want, the most important record of what is already there is the base map.

The Base Map

It may seem a bit excessive to start making a map of your garden when all you want to do is place a few trees and shrubs. But it really is worthwhile. The kind of relationships between plant and plant and between plants and environment that make a forest garden work can only be set up if plants and other features are put in the right places relative to each other. By far the easiest way to do this is with the aid of a map.

The map needs to be to scale, though not incredibly accurate. As well as being a record of what is already there it will act as a template for the new design, and it will only be any use as a template if it is to scale: if you want to know how many fruit trees of a known diameter will fit into a given space you need to know how big the space is – at least to the nearest half metre or so.

To save the expense of buying a long tape measure you can make a reasonably accurate measuring device with a long cord knotted at half-metre intervals. Choosing a simple scale to work to makes the job much easier. 1 centimetre to 1 metre, or 1cm to 2m are much easier to work with than, say, 1cm to 1.25m.

The sample base map on page 143 gives an idea of the kind of things to include. How simple or complex you make it is up to you. Putting symbols on the map which refer to a key is a way of getting more information on there without cluttering it.

Making a map is one of the best ways of getting to know a piece of ground intimately. We often think we know a garden much better than we really do until we come to draw it to scale. One thing in particular that most people get wrong is the spread of the crown of trees. It is usually much wider than we assume at first glance, and it is really important to measure where the crown comes to, not to estimate it.

Other Records

Keeping a garden diary can be a valuable thing to do – both before designing a forest garden and once it is in place and growing. Like making a map, it is a way of getting to know a garden really well. A diary is a good place to record the information on microclimates mentioned above under Collecting Information.

Photographs are useful too. Deep in the winter it is often hard to remember what the garden feels like in summer, and vice versa. A couple of pictures can bring it all back in a moment.

EVALUATION

Two broad categories of things need to be assessed:

* existing vegetation and structures:
    what to keep and what to remove?

* the family's wants:
    do they fit in the available space, and the amount of time you want to give the garden?

Some specific points to check are:

* **Maintenance requirement.** Plants which require more attention should be avoided if low maintenance is a priority. These include: tender fruits such as peaches, fruit trees trained in restricted forms (cordons, fans and espaliers), and self-seeding vegetables as opposed to perennials.

    Planting cooking varieties, or any perishable fruits in quantities greater than the family can eat fresh, means committing yourself to a certain amount of work in preparing or preserving it. It is not a huge job, and can be fun, but preserving perishable fruit must be done when the fruit is ready, not necessarily when you feel like it. You need to be fairly sure you want to do it before you commit yourself to it by planting the trees and shrubs.

- **Food requirement.** This must be matched to the keeping time of the fruit, as well as the size of the trees. Suppose you eat 5lb of apples in a week and want to plant a variety which keeps for only six weeks. You will only be able to use some 30lb of that variety, so there is no point in planting it on an M26 rootstock, which may yield over 100lb of fruit when it comes into full bearing.

- **Availability of plants.** Some of the less common ones may only be available as seed. This should not be a problem for vegetables and herbs, but for trees and shrubs it may mean that you will have to wait a couple of years or more before you have something which you can plant out in the garden.

DESIGN

By now a general idea of what the forest garden will be like should have emerged, including answers to the questions:

- What is the relative importance of food production: beauty, wildlife, playspace etc.?

- Is it to be low-maintenance with a moderate yield or high-maintenance with maximum yield?

- Will it contain tender plants which are marginal in this area, or just hardy ones?

- Will the emphasis be on fruit or vegetables?

You should also have:

- a list of specific things you want to grow in the garden, with quantities;

- the base map and information on microclimates, soils etc.

The task is to fit the former into the latter – to fit the plants into the available space and the environment of the garden.

The Overall Concept
The first thing to do is to make a sketch of what the garden will be like overall, or a number of different sketches representing different options. This should be done on a scale map, perhaps a simplified copy of the base map.

How much detail you go into on this sketch depends largely on the size of the garden. If it is small you may draw in individual trees but put in shrubs and vegetables as blocks. With larger gardens you may sketch everything in as blocks, 'forest garden', 'reedbed', 'fertility patch' and so on.

To some extent this broad-brush designing will be altered by things which emerge from the more detailed work later on. But it is important to start with an overall concept, or you can get bogged down in detail and find you have omitted to leave space for a large component you definitely want.

Trees
It is best to start with the trees, and then design in the shrubs and vegetables round them. You can always go back and change the trees if you find they are not quite right for the shrubs and vegetables.

The first thing to do is to make a list of the sizes of the trees you are interested in. A very common fault in forest garden design is to place the trees too close together. I have seen two chestnut trees planted within 3 metres of each other! The minimum distance apart is the diameter of the mature trees. You may choose to plant them further apart to allow more light into the lower layers, but if they are closer than the diameter of the mature trees, one or more trees will have to be grubbed out before they reach maturity.

The mature diameters of fruit trees on a range of rootstocks are given in detail in Chapter 7, shrubs in Chapter 8. If a tree you want is available on more than

TREE SIZES WHEN MATURE		
Apple	M26	2.5-4m
	M9	2-3m
Pear	QA	3-7m
	QC	2.5-6m
Plum	St.JA	3.5-4.5m
	Pixy	2.5-3m
Sour Cherry Fan	Colt	3m wide
Quince		4m
Hazel		4.5m
Compact Hazel		3-3.5m

one rootstock, check how many of these rootstocks are suitable for your garden. Some may be too big, others may not be suitable for your soil. Don't try to be too accurate at this stage. The list we made when designing Tricia's garden, described later in this chapter, is given in the box as an example.

Some of these trees were not selected in the end. In fact hazel was dropped as a result of making this list, because it is too big for the garden. (There is only one reliably compact variety and this would need at least one pollinator.)

The next step can be done three different ways:

A. **Make a copy of the base map, leaving out all the features that are to be removed, and draw the proposed design on it.**

This is more suitable for smaller gardens. A pair of compasses is an invaluable tool. Always work in pencil and press lightly, so changes can be made without messing up the map. To start with it is as well to use a standard diameter for the trees, say 3m for a typical bush fruit tree. As the design begins to crystalise and you have a better idea of which individual tree is to go where, you can draw the diameters of the trees more accurately according to variety and rootstock.

B. **Make the same map, cut out circles of card to the scale size of the trees you want to include, and pin them to it.**

This is best for larger gardens, with a greater number of trees. As the number of trees rises the number of possible combinations rises by geometric progression. It would be hopelessly complicated to place a large number of trees with a pencil and rubber, whereas the cards can be swapped around and exchanged one for another easily and quickly as many times as you need.

You will need to tape the map to a board. Each kind of tree can be represented by a different colour, green for apples, yellow for pears etc. It is best to cut them out to exact scale to begin with, and have a few in reserve in case you decide to change a rootstock or a variety or even swap an apple for a plum.

C. **Mark the trees out on the ground in the garden.**

This method can be used on its own, at least in small gardens, but it should also be done to complement either of the on-paper methods. It is a check on your mathematics. If you have made any mistake in working to scale on your map it will be revealed when you try to actually lay your plan out on the ground. It also gives a much more realistic idea of what the garden will be like, especially for people who do not find it easy to visualise how things will look from a map.

You need a number of pegs to mark the trunks of the trees, and a compass made with a peg and a piece of string to see where the edges of their crowns will come to. Edges can be marked out by laying a hosepipe or rope on the ground, but it is unlikely that you will have enough of these to mark out the whole garden at once. An alternative is to mark out the edges with sawdust or sand, but these are very difficult to move from one place to another if you change your mind.

An important part of C is looking at the vertical dimension: one person holds a stick vertically on the spot where a tree is to go and the other stands back to get an idea of what it will be like. It is easy to adjust to the expected mature height of the different trees if you lash two or more shorter sticks together to get the length, rather than use a single stick. This not only gives you an idea of where the shade will fall, but helps you to visualise how the new planting will change the appearance of the garden.

Whichever method or methods you use, the design process is a dialogue between the structure of the garden and the choice of plants and varieties. A change in one often leads to a change in the other. For example, if you decide to grow your early apples on cordons instead of in bush form, you may have to drop the idea of a tip-bearing variety; if you decide on a vigorous cooking apple it can enable you to make use of a shady or exposed spot.

At this point it is a good idea to calculate the approximate yield of different fruits which you expect to get from the selection of trees you have made, and see how it compares to the quantities you came up with at the evaluation stage.

Shrubs and Vegetables

The shrubs and vegetables must not be forgotten while you plan where to put the trees. Space needs to be left for them. This means placing the trees sufficiently far apart to allow light into the lower layers when the trees have grown to maturity. It also means leaving space at the edges for planting Sun-loving shrubs and vegetables.

Once the basic arrangement of trees has been designed the shrubs can be added to the map, or on the ground if you are working that way. They should be drawn to scale, in pencil. If you have used method B, using circles of card to represent the trees, it is best to switch to drawing for the shrubs, or the whole process would get too fiddly. This will mean you are drawing partly on the paper and partly on the cards, but that should not be a problem.

Remember that you have represented the trees at the size they will be when mature. They will be smaller than this during the life of soft fruit bushes and canes which are planted at the same time. So you may be able to design a succession, taking a crop of soft fruit for a few years off an area that will eventually become too shady for it.

Once you have drawn in the shrubs it is as well to calculate what yield of soft fruit your design will give you, and see how well it matches the family's needs. At this point you may want to redesign some parts of the tree layer, either to increase or decrease the amount of space allowed for shrubs, or to adjust the amount of light reaching the shrub layer.

The vegetables can be planned in less detail. Unless you have very clear ideas of what you want it is usually enough to designate areas for shade-tolerant perennials, self-seeders, and Sun-loving perennials and leave it at that. But again you do need to have an idea of how much yield you can expect from the space you have allowed.

As there are few reliable figures for the yield of these little-known plants, this may be simply a matter of checking that the areas allowed are realistic. For example, if you find that your plan gives you space for an average of two plants each of the kinds of perennial vegetables you want you will not have enough of each to make a meal. If you find it gives you space for 50 plants of each you can be sure that you will never eat it all.

If you find that your needs for forest garden vegetables can be met by planting only part of the area with vegetables you will need to decide what to plant at ground level on the rest of it. Simply planting the vegetables you want at a wider spacing is the worst possible option: the intervening ground will soon get colonised by weeds and the garden will become a never-ending source of work. The vegetables should be placed at the recommended spacing and the remaining area planted with ground cover.

This is a very important point. Inadequate ground cover, leading to a terrible weed problem, is another very common fault in forest garden design.

Costing

Now is the time to find out just how much the plans you have made are going to cost. The result of your calculation may prompt you to go back and revise the design somewhat. But there is no reason why you should plant the whole garden up at once; and you can spread planting over a number of years according to your budget if necessary.

Fruit nurseries vary in the prices they charge, so it is possible to shop around. But getting good quality planting stock that will grow well and thrive for many years is worth a few extra pounds, and it is certainly not a good idea to go for the cheapest unless you are satisfied that the quality is also good. The best way to check on the quality of a nursery's goods is to speak to previous customers.

Implementation

You can do it all at once, but there are three good reasons for putting the design into action in stages:

- to spread the cost;
- to spread the work;
- because some things need doing before others.

Although a forest garden takes little work to maintain once it is established, the initial planting is a big job. It can be daunting. But splitting it up into 'bite-sized chunks' makes it much more inviting. It also means that you can do it in an unhurried way, giving it the attention it really deserves, so that the plants can get off to the best possible start in life.

Whether you do the whole job at once or over a number of years, some things will dictate their own time sequence. Windbreaks, for example, must be up and functioning before you plant the tender plants they are designed to protect, perennial weeds must be cleared before planting starts and so on. Even if you do not make an absolute timescale, with dates given to particular jobs, a relative timescale, giving the order in which different jobs must be done, is often needed.

A SAMPLE DESIGN:
Tricia's Garden

Collecting Information

The Land
Ecological Value. There is no special wildlife value in the garden. There are a number of wild flowers, and some perennial ground cover. There are few nesting sites for birds, and a resident cat, which makes successful nesting difficult.

Landform. The garden is approximately 20m x 13m. It is uniformly flat, except for the rockery, marked A on the base map (*overleaf*) which is gently domed.

Climate. The garden is in East Devon, with mild, equable temperatures and an annual rainfall of around 900mm (35in).

Microclimate
Light and shade. The area marked E on the base map is shaded by the house in the morning and the mock orange shrub in the afternoon. The area marked A is shaded in the afternoon by the wall to the west, which is about 1.5m high and slightly overtopped by trees growing on the far side. The clump of tall cypresses in the SW corner cast their shadow over the whole

garden for a time each afternoon, but as they are tall and narrow it passes quickly.

Wind. The garden is well protected from all sides except the south-west. When a strong wind blows from this direction the part of the lawn between the cypress trees and the greenhouse is exposed. It also causes strong winds in the passage to the north of the house, where it blows from west to east, and along the west side of the house, where it blows from north to south.

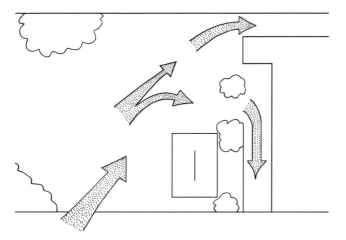

Figure 10.2 Wind directions in Tricia's garden.

Frost. There is no problem with late frosts.

Warm Walls. The western wall of the house has potential for training fruit, though the lower part of it is rather shaded at present, especially towards the southern end. The space between the windows is rather narrow for fan-trained fruit. The north wall of the garden (i.e. south-facing) is 1.5m high and made of brick. It is too low for fan-trained trees but could take cordons, espaliers or soft fruit. The concrete path in front of it will add to the warmth of the microclimate as long as it is not shaded from the south by new plantings.

Soil
This is a free-draining sandy loam, at least a metre deep without differentiation. The dark colour of the soil suggests a high level of organic matter, and the general health of the plants in the garden indicate it is reasonably fertile.

Water
The present water sources for the garden are the tap on the western wall of the house, and the rain water butts filled from the house roof. The grey water downpipe is outside the house and situated east of the rainwater downpipe (*see base map opposite*). The roofs of the shed and greenhouse could be used to collect water.

Existing Vegetation
See base map opposite. Most of the herbaceous vegetation is perennial or self-seeding flowers and herbs. The large cypress trees, judging by the vegetation at their feet, are not inordinately strong competitors.

The ornamental amelanchier overhanging from next door is starting to shade the wall below it. In the bed beneath it the ground cover plants are rose of Sharon and periwinkle, except for the eastern third of the bed which contains various herbaceous plants. These two could prove difficult to eradicate.

The cotinus by the house is too big for its position and has to be pruned fiercely each year to prevent it shading the house excessively. The pittosporum is attractive, but is too big and casts significant shade on the house.

The People
In addition to Tricia herself, the people living in the house are her teenage son, Carey, and her young daughters, Lucy and Rosie. They have two dogs and a cat.

Tricia's wants:
- dessert fruit;
- fruit for bottling and preserving, which she already does;
- nuts;
- some vegetables to compensate for the allotment she is currently giving up;
- a low-maintenance garden;
- to keep plenty of sunshine in the garden;
- ideally to have two woodland glade areas;
- a pond;
- flowers and interesting plants;
- an attractive garden, with a good view from the upstairs windows as well as down; the window most often looked out of is the dining room window, the most northerly one shown on the base map;
- the large cypresses are attractive, and give privacy from the only house that could otherwise overlook the garden.

The Children's Wants
- to keep the large cypresses, which they use for a den;
- Lucy wants her own garden of about 2 square metres;
- the lawn is too small for extensive games and would be equally useful if it were smaller.

Fruits Wanted
Apples, pears, plums, figs, hazel nuts, quinces, raspberries – summer and autumn fruiting, blackcurrants, red currants, gooseberries, elder, grape vine, rhubarb, something unusual and preferably both edible and ornamental.

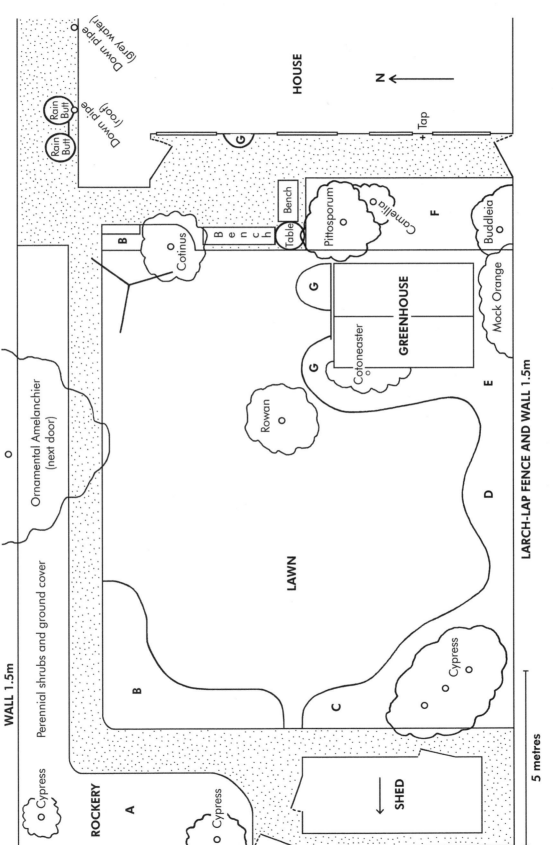

Figure 10.3 Base map

Evaluation

Existing Vegetation and Structures

The clump of large cypresses will remain, but the two smaller ones will be removed. Any new planting on the rockery, where the two smaller cypresses are growing, will only be possible once the rocks have been removed. The rowan, cotinus and mock orange will be removed. The pittosporum will be pruned back and kept at a smaller size.

The neighbour's amelanchier will be cut back to the wall. The rose of Sharon and periwinkle in the bed below it will be difficult to remove completely, but this must be done before perennial plants can be grown there.

The existing vegetation in beds A to E on the base map will be retained.

The existing paths will be retained. The area of hard standing by the shed door is particularly useful as a working surface, e.g. for servicing bikes and for temporary storage of materials.

The Family's Wants

It will be possible to fit all these things into the garden, with the exception of hazel nuts. They would take up too much space (*see pages 139-140*) and are reluctantly dropped from the design.

In order to keep the need for maintenance to a minimum, fruit trees in restricted forms and on the more dwarfing rootstocks will be kept to a minimum. For the same reason no family trees will be included.

Design

Structure

See design map opposite (*Figure 10.4*).

Trees

The trees are kept to the western part of the garden so as not to shade the house. A mixture of upright and more spreading varieties will give visual interest and perhaps reduce competition for light. The four trees on the lawn are placed so that the cherry plum will be visible from the dining room window.

The one tree on a very dwarfing stock is placed to the south-east of the group, a) so that it gets minimal shading from the other three trees and the cypresses, and b) to reduce the amount of shade cast by the trees on the house and lawn area in front of it. The cooking apple is the most vigorous and least light-demanding of the trees, and so it is placed nearest to the cypresses as it will be best able to stand the root competition and shade from them.

No fruit trees are planted in the southern part of the garden, which is most exposed to the wind. One of the functions of the crab apple tree is to reduce the

wind, and prevent a wind tunnel forming between the greenhouse and the other trees. The fence on the southern boundary will be heightened by 60cm with trellis.

Bush pears were ruled out because they are too large: they would take up a good deal of space, as two varieties are needed for pollination; and since they do not keep for as long as apples they would produce more fruit than could be used.

The cordon pears are placed on the south-facing wall, approximately equidistant from both house and apple trees to minimise shading from both, but slightly closer to the house so that they get more afternoon light than morning light. They are also near the existing water butts. This is important as wall-trained pears on this free-draining soil will need watering from time to time.

The fig is placed on the west-facing wall of the house, where it is also well protected from the north. The width available between the two windows is rather restricted for a fig, so it will have to be trained upwards and over the windows. This will entail working from a ladder for picking and pruning, but it is worth the extra trouble for this delicious fruit.

The cherry plum is in a rather shady position, but it is included as much for its decorative qualities as its fruit. Any fruit harvested from it is regarded as a bonus. The hawthorn is already growing behind the small cypress which is to be removed, and should expand to take its place.

Shrubs

All the shrubs grown beneath the apples and plum are gooseberries and redcurrants. None of them are placed near the cypresses to avoid excessive shade and root competition. The tree lupin is included for decorative purposes.

The blackcurrants are given a sunny position, and the autumn-fruiting raspberries one which will be sunny until the trees have grown up. By that time they will be at the end of their productive life, and they can be replaced with something more shade-tolerant. The elder is a longer-lived plant and will make good use of what will eventually be a relatively shady position.

A japonica and a Japanese wineberry are grown up the trellis added to the south fence, mainly for decorative and windbreaking purposes, as this is rather an exposed position for fruiting. But they will produce some fruit, especially in good seasons.

The grape vine is planted outside the greenhouse and trained to grow inside it. Existing climbing roses are allowed to take up the space vacated by the mock orange.

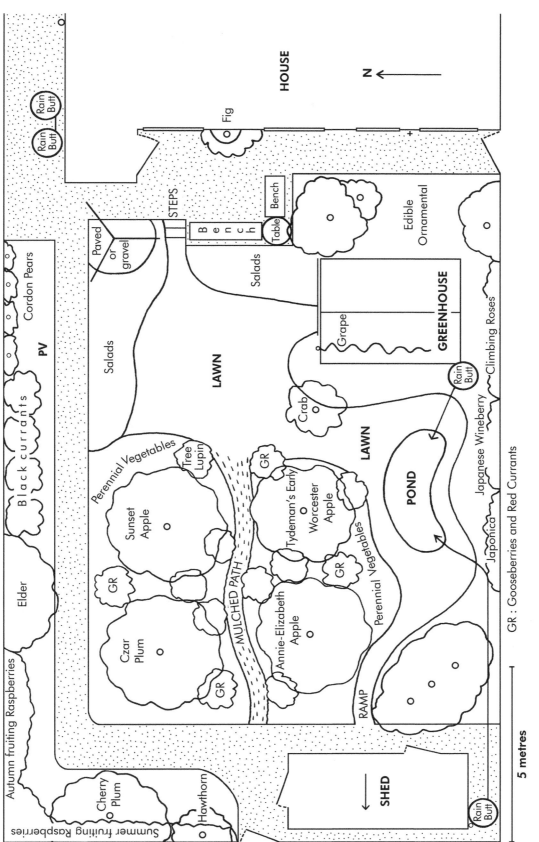

HOUSE

N

Fig

Rain Butt
Rain Butt

STEPS

Paved or gravel

Bench

Table

Salads

B
e
n
c
h

Salads

LAWN

GREENHOUSE

Grape

Edible Ornamental

Cordon Pears

PV

Salads

Crab

LAWN

Climbing Roses

Rain Butt

Blackcurrants

Perennial Vegetables

Tree Lupin

GR

Sunset Apple

MULCHED PATH

Tydeman's Early Worcester Apple

GR

Perennial Vegetables

POND

Japanese Wineberry

Japonica

Gooseberries and Red Currants

Elder

GR

Czar Plum

GR

Annie-Elizabeth Apple

GR

RAMP

Autumn fruiting Raspberries

Cherry Plum

Hawthorn

Summer fruiting Raspberries

SHED

Rain Butt

GR : Gooseberries and Red Currants

5 metres

Figure 10.4 Design map

Vegetables etc.

Areas A to F (*see base map on page 143*), are mainly kept as they are. There are two exceptions. B will eventually become too shady for some of the plants growing there, and these will be moved to the south edge of the trees when necessary. F is enhanced with a ground cover of wild strawberries and some additional herbs. The existing plants in A will continue to grow quite happily as shade levels increase.

The apples and plum are underplanted with a mixture of perennial vegetables, including ramsons, sea beet, perennial kale, Good King Henry and sorrel, together with woodland wildflowers. A rhubarb plant is also planted here. The bed marked PV are planted with Sun-loving perennial vegetables, including nine-star broccoli, sea kale, skirret and Welsh onion, and Sun-loving herbs and flowers.

The salad beds contain mixed annual vegetables and flowers, such as pot marigolds, as well as salad plants. They are placed closest to the house as they need the most frequent attention. This area contains Lucy's plot of 2 sq. m.

Other areas

Water is collected off the shed and greenhouse roofs to feed the pond. The water butts are raised just enough so that this can be done by gravity. The pond must be lined on this free-draining soil. The existing water butts fed from the house roof could be replaced with a larger container, raised off the ground to allow watering to be done by hosepipe, if such a container can be found. Eventually Tricia would like to make use of the grey water.

The ramp leading from the shed to the pond area is to make it easier to get the lawn mower onto the lawn, which at present is difficult as there is a 50cm drop from lawn level to the path.

The area under the clothes line is to be paved or gravelled, and steps put in to make it more accessible. Steps will also be put in to make the lawn more accessible from the house.

Varieties and Rootstocks

All the apples and plums are grown in a bush form with a relatively long stem so as to allow space for underplanting. On the rootstocks chosen there will eventually be a surplus of some kinds at the family's present rate of consumption. But the advantage of having robust, low-maintenance trees with space for underplanting outweighs this. In any case, fruit consumption will rise in the face of such abundance, and the surplus can be traded for foods not grown in the garden. Tricia is a member of the Local Exchange Trading Scheme (LETS), which is a good medium for exchanging surplus produce.

Apples

The cooking apple is Annie Elizabeth, a vigorous, upright variety which should be well able to stand competition from the cypresses. The fruit is attractive to look at, of good quality and moderately prolific, with a long season of use from December to June. Rootstock: M26. Expected yield when mature: 50-60lb. Pollination group: 4.

The maincrop eating apple is Sunset, a Cox type recommended for this area, resistant to scab and moderately vigorous. The fruit is of good quality and keeps from October to December. Rootstock: M26. Expected yield when mature: 60-80lb. Pollination group: 3.

The early eating apple is Tydeman's Early Worcester, earlier-ripening than Worcester Pearmain, juicier and bearing fruit on spurs as well as tips. It is chosen in preference to the Cox-type varieties partly to give some variety of taste. The fruit is ready in September and will keep into October. Rootstock: M9, because the fruit does not keep for long. Expected yield when mature: 40-50lb. Pollination group: 3.

The crab apple is Golden Hornet. It is a multi-purpose tree, providing shelter, pollination, an attractive appearance, and fruit for jam-making. Its small, erect habit will enable it to fit into the space provided without blocking off access or casting much shade.

Plums

The cooking plum Czar has been chosen in place of a dessert type, because Tricia reckons that dessert plums grown in this area do not taste very good. It is a tough, reliable variety, likely to succeed on this soil which is perhaps excessively well-drained for plums. It has an upright habit of growth, so it will not obscure too much of the view of the cherry plum from the house. Rootstock: St. Julien A, as Pixy would be unlikely to do well on this soil. Expected yield when mature: 80lb. Self-fertile.

The cherry plum, Trailblazer, is actually a cross between the Japanese and cherry plums. It is a decorative variety, with purple foliage, masses of blossom and juicy crimson-purple fruit of good size. It is vigorous with a tendency to grow one-sided, which should suit its position. Rootstock: St. Julien A.

Pears

Two varieties are to be planted, two cordons of each. Fertility Improved ripens in October and is a very hardy, disease-resistant pear which bears heavy crops, if not of the finest quality. It also has attractive autumn foliage. Nouveau Poitou ripens in November, has good quality fruit, and is resistant to scab – important here in a wet climate on a light soil. Rootstock: Quince A, as the soil is rather poor for Quince C. Expected yield when mature: 5lb per tree. Pollination group: both 3.

Fig

Brown Turkey is the obvious choice for an outdoor fig.

Elder

Since only one plant is to be grown it must be a native elder, as they are self-fertile. A cutting taken from the wild will do perfectly well.

Raspberries

Two summer fruiting varieties have been chosen, one early and one mid season. Glen Moy is the early one, a heavy cropper, with good flavour and virus resistant. The mid-season one is Malling Delight, very heavy cropping and virus resistant. Autumn Bliss is the autumn fruiting variety, by far the heaviest yielder, and resistant to aphids.

Blackcurrants

Ben Sarek, a new compact variety has been chosen. Four plants can be grown in the space available, rather than the three of other varieties, yet it is said to yield more per bush than them. It is also frost-hardy and of good flavour.

Red Currants

Red lake, a vigorous plant and a heavy yielder is the choice. As it is rather an upright variety care must be taken not to plant it too close to the trees.

Gooseberries

On this very well-drained soil a mildew-resistant variety is essential, and Invicta has been chosen. It is a cooking gooseberry, very high yielding and of good quality.

Grape

Black Hamburg is a good reliable greenhouse grape.

Rhubarb

Reed's Early Superb has been chosen, an old favourite for forcing.

Implementation

This design has been prepared in June. The following outline can be extended over a longer period or compressed into a shorter one according to the amount of time, energy, help and money available.

This Summer

Put up trellis along south fence. Prepare new salad and perennial vegetable beds. Pave under washing line and install steps. Prepare for planting fig. Prepare for planting pears. Start removing periwinkle and rose of Sharon. This will be a long job and should be taken at a steady pace. Hand-digging is the only way, possibly assisted by some poisoning as a last resort.

This Autumn

Remove trees which are to come out.

Plant: apples, Czar plum, pears, fig, gooseberries, red currants, japonica and Japanese wineberry. If at all possible, well-rotted manure or compost should be dug into all planting holes and surrounding soil. If there is not enough to go round the pears should get priority, followed by the dwarf apple, Tydeman's Early Worcester, and the gooseberries. All trees and shrubs are planted with a grow-through mulch. Areas between the trees and shrubs can be left unmulched till the vegetable layer is ready to plant.

COSTING

Trees		£
Apples	3 bush trees @ £10.50	31.50
Pears	4 maidens @ £8.50	34.00
Plum	1 maiden @ £14.00	14.00
Cherry plum		12.00
Crab apple		12.00
Fig		7.50
		111.00

Shrubs		
Raspberries	3 x 10 canes @ £6.00	18.00
Currants	10 plants @ 2.45	24.50
Gooseberries	5 plants @ 2.95	14.75
Wineberry		5.00
Japonica		5.00
Grape		6.00
Rhubarb		4.00
		77.25

Vegetables		
Seeds + plants		25.00

Materials		
Trellis	3 x 6ft x 2ft @ £5.35	16.05
Pond liner	2m x 4m @ £4.50	9.00
		25.05

	Total	£ 238.30

Some help will be needed with the heavy work, including making a root box for the fig and removing stones from the rockery. Tricia will not have to pay cash for this as the work can be done within the LETS bartering system.

Next Spring
Sow seeds of perennial vegetables and herbs, plant out any which are available as plants with a grow-through mulch.

Before Next Autumn
Continue removing periwinkle and rose of Sharon as it regrows. Remove stones from rockery prior to planting cherry plum and summer-fruiting raspberries.

Next Autumn
Plant remaining fruit if the ground is ready. The raspberries in particular should have well-rotted manure or compost dug in before planting.

At any Time
Install pond.

A Note on Maintenance

To some extent the design is a compromise between the desire for low maintenance on the one hand, and the small size of the garden on the other. Trees on relatively vigorous rootstocks, pruned in an unrestricted form require the least maintenance, while more dwarfing rootstocks and restricted forms give smaller sized trees.

The cordon pears will need more looking after than any of the other trees in the garden. They would suffer more from any neglect of pruning, and will need thorough mulching and occasional watering through the summer, and have more need of feeding with nutrients than the other trees. The dwarf apple will come second in line for whatever mulch material and plant nutrients are available.

WEIGHTS & MEASURES

1kg	=	2.2lb	1lb	=	454g
1cm	=	0.4in	1in	=	2.5cm
1m	=	1.1yd	1yd	=	0.9m

Approximate imperial equivalents are given below for some of the metric measurements most commonly used in this book.

5cm	=	2in	1.2m	=	4ft
10cm	=	4in	1.5m	=	5ft
15cm	=	6in	2m	=	6ft
30cm	=	1ft	3m	=	10ft
45cm	=	18in	4m	=	12ft
60cm	=	2ft	4.5m	=	15ft
1m	=	1yd	10m	=	30ft

Simplicity is given a higher priority than pin-point accuracy here, and the same approach has been adopted where imperial equivalents are given for metric weights of fruit yield in the text. Plants are variable things. It is not possible to be very accurate when predicting the ultimate size or yield of a fruit tree, and to give exact equivalents would be to suggest a degree of accuracy that is not possible in practice.

FURTHER READING

BACKGROUND

The Forest Garden
Robert Hart; Institute for Social Inventions; 1991.
This booklet gives a concise account of Robert Hart's pioneering work in his own garden in Shropshire. It also conveys much of the inspiration and spirit behind this kind of gardening.

Forest Gardening
Robert Hart; Green Books; 1996.
An inspiring and stimulating read, this is Robert Hart's personal testament. It explores a wide range of green issues, and is beautifully written in a graceful and readable style. For the practical forest gardener it adds little information to the booklet above. There is a chapter on forest gardens in other countries, mainly in the tropics.

Permaculture in a Nutshell
Patrick Whitefield; Permanent Publications; 2000.
A concise introduction to permaculture as practised in Britain and other temperate countries, it helps to put forest gardening in context.

Orchards, a Guide to Local Conservation
various authors; Common Ground; 1989.
A delightful little book, although not strictly about forest gardening it contains much to interest and inspire forest gardeners, especially those with an interest in maintaining continuity with the past. Appendices include: a list of local apple varieties by county, nurseries, fruit collections and useful organisations. (Available from Common Ground, Gold Hill House, 21 High Street, Shaftsbury, Dorset SP7 8JE.)

GENERAL

Food for Free
Richard Mabey; Collins; 1989.
Undoubtedly the best book about wild food plants, it contains details of 240 edible plants, including fungi, many of which can be grown successfully in forest gardens. Each plant is described and illustrated in colour, there are notes on how to use them plus other interesting information, yet the book is small enough to fit in your pocket.

Fruit
Harry Baker; R.H.S./Mitchell Beazley; 1992.
A beginner's guide to growing fruit at home, *Fruit* gives clear and simple instructions for growing the tree and shrub layers of a forest garden. It gives rather less detail than *The Fruit Garden Displayed* (below), but covers a wider range of plants, also including: mulberries, elderberries, quinces, medlars, chestnuts, walnuts, worcesterberries, grapes, kiwis, low bush blueberries and cranberries. Design considerations, pruning, renovating neglected trees and fruit storage are all covered. **Highly recommended as a companion to *How To Make A Forest Garden*.**

The Fruit Garden Displayed
Harry Baker; Royal Horticultural Society/Cassel; 1991.
This book gives comprehensive growing instructions for: apples, pears, plums, cherries, peaches, apricots, figs, hazels, strawberries, raspberries, blackberries, hybrid berries, black currants, red and white currants, gooseberries and highbush blueberries. General principles of fruit growing and renovation of neglected fruit trees are also covered.

Grow Your Own Fruit
Ken Muir; self-published; (see List of Suppliers).
This is the catalogue for Ken Muir's fruit nursery, but it contains so much information on how to grow the plants offered that it constitutes a concise guide to fruit growing. The information is practical and well presented, covering all the common fruits and some less common ones. It is free from the nursery with first order.

Bob Flowerdew's Organic Garden
Bob Flowerdew; Hamlyn; 1995.
The information on organic pest control for fruit in this book will be of particular interest to forest gardeners who do not want to go along with Harry Baker's chemical approach. It also covers the principles of organic growing, how to grow vegetables, fruit, herbs and ornamentals, with chapters on weed, pest and

disease control, all based on the author's experience in his own garden. The information is less detailed than in either *The Vegetable Garden Displayed* or *Fruit*.

Grow Your Own Vegetables
Joy Larkcom; Frances Lincoln; 2002.
A general guide to growing vegetables by the foremost authority of our times.

The Organic Salad Garden
Joy Larkcom; Frances Lincoln; 2002.
A beautiful, mouth-watering encyclopaedia of salad plants, including many of those mentioned in this book, with full details on how to grow them. Lesser-known plants, herbs, edible flowers, wild salad plants and salad making are all covered. It is a beautifully illustrated and inspiring book.

Gaia's Garden
Toby Hemenway; Chelsea Green Publishing Company (USA); 2001.
A permaculture approach to gardening with much ecological information. Although primarily for North America, it is relevant to forest gardeners everywhere.

Agroforestry News
Periodical; The Agroforestry Research Trust;
(see List of Suppliers).
'News' is a bit of a misnomer; this is a compendium of information on many aspects of agroforestry and forest gardening, including profiles of various fruit and nut trees. The approach is scientific, and the information more detailed than most forest gardeners require, but there is much of interest to the serious student or experimenter.

Permaculture Magazine
Quarterly; Permanent Publications (see address on page 152).
Read worldwide by enquiring minds and original thinkers who care about the environment. Each issue gives practical thought provoking information on: organic gardening, sustainable agriculture, agroforestry, ecovillages, alternative technology, eco-architecture and building, community development and much more.

SPECIAL SUBJECTS

The Book of Apples
Joan Morgan & Alison Richards; Ebury Press; 1993.
The first half of this book is a history of apples, the second half a complete listing of all the apple varieties held by the Brogdale Horticultural Trust. Joan Morgan is probably the only person alive to have tasted almost every one of the world's apple varieties, and this book contains the

wealth of her experience. It is an invaluable companion to choosing apple varieties, with some cultural information for each one (flowering time, vigour, tip/spur bearing, disease resistance, picking time and eating season etc.) as well as notes on its taste and culinary qualities.

Directory of Apple Cultivars
Martin Crawford; Agroforestry Research Trust; 1994.
Details of over 2,650 apple varieties are given, including where the trees can be bought. Slightly more information on each one is given than in *The Book of Apples*, and there are 19 separate lists of varieties for specific purposes, including: forest gardens, no-prune growing, organic growing, high rainfall, late frosts, Northern Britain, chalk soils, fruit for drying and for juicing.

Directory of Pear Cultivars
Martin Crawford; Agroforestry Research Trust; 1996.
This has details of over 600 varieties, including perry pears and Asian pears. It is similar to the *Directory of Apple Cultivars*, but the lower number of varieties, and comparatively less information about them, reflects the lesser importance of pears generally. As ever, Martin Crawford gleans all the information there is to be had on the subject.

Plums
Martin Crawford; Agroforestry Research Trust; 1996.
This is both a guide to growing plums and a directory of varieties. The directory contains less information than the above two, but does give all the available information on disease resistance – something which is often missing from nursery catalogues.

Hazelnuts
Chestnuts
Walnuts
Martin Crawford; Agroforestry Research Trust; 1995-6.
These three booklets probably represent the fullest information available in English on the cultivation of these nuts. Comprehensive variety lists are included.

Plants For A Future
Ken Fern; Permanent Publications; 1997.
Subtitled 'Edible and Useful Plants for a Healthier World', this is a compendium of unusual plants for those who want to experiment. They are almost all perennials, including trees, shrubs, climbers, perennial vegetables, edible flowers, water plants, ground covers and even edible lawn plants. Many of them are suitable for forest gardening. Instructions for using the plants, as well as growing them, are given.

Planting A Natural Woodland
Charlotte de la Bédoyère; Search Press; 2001.
A full colour guide to selecting and planting native trees, shrubs and woodland herbs.

Mushrooms in the Garden
Hellmut Steineck; Mad River Press; 1984.
This is a comprehensive and detailed account of the subject for anyone who is seriously interested in making the most of the mushroom-growing potential of their forest garden.

Soil Care & Management
Jo Readman; HDRA/Search Press; 1991.
An excellent practical guide for gardeners, including forest gardeners.

Pests
Healthy Fruit & Vegetables
Pauline Pears & Bob Sherman; HDRA/Search Press; 1990-1.
Sound practical advice. Organic pesticides are included as a last resort when all else fails.

Lifting The Lid
Peter Harper and Louise Halestrop; Centre of Alternative Technology Publications; 1999.
All you need to know about dealing ecologically with your domestic sewage, including detailed plans for a compost toilet.

The books in this Further Reading list, plus many others, are available through *Permaculture* Magazine's Green Shopping website:

www.green-shopping.co.uk
Tel: (01730) 823 311
Overseas: (int. code + 44 - 1730)
Email: orders@green-shopping.co.uk

LIST OF SUPPLIERS

This list is by no means exhaustive. The more common plants used in forest gardening can be bought from many different suppliers, and there is not space here to include them all. The omission of any supplier from this list should not be taken as adverse comment. But the less common plants can be difficult to find, and the sources listed here should between them be able to provide all the plants mentioned in this book. *PW*

Agroforestry Research Trust
46 Hunters Moon, Dartington, Totnes,
Devon TQ9 6JT
01803 840 776
mail@agroforestry.co.uk
www.agroforestry.co.uk
Seeds and plants of many shrubs and trees suitable for forest gardening, mostly unusual kinds. Will search for plants or varieties not in their catalogue on request.

Buckingham Nurseries
Tingewick Road, Buckingham MK18 4AE
01280 813 556
web-enquiries@hedging.co.uk
www.hedging.co.uk
Self-fertile kiwis, a small range of fruit and several of the edible ornamentals mentioned in this book.

Chiltern Seeds
Crowmarsh Battle Barns, 114 Preston Crowmarsh,
Wallingford OX10 6SL
01491 824 675
info@chilternseeds.co.uk
www.chilternseeds.co.uk
Seeds of uncommon vegetables, herbs, trees and shrubs, some of which are useful for forest gardening. Informative catalogue.

Chris Bowers & Sons
Whispering Trees Nurseries, Wimbotsham,
Norfolk PE34 8QB
01366 388 752
info@chrisbowers.co.uk
www.chrisbowers.co.uk
Good range of fruits, especially soft fruit, including traditional varieties. Informative catalogue.

Christies of Fochabers
The Nurseries, Fochabers, Moray IV32 7PF
01343 820 362
info@christiesoffochabers.com
www.christiesoffochabers.com
Fruit varieties suitable for Scotland, plus trees for forestry, hedging etc.

Clive Simms
Woodhurst, Essendine, Stamford,
Lincolnshire PE9 4LQ
01780 755615
Unusual nut trees and uncommon fruits – a small range, but including some not readily available elsewhere. Mail order only. 2 x 1st class stamps for descriptive catalogue.

The Conservation Volunteers (TCV) Online Shop
Sedum House, Mallard Way,
Doncaster DN4 8DB
01302 388 828
retail@tcv.org.uk
www.store.tcv.org.uk
Native trees, shrubs and wildflowers.

Future Foods
Luckleigh Cottage, Hockworthy, Wellington,
Somerset TA21 0NN
01398 361 347
Specialists in unusual foods, supplying seeds or tubers of many trees, shrubs, vegetables and herbs which are useful for forest gardening and hard to obtain elsewhere. Also spawn of a number of edible mushroom species, including those mentioned in this book. For informative catalogue send 4 x 1st class stamps.

John Chambers Wildflower Seed
Rabbit Hill Park, Great North Road, Arkendale HG5 0FF
01423 332 130
sales@johnchamberswildflowers.co.uk
www.johnchamberswildflowers.co.uk
Specialist in seeds of wild plants, including most of the
edible ones mentioned in this book.

Ken Muir
Honeypot Farm, Weely Heath, Clacton-on-Sea,
Essex CO16 9BJ
01255 830 181
www.kenmuir.co.uk
Fruit – not the widest selection, but the catalogue gives
full instructions for growing the fruits offered for sale.
(See Further Reading.)

National Fruit Collection
Crop Technology Centre, Brogdale Farm,
Brogdale Road, Faversham, Kent ME13 8XZ
01795 533 225
contact@nationalfruitcollection.org.uk
www. nationalfruitcollection.org.uk
Rare varieties of apple, pear and cherry; any variety
from the collection grafted onto the rootstock of your
choice, with aftercare instructions. Also supply graftwood
and budwood for you to propagate at home.

Organic Gardening Catalogue
Heritage house, 52-54 Hamm Moor Lane, Addlestone
Hersham, Surrey KT15 2SF
01932 878 570
enquiries@organiccatalogue.com
www.organiccatalogue.com
A range of seeds, including many vegetables mentioned
in this book plus comfrey plants and a small range of
organically grown apple trees. (Most perennial vegetables
are listed under 'Herbs'.)

Plants For A Future
Chris Marsh (Secretary), 9 Priory Park Road, Dawlish,
Devon EX7 9LX
01626 888 772
admin@pfaf.org
www.pfaf.org
Permaculture specialists, supplying plants of trees, shrubs
and perennial vegetables, a selection of the most useful from
the 1,800 kinds grown at this remarkable research site.
Many plants, including perennial kale, are unobtainable
elsewhere to my knowledge. Informative catalogue.

Poyntzfield Herb Nursery
Black Isle, by Dingwall, Ross & Cromarty IV7 8LX
01381 610 352
info@poyntzfieldherbs.co.uk
www.poyntzfieldherbs.co.uk
Herbs grown organically in tough Scottish conditions.

Reads Nursery
Douglas Farm, Falcon Lane, Ditchingham, Bungay,
Suffolk NR35 2JG
01986 895 555
www.readsnursery.co.uk
Grape and fig specialists, with a very wide selection of
varieties. Good selection of hazels.

R.V. Roger Ltd
The Nurseries, Malton Road, Pickering,
North Yorkshire YO18 7JW
01751 472 226
sales@rvroger.co.uk
www.rvroger.co.uk
Fruit suited to the north of England.

Suffolk Herbs
Monks Farm, Coggeshall Road, Kelvedon,
Essex CO5 9PG
01376 572 456
Seeds of many of the vegetables and herbs mentioned
in this book, including a wide range of chicories.
Informative catalogue £1.

Thornhayes Nursery
St. Andrews Wood, Dulford, Cullompton,
Devon EX15 2DF
01884 266 746
trees@thornhayes-nursery.co.uk
www.thornhayes-nursery.co.uk
Edible hawthorns, wide range of apples. (Mainly wholesale,
but open to 'discerning gardeners'.)

**As far as I am aware all the suppliers in this list do their
best to provide a first-class service, but I cannot take
any responsibility for the quality of any goods or services
supplied. PW**

PLANT INDEX

SUBJECT INDEX